A HISTORY OF
NEW YORK

D0112397

A HISTORY OF
NEW YORK

François Weil

Translated by Jody Gladding

COLUMBIA UNIVERSITY PRESS

New York

Columbia University Press
Publishers Since 1893
New York Chichester, West Sussex
Histoire de New York de François Weil
© Librairie Arthème Fayard, 2000
Translation copyright © 2004
Columbia University Press

Library of Congress Cataloging-in-Publication Data
Weil, François.
[Histoire de New York. English]
A history of New York / François Weil ; translated by Jody
Gladding.
     p.   cm. — (Columbia history of urban life)
Includes bibliographical references and index.
ISBN 0–231–12934–3 (acid-free paper) —
ISBN 0–231–12935–1 (pbk. : acid-free paper)
1. New York (N.Y.)—History. I. Title. II. Series.
F128.3.W4413   2004
974.7'1—dc21   2003055174

∞

Columbia University Press books are printed on
permanent and durable acid-free paper.

Printed in the United States of America

c 10 9 8 7 6 5 4 3 2 1
p 10 9 8 7 6 5 4 3 2 1

For Jean Heffer

CONTENTS

ILLUSTRATIONS

PREFACE

The terrorists who hijacked two airplanes and crashed them with their human cargo into the north and south towers of the World Trade Center on the morning of September 11, 2001—causing death, fear, confusion, sorrow, and destruction of a magnitude never experienced before in New York City, trying New Yorkers' individual and collective souls at the moment and ever since, and prompting many private or public acts of bravery and sacrifice—did not choose their target at random. In the eyes of many throughout the world, since its official inauguration in 1973, the World Trade Center had symbolized New York's immense financial power and embodied the global outreach of American capitalism, as its name appropriately suggested.

The Twin Towers also symbolized New York's ethnocultural diversity—what we now call multiculturalism. The victims of the September 11 attacks included men and women from various backgrounds who worked there and made the World Trade Center a place of racial, social, ethnic, and national diversity on a scale representative of the metropolis as a whole.

In a sense, then, the Al Qaeda terrorists' attack on the Twin Towers was an assault on capitalism and multiculturalism—the perpetual and often uneasy tension between them representing, in my view, the central theme of New York City's history and identity. Although the pages that follow (originally published in French in 2000) do not directly address September 11 and conclude with an account of the millennium celebration on December 31, 1999, I recount the long history of New York City simultaneously as a local community and a global city, and I attempt to show the changing meanings of these terms over time. In elaborating, for each period of New York's history, on the mixture of functions, classes, and cultures that characterized the city, this book is intended to explore New York both as a unique space and one which exemplifies American diversity, thus to contribute to a better understanding of September 11, its aftermath, and the present and future of New York City.

While researching this book I often wondered why understanding (and explaining!) New York was so difficult, and I have come to the conclusion that the reason lies in the symbolic power that the city slowly acquired over its almost four-century history and in the fascination that it came to exert worldwide.

For New York *is* fascinating—its energy, the hieroglyphs its skyline etches on the face of Manhattan, the hubbub that resonates from the Battery to the heights of Harlem, the incessant movement that makes the whole metropolis shudder with violent contractions. An infinite kaleidoscope of images and sensations, New York is the stuff of dreams. It is also a radical city—the whirlwind one person describes, the delirium another diagnoses, the worldwide proclamation of a triumphant modernity. New York is not America but a potentiality of America, perhaps its most intense one.

But the magnetism and the brutality of the metropolis have their price. An immense palimpsest, New York is always rewriting itself, risking the loss of its past meanings. New York lives in the moment, even if that means it will sometimes seem incomprehensible. Condemned to a perspective without history, swept along by its movement, the city's spectators and actors, those who pace its streets, are prisoners of the contemporary, of the immediacy that its name evokes.

I recognize New York's powerful magnetism and its present- and future-mindedness, but I have endeavored to treat them as historical subjects. I have therefore conceived this book as an attempt to temporarily break New York's spell in a search for meaning, and as a historian's reading intended to decipher the writings of the past beneath the overlay of today's metropolis.

I do not hold New York's destiny to be self-evident. Whether at the time of the Dutch colonial trading post, the British colonial port, or the nineteenth and twentieth centuries' American city, the city's history could easily have taken another path. For the city on the Hudson to become the all-powerful and mythical New York, it took many New Yorkers to demonstrate their ability to innovate, adapt, take advantage of circumstances, and create the appropriate conditions for spiraling growth. New Yorkers' commercial virtuosity, industrial flexibility, and financial networking capacity made New York the opportunist city *par excellence*.

Therefore I describe how the city was born to capitalism and how, from its beginnings in the 1620s, it followed the rhythm of phases and fluctuations in the Atlantic world—long remaining secondary in importance, its growth slow and halting before everything changed within just a few decades in the mid-eighteenth century. I show how and why thereafter the wars, the maturation of the colonial economy within the British Empire, and the rise in power of the young American republic made early nineteenth-century New York the gateway to a continent. I explain how, from then on, the city's success led it to take over the island of Manhattan, Brooklyn, the Bronx, Queens, and Staten Island during the course of the nineteenth and twentieth centuries—and how, not content with the sea, it turned to the sky, an element its highest buildings became so familiar with.

New York's capitalist growth was inseparable from its inhabitants' ethnocultural diversity, itself the product of forced or voluntary migration to the city on the Hudson during most periods of its history. Immigration (from elsewhere in the United States and from all over the world) provided the much-needed labor force that made New York an economic success and some New Yorkers rich. It fed into the city's cultures, stimulating cultural practices, at times provoking violent confrontations, and overall making much of materialistic New York (and many New Yorkers) culturally self-conscious. Diversity also made New York important symbolically—as a mythic haven of freedom, the object of millions of immigrants' perpetual desire, in whose eyes it embodied the vast realm of possibility.

This book tells the history of the tension between capitalism and diversity that has allowed New York to overcome many tragedies and contradictions, even as it has nurtured the dynamics, energy, and symbolic dimension that give the city its place in American and world culture.

ACKNOWLEDGMENTS

It was more than ten years ago that I set out on the adventure of this book, and over those years, I have accumulated many debts, which I am happy to acknowledge here.

My gratitude goes first of all to the Thiers Foundation, where I was able to begin to think about this project, and to my academic home, the École des hautes études en sciences sociales, where, since 1993, I have found a stimulating intellectual and collegial environment, as well as opportunities for carrying out research abroad. On several occasions, I have presented ongoing research in my seminars at the EHESS, and I would like to thank the participants for their critical comments and suggestions.

I am also deeply indebted to the library staffs of the École normale supérieure, the Maison des sciences de l'Homme, the Bibliothèque nationale, Harvard and Columbia Universities, Louisiana State University, New York University, the University of Virginia, the Museum of the City of New York, and the New-York Historical Society.

This books owes its existence to the temerity of Agnès Fontaine, then literary director of Fayard, who proposed the project to me, and was then able to demonstrate the patience necessary for its preparation and the impatience indispensable to its completion. For the former and the latter, as well as for her expert rereadings, she must be warmly thanked, along with her assistants Mathilde Puech and Virginie Bressis.

My gratitude goes as well to all the researchers who have devoted their labors to the history of New York. Without them, without the knowledge that they have collectively accumulated, I would never have been able to carry through with the undertaking that I assigned myself. The bibliographical essay at the end of this book gives only a partial idea of my debt in this regard, which is immense.

I owe more personal thanks to my family, which has

stoically lived with this book for years, as well as colleagues and friends too numerous for me to name here—but in particular, Caroline Béraud, Louis Bergeron, Alan Brinkley, Nancy L. Green, Vincent Michelot, Gilles Pécout, and Jacques Revel. Laurent Dappe, Jean Heffer, Janet R. Horne, Jennifer Merchant, Pap Ndiaye, and Olivier Zunz read and criticized each chapter of the book, and I am deeply grateful to them for that.

This book was originally published in French in 2000. This American edition owes much to the initiative and advice of Daniel T. Rodgers, who was among the first to read it and suggest that it should be translated into English. I am deeply indebted to him, as well as to Thomas Bender, Alan Brinkley, and Olivier Zunz, outstanding friends and colleagues who helped bring this project to fruition. I thank them and the anonymous readers who encouraged this translation. At Columbia University Press, I am grateful to Kenneth L. Jackson for welcoming this book in his series. Working with senior executive editor Peter Dimock and associate editor Anne Routon has been a pleasure. I owe Jody Gladding, who translated my prose into English, a particular gratitude for her sense of rhythm, clarity, and precision. The final product was much improved by the attentive copyediting of William Meyers and the skills of manuscript editor Leslie Kriesel.

Finally, I want to express all my gratefulness to James F. and Jimmie Holland, as well as their children, with whom I have always found a home in New York for twenty years now, and who were the first to introduce me to the history of their city.

Over the last fifteen years, Jean Heffer has shared with me his friendship, his knowledge, and his intellectual generosity. This book is dedicated to him, with gratitude.

Paris, March 2000, and New York, July 2003

A HISTORY OF
NEW YORK

I
THE PROVINCE
1620–1820

FIGURE 2
New Amsterdam on the Isle of Manhattan in America
© Hachette Livre

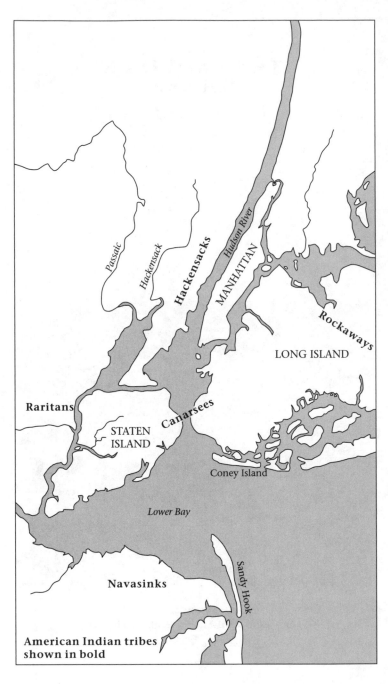

MAP 1
New York Bay

1

THE OCEAN

In the beginning, a large bay scattered with islands, a veritable archipelago teeming with oysters and pike, eel and sturgeon, Canadian geese and wild turkeys, ducks and wild geese. . . .

At the end of the sixteenth century, several thousand sedentary Amerindians were established there—Munsees, Lenapes, Rockaways, Hackensacks, Nayacks, Raritans, Navasinks, and other Canarsees coming from the Delaware branch of the Algonquin family. Some fished in the well-stocked waters or cultivated Indian corn and beans, others hunted deer and bear in the surrounding forests. Their camps, sometimes comprising several dozen families, were scattered along the banks of the Hudson and the Raritan, as well as on the islands we now call Manhattan, Long Island, and Staten Island.

BEAVERS AND SAILING SHIPS

Beginning in the early seventeenth century, Dutch sailors made many voyages to explore the region. Following decades of conflict with the Spaniards, the seven United Provinces of Holland, Zeeland, Utrecht, Gelderland, Overijssel, Friesland, and Groningen won their independence in 1581. They wanted to build an empire, to thwart their Spanish enemy, and also to support the expansion of their cities and the growing profits of their merchants. Unlike the Spanish, this empire had no territorial aspirations. The Dutch objective was to establish commercial networks supported by strategically located trading posts, from which they hoped to earn quick profits.

The Dutch turned first to Asia. In 1602, they founded the United East India Company, to develop trade with India as well as with Japan and China. Paradoxically, their Asian policy was also the origin of their explorations of the North American coast—the market fever experienced in Amsterdam stimulated new initiatives, both individual and collective. Merchants and politicians dreamed of discovering a northern maritime route, through the Arctic, that would allow Dutch ships access to Asia while avoiding the long and dangerous journey around the Cape of Good Hope.

Early in 1609, the Amsterdam Chamber of the East India Company entrusted this mission to an experienced navigator, Henry Hudson, an Englishman who had just completed two fruitless expeditions for a London company in search of a northwest passage to Asia. In April, Hudson left Amsterdam on his expeditionary ship, the *Halve Maen* (Half Moon).

First he headed north and rounded the coast of Norway, but then he changed his course. Probably influenced by his Dutch contacts, the merchant Isaac Le Maire and the theologian and geographer Petrus Plancius, he decided to start out in search of a northwest passage. The *Halve Maen* thus reached the New World, following the northeastern American coast south to the Chesapeake Bay, and then headed north again—exploring in passing the bay of the "South River" (the Delaware River today).

In September, Hudson passed the Narrows, entered the Upper Bay, and sailed up the "Great River," or the "North River," later given his name. There, the Dutch established friendly relations with the Amerindians, and supplied themselves with tobacco, provisions, and furs. Reaching as far upriver as present-day Albany, Hudson convinced himself that he had not found the passage he was looking for and turned back. The *Halve Maen* returned to Amsterdam.

In the United Provinces, the sponsors of the expedition did not hide their disappointment. But Hudson never lost his belief in the existence of a northwest passage, and he managed to persuade the Company to finance another expedition in 1610. He died in the midst of it, the victim of his mutinous crew, after exploring the great Arctic bay that would henceforth bear his name.

Nevertheless, the autumn 1609 voyage was not without consequences, unlike the incursions into that region by the sixteenth-century explorers who preceded Hudson— Giovanni da Verrazano in 1524, Esteban Gomes in 1525, and an anonymous English navigator in 1568. Hudson describes a land of plenty, a valley rich with game. "The people of the Countrie came flocking aboord," and "many brought us Bevers skinnes and Otters skinnes, which wee bought for Beades, Knives and Hatchets," noted one of his companions, Robert Juet, in his ship's log.[1]

Attracted by the fur trade, many groups of merchants from Amsterdam and Hoorn resumed exploration of this still unknown region. For example, Adriaen Block, who was probably present in the area in 1611 as a supercargo on a ship chartered by the Amsterdam admiralty, returned there as a captain in 1612 and 1613. He explored the Atlantic coast as far as Cape Cod, sailed up the Connecticut River, and conducted a profitable bartering trade with the Amerindians.

The furs from the Great River—which the Dutch christened the Mauritius in honor of Prince Maurice of Nassau, *stadholder* (governor) of the United Provinces—became the object of fierce competition among the merchants. In the autumn of 1613, five ships financed by different sponsors found themselves on the river at the same time. One of them, Adriaen Block's *Tyger*, was destroyed by fire. His crew had to disembark on a large island and cut down trees there to build a makeshift vessel. These sailors were probably the first Europeans to tread upon Manhattan soil.

In order to minimize the rivalry and the dangers of the voyages themselves, several merchants joined forces in 1614 to form the New Netherland Company. The States General granted them a monopoly, beginning on January

1, 1615, over trade on the Mauritius River. But by 1618 this privilege came to an end.

A NEW NETHERLAND

In 1621, while commercial initiatives—and sometimes conflicting ones—multiplied, the States General chartered a new enterprise, the West India Company, which was granted important privileges: a commercial and sailing monopoly over the Americas and western Africa; military, legal and administrative privileges; and the right to populate and colonize conquered territories. The Company had grand designs. It was supposed to be the vehicle for, and the military force behind, Dutch expansion in the world of the Atlantic, dominated until now by the Portuguese and the Spanish. The idea for such an enterprise was not new, but the end of the twelve-year truce that the United Provinces had made with Spain in 1609, and the East India Company's success in Asia, allowed the Dutch to enlarge their commercial networks.

The Amsterdam sponsors dreamed of conquering Brazil, of seizing the island of Curaçao, and of capturing Spanish silver fleets. But the good deals that sailors and merchants had made in the 1610s in the Mauritius River region convinced them that the fur trade could be a rich source of profits. So, in 1624, hardly a year after the beginning of its activities, the Company decided to establish a permanent trading post in New Netherland.

The first colonists, about thirty families, crossed the Atlantic on the modest *Nieew Nederlandt*. They were not Dutch, but Walloon, and had gone into exile in the United Provinces because of their Protestantism before crossing the Atlantic. For the most part, they settled in the Mauritius River valley, at the site of Fort Orange (now Albany). A few remained in New York Bay, on a little island south of Manhattan (today's Governor's Island); others reached the "South River" (the Delaware) and founded Fort Nassau. A small group may have ventured to the mouth of the Connecticut River. The colonists were widely scattered, and the Company soon felt the need for a commonly shared district, easily accessible by sea and easily defensible against

FIGURE 3
The Hartgers View, First View of New Amsterdam, ca. 1626. Joost
Hartgers. Engraved in 1651. Museum of the City of New York

possible incursions by Amerindians. Thus it planned to
regroup its forces and create a fortified trading settlement
at the southern end of the island of Manhattan.

In the spring of 1626, this project became a reality. Under
the leadership of Willem Verhulst and then his successor
Peter Minuit, the trading post, named New Amsterdam,
assembled builders, furriers, soldiers, farmers, and artisans
employed by the Company. The engineer Cryn Fredericks
began the construction of Fort Amsterdam, designed to
control the bay and the river with its guns, and to shelter
the stores, the storerooms and the offices of the Company.

This settlement entailed negotiations with the Amerindians who lived on the island. The Dutch knew they were
threatened. They had to win the goodwill of the inhabitants
of the region if they wanted to establish their presence there
permanently. In accordance with the Company's instructions, they recognized the property rights of the Amerindians, and in the spring of 1626, before settling on it, they
bought Manhattan "for the price of sixty florins." This
famous transaction, documented only by a single mention
in a contemporary letter, symbolically marks the beginning

of the Dutch period of Manhattan. Undoubtedly it meant two different things for the Amerindians, who had no notion of private property, and for the Dutch, who wanted to follow the rules in order to have incontestable property titles, should they need them.

The *Wapen van Amsterdam*, the Company's ship "which sailed from New Netherland, out of the River Mauritius on the 23rd September," brought the news of the island's acquisition to Amsterdam in early November 1626. On board was important cargo: thousands of beaver skins, hundreds of otter skins, dozens of mink and wildcat skins, meant to reassure the Company's directors about the new colony's resources.[2]

But their satisfaction was short-lived. During the four decades of its history, the colony reflected in miniature Holland's lack of success in the New World. The Company was losing money by the end of the 1620s. The furs its ships brought back to Amsterdam from New Netherland hardly covered the cost of its operations there. That profits did not meet expectations is explained in part by some unfortunate choices: the Amerindians did not want the copper cauldrons and other objects sent to New Netherland to use as barter for skins. Most importantly, the Company proved itself incapable of retaining, even among its own employees, the monopoly it held on fur trading.

Added to the difficulties in New Netherland were those the Company experienced in its other theaters of operation in the New World. In Brazil, the Spaniards took São Salvador back from the Dutch in 1625, the capital that they had relinquished to them a year before. Nevertheless, in 1628 at Matanzas, a port located east of Havana, Admiral Piet Heyn seized a Spanish fleet heavily loaded with gold and silver. The 11.5 million or so florins that this prize provided reassured the Company's shareholders and financed its operations for the next decade. But New Netherland remained more costly than profitable.

Under pressure from its stockholders, the Company then adopted a plan for private colonization. While retaining its monopoly over navigation, it granted large property owners (called patroons) huge territories in the Connecticut, Delaware, and Hudson Valleys, as well as authorization to conduct fur trading. Five investors had signed on by 1629: Albert Burgh and Samuel Godijn wanted to locate along the Delaware, Samuel Blommaert and Michael Pauw near the Connecticut, and Kiliaen Van Rensselaer in the Hudson Valley. In exchange for these lands, they all had to recruit colonists and make their properties profitable. For its part, "the Company reserves the island of Manhattes to themselves," noted the Dutch chronicler, Nicolas Van Wassenaer.[3]

These private colonization projects failed in their turn. In accordance with subsequent negotiations and two successive compromises, the Company agreed to limit its monopoly, but in fact, it found itself competing with the large property owners. By the mid-1630s, the Company's attitude and Indian threats prompted four of these large property owners to renounce their claims. Only Rensselaerswyck survived, a vast stronghold in the Hudson Valley, near Fort Orange (Albany) and property of the Amsterdam merchant and jeweler, Kiliaen Van Rensselaer.

After trying monopolies and private colonization, New Netherland then adopted a third approach, open trade. In 1638–39, the Company relinquished its monopolies on navigation and commerce, including the fur trade. Henceforth it was content to regulate and administer its colony, but not without sporadic tensions and rivalries.

This solution was only a stopgap measure, but for a quarter century, New Netherland experienced prosperity nonetheless. Between 1640 and 1664, New Amsterdam grew from 400 to about 1500 inhabitants. The colony owed its expansion to private initiatives—slowed down at first by the Indian wars set off by the heedlessness and brutality of the director-general Willem Kieft in the early 1640s. These ended with a hard-won Dutch victory.

Many Amsterdam firms (Verbrugge, De Wolff, Van Rensselaer, Van Hoornbeeck) specialized in trade with the colony and prospered by increasing maritime relations with New Amsterdam. Between 1641 and 1662, Gillis and Seth Verbrugge financed twenty-seven voyages between Amsterdam and New Netherland all by themselves, as well as exchanges with the English colony of Virginia. In the 1650s, when the English laws of navigation prohibited direct maritime traffic with Virginia, the Verbrugge galliots, laden with tobacco leaves, maintained coastal navigation between New Amsterdam and Virginia. Dirck De Wolff, a former Haarlem baker who made his fortune in the grain trade between Friesland and Amsterdam, adopted a different strategy. He rented space for his merchandise in the holds of ships that belonged to others and delegated management of the operations to his son Abel and his son-in-law Gerrit Jansz Cuyper, whom he sent to New Amsterdam to procure furs, tobacco, and wood for distribution in the United Provinces.[4]

At the same time, New Amsterdam played an ever-growing role in the commercial network the Dutch had woven across the Atlantic and throughout the New World. It ceased to be simply a trading post for Amsterdam and became an essential entrepôt in the connections that were established with the English colonies in the West Indies and on the North American continent, and with the Dutch settlements in the Lesser Antilles (Saint Martin, Saint Eustatius and Saba) and the island of Curaçao, off the coast of New Granada.

Dutch merchants hoped to profit from the civil war then tearing England apart by taking over the English colonial markets, from Massachusetts to Barbados. True to their reputation of seaborne traders, they became transporters, always ready to replace the English merchant ships and bring the precious "Virginia leaves," or tobacco, to Amsterdam. Elsewhere, as in Barbados, they assisted in the sugar revolution (a major phenomenon of the 1640s) by offering the English planters the knowledge they had acquired in Brazil— their expertise in sugarcane, credit, slaves, and the commercial outlets that the planters needed.

New Amsterdam found itself at the crossroads of numerous commercial circuits. The oldest one linked it directly to Amsterdam: from Holland, the port received glassware, alcohol, gun powder, firearms, and objects needed to sustain the fur trade, as well as livestock, other provisions, and many manufactured products destined for the inhabitants of New Netherland or the English colonies. Thus the *Valke-*

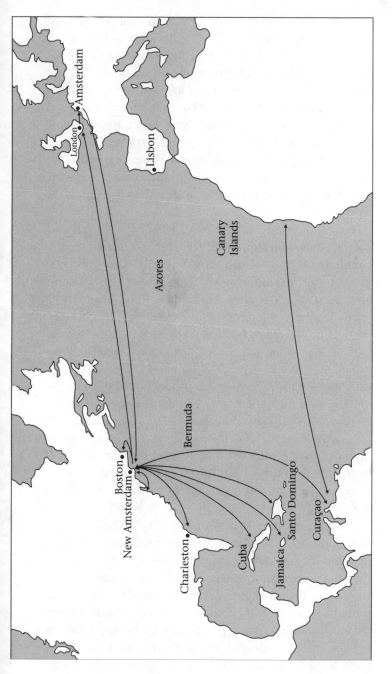

MAP 2

New Amsterdam commerce (about 1650–1660)

nier, chartered by Abel De Wolff and Jan Baptist Van Rensselaer, left Amsterdam in 1650, laden with leather boots,
books, woolen goods (including the famous Duffel cloth,
dear to the Indians who made it into blankets), farming
tools, lace, and scented soap. For its part, New Amsterdam
sent to the United Provinces tobacco from Virginia, wood
from the Hudson Valley and New England, and most
importantly, furs from the Fort Orange furriers. "This country does a large trade in furs, especially beavers, which are
sold to us by the savages by the thousand for Dutch merchandise. All the people here are traders," noted Nicasius De
Sille in 1654.[5]

A second circuit placed New Amsterdam at the crux of
coastal navigation trade with the English colonies on the
continent: tobacco from Virginia, fish, flour, biscuits,
salted meats, oakum, tar, and wood from New England
accumulated in the New Amsterdam storerooms. These
goods had been obtained in exchange for manufactured
products from Holland, and sometimes from New Netherland, along with sugar, molasses, and rum from the West
Indies. A third circuit, precisely, was West Indian: in
exchange for the highly prized products of the sugar revolution, New Amsterdam provided Jamaica and the Lesser
Antilles with miscellaneous provisions (grain, flour, biscuits, salted meats, and fish) and manufactured objects
intended for the planters. Finally, a fourth circuit, no less
important than the others, linked New Amsterdam to the
slave entrepôt of Curaçao, and from there, directly to
Africa and to the Spanish Main.

All this merchandise passing through the New Amsterdam port substantially enriched the Dutch merchants who
financed the transactions, and it provided a livelihood for
the sailors, artisans, innkeepers, and longshoremen of the
town. The desire for free trade that impelled them contrasted sharply with the many restrictions imposed upon
the local economy. In fact, the great majority of occupations
in New Amsterdam were very strictly regulated, whether it
was a matter of making or selling beer, wine, or other forms
of alcohol, or baking, butchering—almost any trade. These
regulations existed in the English colonial towns as well as
in most European cities at the time.

But New Amsterdam was the scene of an ongoing conflict between the directors of the West India Company, in Amsterdam, and their representative in the colony, the director-general. Peter Stuyvesant, who held this position from 1645 to 1664, tried hard to increase regulations over matters of price, weights, measures, and trade. For its part, the Company balked at strict controls, because in the long term they could hinder the colony's interests. The Company was opposed, for example, to granting any trade monopoly in the colony, a paradoxical decision considering the monopoly it had itself enjoyed in 1638–39, but logical in view of its support for unrestrained commercial development.

THE ENGLISH CONQUEST

New Amsterdam was a booming port when the English took possession of it in 1664, thus putting an end to the commercial and maritime rivalry between England and the Netherlands that had spanned many decades.

By 1610–20, English merchants had made up their minds. London must replace Amsterdam as the hub of international trade, and to achieve that, the Dutch must be prevented from playing the role of intermediary at which they excelled. The Navigation Act that the Cromwell Parliament passed in October 1651 constituted the first response to the arrogant supremacy of Dutch merchantmen. In accordance with this law, only English ships were authorized to import merchandise into English ports, with the exception of foreign vessels bearing products from their own countries.

This attempt to put into practice the well understood principles of mercantilism started the first Anglo-Dutch war of 1652–54. Thus the English, whose New England colonies had gained increasing prominence since the 1630s, seriously considered seizing New Netherland. But the announcement of a truce in spring 1654 prevented the fleet assembled in New England from sailing to the mouth of the Hudson. The truce brought only a brief pause, however. In 1660, and again in 1663, King Charles II reinforced mercantilism's legislative arsenal. Two trade acts were introduced that reserved for English ships alone, sailing from the metropolis or the colonies, all colonial commerce in a certain number of products: sugar, tobacco, cotton, indigo, ginger, and dyewood were affected by these measures, but not wheat or flour.

It was then that the English decided to put an end to the Dutch presence in North America. Without even an official declaration of war, Charles II resolved the old territorial rivalry between England and Holland, and New England and New Netherland, in his own way. In March 1664, he presented his brother James, Duke of York and Albany, and heir to the throne, with all the lands located between Virginia and New England, over which, in his eyes, the Dutch had no rights.

In the summer, an English squadron commanded by Colonel Richard Nicolls anchored near the entrance channel to New York Bay and demanded the surrender of the "Towne, Scituate upon the Island commonly knowne by the Name of Manhatoes, with all the forts thereunto belonging."[6] Stuyvesant considered resisting. But he decided against it, under pressure from the municipal authorities and the inhabitants of New Amsterdam, who were concerned about protecting the city from plunder and destruction. The surrender was signed on September 8, 1664. The small Dutch garrison left the fort in an orderly manner to board the *Gideon*, while the English took possession. That was the end of New Netherland and New Amsterdam, relinquished by the United Provinces in the Treaty of Breda (1667). Having become a ducal possession, the city was immediately renamed New York, in honor of its new master.

IN THE EMPIRE

Under the leadership of the first governor of the new colony, Richard Nicolls, New York entered the English Atlantic colonial system. In 1673, during the third Anglo-Dutch war, the Dutch took possession of the city and renamed it New Orange. But the English recovered it the following year through the Treaty of Westminster.

The transfer of sovereignty meant that London had to eventually replace Amsterdam. In fact, this transfer evolved slowly because New York was still a Dutch city in which the English were very much the minority. New York's demographic and economic growth remained limited until the mid-eighteenth century. In 1737, it counted hardly more than 10,000 inhabitants, and only ranked third among colonial cities, behind Boston and Philadelphia, and just ahead of Charleston, in South Carolina, and Newport, in Rhode Island.

New York's low standing can be explained first of all by its rivals' advantages. Boston was the colonies' main port and largest city thanks to its seniority and its vital commercial ties with England and the Caribbean. Despite its recent founding (1682), Philadelphia benefited from Pennsylvania's spectacular population growth and from the rich farm lands that surrounded it. New York's resources were more meager. With the exception of furs, the province did not have great quantities of easily exportable staples, as the Chesapeake Bay region had tobacco or Pennsylvania had wheat. The New York hinterlands included only Long Island and the Hudson Valley as far north as Albany. The Mohawk Valley was solidly held by the League of the Five, soon-to-be Six Iroquois Nations, and the French in Canada posed a continual threat to the colony. Also, unlike Boston, New York had only recent ties to England.

These weaknesses dictated the directions taken by the New York economy in the years between 1670 and 1740: first of all, as in the past, commerce with the upper Hudson Valley, the West Indies, and other continental colonies; then, to a lesser extent, the new motherland. "New York and Albany live wholly upon trade with the Indians, England and the West Indies," reported Governor Thomas Dongan in 1687.[7] After the departure of the Dutch, the old commercial networks of the United Provinces functioned as well as could be expected for a time. Abel de Wolff, for example, or Gillis Van Hoornbeeck briefly attempted trade with New York from Amsterdam, but they soon had to give up because of the high duties that the English imposed on their merchandise.

The Amsterdam merchants gradually disappeared, replaced by colonial merchants of Dutch origin, but also Huguenots and English, who arrived in the 1670s and 1680s. The commercial networks that they established gave New York commerce a dual aspect, both licit and illicit, public and clandestine. Importing, exporting, reexporting—in short, New York fulfilled the function of entrepôt as it had done in the Dutch period, serving intercolonial, transatlantic, and West Indian trade, within the framework defined by the principles of English mercantilism. Like Philadelphia and Boston, which offered fierce competition, New York supplied Barbados, Jamaica, Antigua, and the other English islands with essential foodstuffs (flour, bread, grain, corn, biscuits, barrels of dried meat) as well as lumber, planks, and staves. In exchange, the port received cargoes of sugar, molasses, tafia, syrup, dyewood, and slaves, with cash or notes to be cleared in London. "For the goods which are sold in the West Indies either ready money is accepted or West India goods, which are either first brought to New York or immediately sent to England or Holland," observed the Swedish scholar Peter Kalm, on a visit to New York.[8]

New York also continued to specialize in intercolonial coastal navigation. It exchanged West Indian products with Boston for fish and English imports, as well as with Charleston for rice from the Carolinas. At the same time, it endeavored to establish and maintain relations with London, where it sent its wheat, flour, whale oil, furs, "sugar, logwood, and other dying woods, rum, mahogany and many other goods which are the produce of the West Indies." For its part, London sent to New York "all sorts of English manufacture for Christians and blancketts, Duffells etc., for Indians," according to Governor Andros. As for Ireland, it received linseed, in great demand on the island, and West Indian products. "I have been assured," wrote Peter Kalm, "that in some years, no less than ten ships are sent to Ireland, laden with nothing but linseed, because it is said that the flax in Ireland does not give good seed."[9]

These commercial ties accelerated New York's takeover of the economy of its province. Its domination was not

FIGURE 4
View of the New York port in the eighteenth century
© Hachette Livre

yet established in the 1660s when Albany still controlled the fur trade. But New York profited from the political favor it enjoyed during the first years of the English regime. Between 1678 and 1694, the benevolence of Governor Andros and his successors earned it a monopoly over flour processing throughout the province, to the great displeasure of merchants and farmers in the Hudson Valley and on Long Island. Strengthening its position at the expense of its rival, Albany, New York developed the milling trade and became "ye chief Grainery for most of ye West Indian islands."[10]

Nevertheless, within the mercantilist framework, stiff competition from other colonies hurt New York merchants, who had neither Philadelphia's grains nor Boston's merchant fleet and powerful London connections. Thus, during the colonial period, New York commerce remained much inferior to that of Boston, Philadelphia, and even Charleston, a port that benefited from vast exports of rice and indigo grown on Southern plantations.

THE PROFITS OF PRIVATEERING AND WAR

New York's relatively weak position prompted interest in diversification which would help to make its fortune. The commercial appetites of New Yorkers, combined with the constraints they were under, led them to resort to practices as lucrative as they were illegal. In the 1690s, New York was, in effect, a port of registry for illicit merchandise, even a refuge for pirates.

Piracy depended upon accommodating harbors, where pirates could get water and provisions, repair their ships, and perhaps spend their shares in the taverns, brothels, and shops. At the end of the seventeenth century, the governor of the colony, Benjamin Fletcher, very mindful of the gifts systematically bestowed upon him by the outlaws, often proved inclined to provide them with the commissions that transformed them, when necessary, into privateers. Thanks to him and to the merchants who were always ready to sell pirates the weapons, supplies and spirits they wanted, New York became one of piracy's favorite ports—as pressure from the English, Spanish, and French, who were determined to end the era of the buccaneer, eventually forced piracy to operate more in the Indian Ocean and the Red Sea than in the West Indies.

It was no accident then, that New York sheltered an old buccaneer of the West Indian seas in this period: William Kidd, who had no qualms about consorting with New York notables like the merchant Robert Livingston. In 1695, Captain Kidd obtained a royal commission to hunt pirates in the Indian Ocean. A short time later, he began pirating again himself, but was arrested in 1698 and hanged three years later. His fate embarrassed his protectors, Livingston and Lord Bellomont, who succeeded Fletcher as governor of New York. But in truth, they were mainly embarrassed by Kidd's indiscretion, in not confining himself to the role of intermediary.

Piracy was first of all a source of considerable profits.

Consider the New York merchant Vledrick Flypsen, alias Frederick Philipse. Born in Holland in 1626, a carpenter by trade, he arrived in New Amsterdam in the early 1650s, became a merchant, married a rich widow, anglicized his name following the English conquest, and became one of the chief merchants of his time. At the end of the seventeenth century, he was undoubtedly the largest slave trader in New York, thanks to slave purchases made at very low cost in Mozambique and Madagascar. He was also a member of Governor Fletcher's council and, like the governor, only saw advantages in pirates' laying over in New York. When Governor Bellomont decided to forbid them from entering the port, Philipse devised a way to draw profits from concurrently trading with and supplying the pirates. His ships left New York with cargoes destined for pirates from Madagascar or neighboring Sainte-Marie, and then returned to their point of departure loaded with slaves. Thus Philipse sold at a good price the kegs of beer, casks of rum and wine, and barrels of lemon juice (to ward off scurvy), as well as the sugar, salt, gunpowder, tobacco, cloth, pipes, hats, shoes, scissors, combs, knives, and cord that the pirates wanted. After 1698, when, at the East India Company's request, the London Parliament severely restricted trade beyond the Cape of Good Hope, Philipse continued his activity unabated, even though it meant running the risk of being convicted of contraband and having cargo and boats confiscated.

Authorized or forbidden, this trafficking constituted only one facet of the New York economy at the time, because the city was becoming more important to the English in their strategies against the Spanish and the French. New York was the only colony where London maintained a permanent garrison, and its location, at the heart of the continental colonies and in contact with Canada through the upper Hudson Valley, made it a nerve center for the empire.

Unlike the Bostonians, New Yorkers cleverly avoided getting caught up in the rash of military operations during the various wars from 1690 to 1750: King William's War between the French and the English in America in the 1690s; Queen Anne's War concluding with the Treaty of Utrecht in 1713; the English-Spanish war known as the "War of Jenkin's Ear" in 1739; and the War of the Austrian Succession (or King George's War) of 1740–48.

In Boston, these wars stimulated activity at naval yards, but they also led to inhabitants being pressed into service in the regiments and on the navy vessels, prompting a serious monetary inflation and dramatically increasing urban poverty. New York, on the other hand, showed little taste for the expeditions that Massachusetts repeatedly launched against Acadia and Canada—costly in terms of money and human lives and futile in military terms. New Yorkers limited themselves to profitable commercial engagement, an attitude explained first by the ties that existed between Albany and Montreal, and second by the proclaimed neutrality of the Iroquois, without whose aid any military enterprise would be futile. New York preferred the advantages of the wars to their disadvantages: its merchant ships grew in number from 35 in 1689 to 124 in 1700, and many suppliers were kept busy providing supplies to the English fleets in the Caribbean. With the same zeal, the suppliers equipped some 6,000 English soldiers in 60 ships for a 1711 expedition launched against Quebec—an effort that resulted in a resounding fiasco but brought them financial profits.

The rewards of legalized piracy continued to augment the profits of war. By the late 1680s, the New York port harbored several privateersmen, but privateering developed especially during the English-Spanish war of the 1740s. Attracted by Spanish colonial treasures, New Yorkers armed dozens of vessels, some of which returned to the port after successful campaigns and profitable marauding. A New York newspaper of that time, the *Post-Boy*, published triumphal lists: 32 prizes between 1739 and 1744, 213 prizes between 1744 and 1748, all declared legally sound by the Admiralty Court and sold at auction. "This is the fifteenth vessel taken by this ship," exulted the *Post-Boy* in 1744 upon the arrival of the *Launceton*, commanded by Peter Warren, and his prize, the *Saint François Xavier*, a three-hundred-ton ship. "She was saluted by all our Privateers, and several other vessels, and the general Acclamation of the People, as a Testimony of the Sense they have of the signal Service done by this gentleman [Warren] during the continuance of the war."[11] The hundreds of thousands of pounds sterling that these prizes brought in not only enriched the privateers but also the merchant shipowners, unleashing a speculative fever for outfitting the corsairs.

THE AMERICANIZATION OF NEW YORK

Beginning in the mid-eighteenth century, New York experienced increasingly rapid growth. In 1755, during the last conflict between the English and the French in North America, the so-called French and Indian War, the city found itself assigned the role of "general store," and served as headquarters for the English troops attacking Canada via the Hudson and Mohawk Valleys, Lake Champlain, and Lake Erie. Thousands of soldiers and sailors had to be armed and provided with clothes and footwear, food and drink, greatly profiting the New York merchants who successfully bid for the lucrative contracts and the suppliers who filled those merchants' orders. Thus after eighteen months, London owed some 115,000 pounds sterling to Robert Livingston alone. "I can plainly see that New York is growing immensely rich, by Money brought into it from all Quarters for the Pay and Subsistance of the Troops," noted the very Philadelphian Benjamin Franklin.[12] The prosperity engendered by the war economy profited all New York enterprises, from merchants to innkeepers and artisans.

New Yorkers also continued to passionately devote themselves to maritime privateering. In 1758, Governor James DeLancey wrote to William Pitt that a "kind of madness to go privateering" reigned in the port and that he himself was besieged by requests for commissions.[13] Privateer outfitting proliferated (224 ships during the French and Indian War, or three times more than during the King George's War), and the prizes, sold at auction, brought the privateers and their sponsors more than two million pounds sterling, which was reinvested in the urban economy.

After 1759, when the Anglo-Americans were the masters of the seas, New York privateers—like their Boston and Philadelphia rivals—became merchants and began illegally to resupply the French sugar islands, then deprived of any contact with their home country. Of course commerce with the enemy was not without risks—the merchant Peter R. Livingston learned this expensive lesson in 1761, when his *Dove*, returning from the French islands, was inspected, seized and confiscated by the English navy, leading to its owner's ruin. But the hoped for, and sometimes realized, profits could be immense.

After 1763, once peace was reestablished by the Treaty of Paris, which sanctioned the transfer of Canada to Great Britain, New York became increasingly involved in the Revolution. It became one of the centers for colonial dissent in the 1760s and 1770s, conducted in the name of political and economic autonomy. Such principles ran counter to Great Britain's desire for imperial domination over its colonies and threatened its already shaky finances. London's 1764 decision to enforce an old law, which had never been put into practice, taxing the importation of molasses, and especially Parliament's adoption of the 1765 Stamp Act, imposing a stamp tax on all colonial publications, provoked the wrath of New Yorkers, the boldest of whom christened themselves the Sons of Liberty. By autumn, they mobilized, resulting in demonstrations and a riot during which the governor was hanged and burned in effigy. Soon London relented.

In 1767, New Yorkers protested new customs regulations by organizing a very widely adopted boycott of merchandise imported from Great Britain. Once again the British government reversed its decision, except with regard to tea. Three years later, in January 1770, six weeks before the first shots were fired in Boston, a skirmish dubbed "the battle of Golden Hill" set the New York Sons of Liberty, led by merchants Alexander McDougall and John Lamb, against the British garrison. The affair grew out of the resentment prompted by the obligation to accommodate soldiers possessing bills of lodging and was further provoked by the troops who pulled down the liberty poles (symbols of resistance to British authority) erected on Golden Hill. Tensions then subsided for some time, but resurfaced in April 1774 when a group of New Yorkers threw crates of English tea into the harbor, Boston-style.

In the spring of 1775, when the American Revolution broke out in New England, New York was deeply divided between loyalists and patriots. At the announcement of fighting in Lexington and Concord, the patriots rejoiced. Thousands of loyalists left the city over the months that followed, while the New Yorkers who remained issued increasingly impassioned proclamations and participated in ever more extensive military exercises.

Early in 1776, the Continental Army encamped in New York, fortified by General George Washington's and Major General Charles Lee's soldiers in anticipation of the English attacks to come. During the night of June 28–29, 1776, a hundred English vessels came to anchor in the bay. They formed the vanguard of an expeditionary corps of several hundred ships, with 10,000 sailors and 32,000 soldiers, who disembarked on Staten Island. On July 6, the news of the proclamation of American independence reached New York. Three days later, the text of the Declaration was read aloud there for the first time before an exultant crowd of soldiers and patriots, who celebrated the news by toppling a statue of George III on horseback

On August 22, 20,000 English and Hessian soldiers, under the command of General Howe, launched the attack. They disembarked at Gravesend Bay, on Brooklyn's southern shore, and advanced toward the East River. From August 26 to 29, Washington's approximately 7,000 soldiers tried to resist but failed. Less numerous, less experienced, the Americans were quickly overwhelmed and driven back to the East River. More than 2,000 of them were left behind on the battlefield. Risking an audacious maneuver, Washington managed to evacuate the others, who were transported silently by boat to New York during the night of August 28. Forced to relinquish the city, he retreated slowly across Manhattan over the course of September and October. Howe entered New York as early as September 15, but Washington's forces did not leave the island until November.

FIGURE 5
"The Destruction of the Royal Statue in New York": representation
of the July 9, 1776 episode, as conceived by a Parisian engraver
© Hachette Livre

Until 1783, New York was occupied by the British, who
made it their headquarters. Thus the city accommodated
a great number of loyalists. The war disrupted all the New
York commercial circuits, but it stimulated relations
between New York and Liverpool, London, Cork, and
Belfast. This reinforced a tendency already apparent in 1755,
when London had decided to make New York the destina-
tion of the postal brig that weighed anchor each month
from Falmouth. The Hudson port found itself in a privileged position regarding matters of political and economic
information, and it profited from the deterioration of
Boston's special relationship with England.

In this respect, the American victory concluding the
War of Independence marked only a temporary rupture.
After the English troops were evacuated and a triumphant
George Washington returned to New York on November
25, 1783, commercial ties with Great Britain ended for a

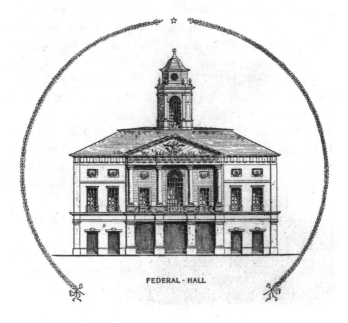

FEDERAL · HALL

FIGURE 6
Federal Hall, seat of the Congress (1789)
© Roger Viollet

time, but New York's preeminence over Boston was henceforth accepted—all the more so when the Continental Congress established itself on the shores of the Hudson in 1785.

Four years later, once the Federal Constitution was ratified, George Washington took the oath of office as President of the United States on the balcony of City Hall on April 30, 1789—Inauguration Day. The building was renamed Federal Hall and became the seat of the first Congress of the United States. New York was the official capital of the country, but the following year, under pressure from Thomas Jefferson, it lost this distinction to Philadelphia, which soon lost it to the new city of Washington.

New Yorkers quickly got over this disappointment. Commerce at the port regained its vitality beginning in 1790. Revolutionary wars were disrupting Europe, and the Americans, who had proclaimed their neutrality, reaped the rewards. Taking advantage of the forced immobilization of Europe's merchant fleets, New York ships rushed to ports in the Americas, Europe, and Asia. Growth in New York exportation doubled between 1792 and 1794, again between 1794 and 1797, and once more between 1797 and 1807: from 2.5 million dollars in 1792, it grew to more than 26 million in 1807! Foreign observers noticed; La Rochefoucauld-Liancourt, who visited New York in August 1797, remarked on the way in which the city "grew" and "became more beautiful with unprecedented speed." He attributed the phenomenon "in very great part to the immense profits that present circumstances in Europe made possible" for New York commerce "in the last two or three years."[14]

The Chinese market opened slightly in the 1780s, following the voyage of the *Empress of China*. This 360-ton three-master sailed from New York on February 22, 1784, reached Macao in August, departed from there four months later, and returned to New York the following May. The profits from the operation, estimated at a third of the initial outlay, drew shipowners' attention to China. Soon, New Yorkers were scurrying to Canton, in search of tea, cassia, nankeen, silk, and porcelain. In exchange, they worked hard to locate merchandise that might interest their Cantonese counterparts, like otter skins from the Northwest, seal skins from the southern seas, sandalwood from the Pacific islands, and the sea cucumbers that were favored in China. Otherwise, they would have had to pay in cash.

After 1807, Anglo-American tensions that culminated in the War of 1812 temporarily put an end to this prosperity, but when peace was restored in 1815, New York's commercial supremacy was even greater. On February 11, the city celebrated the announcement of the end of hostilities. New York, with its long tradition of auctions, welcomed English merchants who were eager to sell—as quickly as possible and at reduced price—their stocks of wool and cotton fabric that had accumulated during the war. To the sellers' dismay, the rapidly saturated market lowered prices, and buyers coming from other states greatly benefited. Bargains proliferated, and even more so after 1817, when a new law prohibited sellers from withdrawing their goods from auction when the prices offered seemed too low to them.

In the autumn of 1817, New York's place in transatlantic relations was further strengthened by the creation of a regular shipping line between Liverpool and New York, the Black Ball Line. Its owners, the American merchants Isaac and William Wright and their English associates Francis and Jeremiah Thompson and Benjamin Marshall, had the idea of ships sailing on a fixed schedule, without necessarily waiting for the holds to be full. Their first four packets, the *Amity*, the *Courier*, the *Pacific*, and the *James Monroe*, garnered the most time-sensitive cargo, such as cabin passengers and the mail: the *Courier* was to sail from Liverpool on January 1, 1818, and the *James Monroe* from New York on January 5. The success of these imaginative entrepreneurs—the Black Ball Line operated for sixty years, until 1878—transformed the crossing of the Atlantic into a slightly more predictable adventure than it had been in the past. This connection confirmed New York's preeminence in matters of news and information within America's emerging urban system.

Around 1800, New York had also staked a claim on the cotton export business, then in full expansion. The city sent manufactured products imported from Liverpool to the southern ports of Savannah and Charleston. In return, coastal fleets sent raw cotton, which was then loaded onto transatlantic vessels. The operation offered only advantages to New Yorkers. They were able to increase the volume of imports and especially of exports that passed through the port's quays; and they had access to enough freight to fill the holds of returning ships that had arrived loaded with immigrants or manufactured European products. At the same time, New Yorkers thus prevented the development of Southern coastal ports, which abandoned their direct ties to Le Havre and Liverpool, and saw their dependence increase.

This commercial vitality was accompanied by the expansion of local manufacturing and craft industries. In existence since the 1640s, the artisanal sector primarily satisfied local demand. New Amsterdam, and then New York, counted among its many skilled workers carpenters and blacksmiths, masons and tailors, cobblers and bricklayers, bakers, harness and saddle makers. The commercial links that New York merchants maintained with the sugar islands even led some of them to invest capital in sugar refineries. John Van Cortlandt and Peter Livingston entered into such a venture, Nicolas Bayard owned a large refinery on Wall Street in 1730, and William Rhinelander founded the famous Rhinelander's Sugar House.

By the late seventeenth century, New York also boasted a number of skilled artisans, who produced fine work to respond to the demands of the ever wealthier urban elite as well as the sugar island planters and the Southern colonies. For example, members of the Huguenot dynasty of Le Roux became famous silversmiths: Bar-thélemy (1663–1713), who settled in New York beginning in 1687, and his sons John and especially Charles (1689– 1745), silversmith for the municipal council from 1720 to 1743.

The craft sector changed scale beginning in the mid-eighteenth century. Its reorganization, varying according to the craft, extended over more than a century. The first signs of a change appeared when certain New York artisans—cobblers, cabinetmakers, and tailors—began to produce goods for the markets of the Southern colonies and the sugar islands. Other occupations, especially those associated with the building trade, were transformed as the city grew. For all these occupations, the workshops were always directed by a master, who was assisted by a few journeymen and apprentices. The same was true for occupations that hardly evolved at all, such as butchering, baking, and all the specialized trades involved in shipbuilding, such as framing and sail making.

Certain craft enterprises gradually expanded, so that by 1820, a few New York firms counted more than twenty-five employees—not a negligible size for that period. In these manufacturing shops, increased production and division of labor brought traditional practices into question. Some master craftsmen became real entrepreneurs. One of the most famous was the cabinetmaker Duncan Phyfe. Scottish by origin, he grew rich thanks to his neoclassical-style furniture, which, beginning in 1800, met with great success. His example was imitated—with mixed results—by numerous carpenters, cabinetmakers, gilders, engravers, and upholsterers, who created luxury furniture intended for the New York elite and Southern plantation owners, as well as standard products more widely distributed to the West Indies, Latin America and the towns and rural areas of the United States.

In shipbuilding, where, despite strong growth, traditional production methods remained intact, a master sail maker like Stephen Allen, who became mayor of New York in 1821, or a builder like Noah Brown, directed major enterprises that could no longer be called craft workshops. At the end of the eighteenth century, master artisans, journeymen, and apprentices constituted nearly half the workforce of New York. They formed "one of the firmest pillars of our social Edifice," proclaimed the master baker Thomas Mercein in 1821.[15]

The regional context also changed. Even while overtaking Boston by the mid-eighteenth century, New York remained behind Philadelphia until the 1790s, because of differences in the lands surrounding the two cities. Between 1740 and 1780, the population of Pennsylvania grew from 52,000 to 327,000 inhabitants, while provincial New York's population experienced weaker growth, from 49,000 to 211,000 inhabitants. Nevertheless, the New York region gradually expanded. Waves of British immigrants, many of whom were Scottish, arrived after 1760. With this boost, the colony's population grew nearly 40 percent in the 1760s and 30 percent in the 1770s. Between December 1773 and March 1776, for example, forty-two ships filled with immigrants arrived in New York.

At the same time, the French threat had subsided, and clever speculators negotiated with the Iroquois for lands north of the Mohawk Valley around Lake Champlain, as well as to the west of the Hudson Valley. Some were New York merchants, like Lawrence Kortright; others were English, like John Wetherhead. One of the most imposing figures was William Johnson, the longtime intermediary between the Amerindians and the British, who carved out a kingdom for himself in the Mohawk Valley and took advantage of his position as privileged representative to conduct profitable land negotiations with the Amerindians.

In 1779, the Iroquois decision to support the English against the colonies during the War of Independence prompted an American expedition commanded by James Clinton and John Sullivan to ravage the Iroquois country, for the greatest profit of later land speculators. When peace was restored, the Iroquois were forced to sign a series of treaties over the course of the 1780s. They ceded almost all their lands to the State of New York before withdrawing to Canada or the reservations granted to them. This cleared the way for colonization and land speculation. Between 1790 and 1820, the population of New York State quadrupled, growing from some 340,000 to nearly 1.4 million inhabitants.

This growth found its historic symbol in the November 1825 opening of a canal linking Lake Erie, at Buffalo, with the Hudson Valley, at Troy, north of Albany. The idea had been in the air a long time when the mayor of New York, DeWitt Clinton, took up the cause himself around 1810. This huge project, quickly nicknamed "Clinton's Ditch" by contemporary critics, gave his city access to western markets. An untiring promoter, Clinton obtained consent from the state legislature in 1817. Work began in the month of July, three days after Clinton took office as state governor. It lasted eight years. According to an anonymous author of a guide intended for French travelers, the canal "will have no equal in the world" and "will render the lakes and forests beyond, even in upper Canada and Pennsylvania, dependent on this magnificent port."[16]

Digging a 363-mile canal was a major technical feat: eighty-three locks had to be constructed, as well as an aqueduct to cross the Genesee River at Rochester, and a mountain near Lake Erie had to be cut through. The central section, the easiest to dig, was completed in 1820. In October 1823, the canal already linked Rochester to Albany. Two years later, it reached Lake Erie.

The canal was then inaugurated in grand style. On October 26, 1825, the canal boat *Seneca Chief* left Buffalo amidst great ceremony and entered the new canal. Greeted with cheers, it soon passed Rochester, Syracuse,

FIGURE 7
Erie Canal Celebration, 1825
Anthony Imbert. Museum of the City of New York

Rome, Utica, Schenectady, and finally Albany, before going down the Hudson to drop anchor at the tip of Manhattan, in the middle of a flotilla of boats decked with flags. On November 4, 1825, with Governor Clinton aboard, the *Seneca Chief* and its escort of schooners, harbor vessels, and small boats reached the ocean. There, Clinton solemnly poured into the Atlantic a small cask of water the *Seneca Chief* had carried from the Great Lakes, and proclaimed the Erie Canal open. The new Venice, New York's union with the ocean and the interior of the continent was symbolically sealed.

New York now dominated America's new urban system, thanks to its essential role in commercial relations and its access to information. Again, observers of the time took notice. From 1790 to 1820, predictions of the city's glorious future multiplied. It was an impression shared generally, in Boston, Philadelphia, and Europe. "Of all the cities on the continent, New York is the one called by its position to the greatest destiny," La Rochefoucauld-

Liancourt declared. Although Philadelphia probably tried to catch up to its rival during the years that followed, its development was relatively slow, due to structural reasons, apparently, and not only economic ones. "New York has been the commercial center of the United States for a long time and over many years," another visitor noted.

New Yorkers had much to say themselves, of course. "That city," prophesied the eloquent DeWitt Clinton, "will in the course of time become the granary of the world, the emporium of commerce, the seat of manufactures, the focus of great monied operations, and the concentrating point of vast, disposable, and accumulating capitals which will stimulate, enliven, extend, and reward the exertions of human labour and ingenuity, in all their processes and exhibitions."[17]

2

THE COMMENCEMENT OF A TOWN

In the autumn of 1825, New York celebrated. The inauguration of the Erie Canal gave rise to an impressive ceremony. The newspapers of the day and the official chroniclers outdid one another in describing the parade of ships and the "Grand Procession" that attracted tens of thousands of spectators from the Battery to the Bowery. More than seven thousand people marched for the occasion. First came the guilds, masters, journeymen, and apprentices lined up behind their banners: printers, tailors, coopers, wool combers, hat makers, bakers. . . . The merchants and barristers marched behind them, then the carters and butchers, the fire companies, local militia units, and the city guard. If some New Yorkers were not represented in the celebration, which was largely dominated by the white, male population, everyone was probably willing to recognize that the splendor displayed before their eyes symbolized the greatness of their city.

EARLY STAGES

Such public acclamation would have seemed laughable two centuries earlier when New York was still New Amsterdam. At that time, only its name evoked the splendors of the European metropolis on the shores of the Amstel River. The anchorage chosen by the Dutch at the tip of

Manhattan was hardly a village, just the start of a fortification surrounded by a few huts.

The earliest surviving accounts, dating from 1626 and 1628, emphasize Fort Amsterdam's mediocrity, in addition to its unfinished state. Four earthen bulwarks topped by bare fence boards sheltered the colony director's quarters and the precious stores of provisions, merchandise, and furs that were the reason for the settlement. Near the fort stood a stone structure meant to accommodate transactions for employees of the West India Company: about thirty bark houses covered with cut reeds, a mill, the first floor of which served as a place for worship, and a few farms. No concern for planning governed the first buildings, despite the orders received by the Dutch engineer Cryn Fredericks. In short, the prophetic judgment issued in 1628 by the Reverend Johannes Michaelius seemed very optimistic in perceiving Manhattan Island as "the key and principal stronghold of the country."[1]

The capital of New Netherland hardly changed over the course of the 1630s, even though a Dutch reformed church was erected in the fort and a few more solid houses were built for some artisans. The island began to be urbanized after the West India Company decided—or was forced—to relinquish its various monopolies. In 1643, Father Isaac Jogues, a Jesuit missionary passing through New Amsterdam after being released from captivity by the Mohawks, thought he observed there the "commencement of a town."[2] This "commencement" was confirmed thanks to the initiatives of New Netherland's last director-general, Peter Stuyvesant (from 1647 to 1664), his English successors, and New Yorkers themselves.

Early on, the colony was administered in a discretionary manner by the director-general, assisted by two Company officials and a council of nine members, whom the director-general appointed and dismissed as he pleased. The director-general, who governed by decree, held both executive and judicial powers without concern for a code of law. But in the 1640s, economic growth and social diversification—as well as the emergence of villages on Long Island inhabited by colonists from England and New England who were very attached to the political model of the town meeting—led to a demand for municipal autonomy within the colony that had been inconceivable fifteen years earlier. From then on, certain colonists rebelled against a system of government they considered intolerable, and demanded that the Company change it.

Their wishes were granted in 1653. Against his will, the imperious Stuyvesant, nicknamed "the Grand Duke of Muscovy" by one of his enemies, received instructions to grant New Amsterdam a charter establishing a town body composed of two burgomasters, five aldermen, and a sheriff. All were appointed or dismissed by the director-general, who fully intended to retain and exercise his authority, but henceforth he had to reckon with this municipal counterforce, despite its uncertain and fragile nature.

After the English conquest, the existence of a municipality was confirmed in the charter granted in 1665 by Governor Nicolls. The new "corporation of the city of New York"—that is, "the mayor, aldermen and citizens"—saw its function and the nature of its authority adapted and clarified by many successive charters that bore the names of governors Dongan (1686), Cornbury (1708), and Montgomerie (1731). Until the end of the colonial era, except for a period of insurrection in 1689–91, the mayor of New York was appointed each year by the governor of the colony. Beginning with the Dongan Charter, New York was divided into six districts or wards (five inner wards: South, North, East, West, Dock, plus an Out Ward), where the electors (the bourgeoisie or freemen) chose the alderman and assistant alderman each year who would represent them in the municipal council. The 1731 charter created a seventh district that was named after Governor Montgomerie.

The development of a municipal institution carried over into the urban landscape. New Amsterdams's oldest tavern was turned into a town hall in 1653. Half a century later, between 1699 and 1704, a new municipal building was constructed in the English style in the center of a district then undergoing full expansion: Wall Street. That was also where the province's assembly met, elected for the first time in 1691 by the colony's twelve counties. The governor himself resided at the tip of Manhattan, in the middle of a garrison, in the fort renamed successively throughout the colonial era for King James, King William, Queen Anne and King George.

Under the supervision of the governors, New York's mayors and aldermen—and in the eighteenth century, members of the provincial assembly as well—looked after policing the city and regulating its economic life. At Stuyvesant's instigation, New Amsterdam protected itself against possible incursions by building a wall that barricaded the island from the Hudson to the East River and gave Wall Street its name. Stuyvesant also had Fort Amsterdam repaired, which he had described dryly as a "molehill" in 1647. In the late 1640s, to protect against fires, the authorities established a watch maintained voluntarily by city inhabitants and then by paid watchmen. About 1730, this protection seemed insufficient. The city acquired fire engines, and the provincial assembly provided it with thirty volunteer firemen. To protect property and individuals, a militia was also created in the 1640s. At the end of the century, the streets began to be lit at night.

The aldermen decided the price of bread and regulated how the markets operated in the city. They also tried to restrict pigs and other animals from roaming untethered—Manhattan counted at least a thousand dogs about 1750, according to an exasperated correspondent for the *Independent Reflector*, who considered them "truly noxious."[3] They acted to reduce the pollution resulting from cottage or craft industries like tanning or slaughtering cattle, and, after 1675, arranged for the weekly collection of trash.

The visual aspect of the town also changed beginning in the 1640s. New Amsterdam began to resemble a Dutch town. A canal, dug in 1654 and spanned by three wooden bridges, called to mind the Dutch metropolis. So did the gabled brick facades and the red and black tile roofs of the high, narrow houses that New Amsterdam inhabitants had built. In 1660, a remarkable map, prepared by the colony's surveyor, Jacques Cortelyou, registered the extent of the transformation that had taken place in a quarter century.

In 1670, a few years after the English conquest, New York was, according to John Ogilby, "compact and oval, with very fair Streets and several good Houses; the rest are built much after the manner of Holland, to the number of about four hundred Houses, which in those parts are held considerable."[4] In the mid-eighteenth century, according to Thomas Pownall, again, it had "the general appearance of a Dutch town."[5] But it had grown considerably. From about 1,500 inhabitants in 1664, its population grew to some 5,000 by 1700, 7,200 in 1720, 11,000 in 1740, and 13,000 in 1750. This eightfold increase in the number of New Yorkers in less than a century led to an expanded area of habitation and a higher population density in the old districts. In 1676, the canal was filled in; in 1689, the wall of the Dutch town was dismantled.

More spectacular was the emergence of an "English style," first noted by visitors at the end of the seventeenth century. In 1698, a doctor from Boston, Benjamin Bullivant, admired the brand new Anglican church, Trinity, "of good brown square stone and brick, exactly English fashion." The wealthiest merchants had beautiful "English style" houses built in the new districts, along the East River and north of the Dutch village. More attentive to architectural crossbreeding, Sarah Kemble Knight, another visitor from Boston, noted in December 1704 that the brick buildings, even though "very stately and high," were in fact "not altogether like ours in Boston. The Bricks in some of the Houses are of divers Coullers and are laid in Checkers, being glazed look very agreeable."[6]

TOWARD NEW HEIGHTS

Beginning in the mid-eighteenth century, New York's development accelerated. In seventy years, its population increased almost tenfold. From 13,000 inhabitants in 1750, it rose to 22,000 in 1770, 33,000 in 1790, 60,000 in 1800, 90,000 in 1810, and 123,000 in 1820. Thus, in the first years of the nineteenth century, New York became the largest city and the largest American port.

Beyond its three original axes—Broadway, Chatham Street, and the Bowery—New York extended along the East

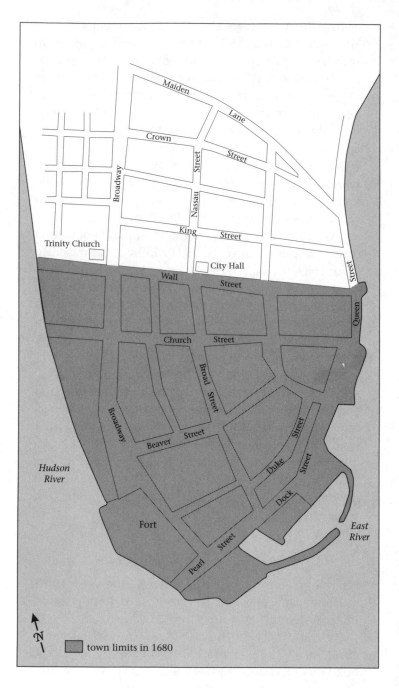

MAP 3

New York in the early eighteenth century

River. It reached Grand Street and Corlear's Hook shortly after 1800, and, to the west, Canal Street. In the early nineteenth century, it experienced a spectacular boom with the development of the area located between the town hall, Greenwich Street, Broadway. and the Bowery. To the northwest, the city reached almost as far as Fourteenth Street.

This expansion paid off. During these decades, landownership became subject to speculation. The territory north of the inhabited zone belonged to large landowners who had received it from the Dutch West India Company and English governors anxious to reward their local supporters. Since the Dongan Charter of 1686, the corporation of the city of New York held the remaining unused lands. The large landowners built beautiful country homes on their estates, modestly called "farms." Manhattan counted nearly 140 of these in the late 1760s. These properties, which were one of the most visible signs of the New York elite's wealth and social pretensions, won the admiration of La Rochefoucauld-Liancourt: "The island is covered with country houses belonging to the rich inhabitants of New York, and the closer to the city, the more beautiful and more numerous they are," noted the French aristocrat in 1795, who particularly appreciated "the lovely country house of Colonel Burr," then senator and soon to be vice president of the United States.[7] Greenwich, the property of Admiral Peter Warren, Bloomingdale, Oliver De Lancey's retreat, and many others lined routes along the Hudson.

Now these large landowners set about increasing the value of their lands by dividing them into lots meant to be leased. In the 1750s, the Trinity Church wardens put lands on the market that the parish had acquired through the munificence of Queen Anne and the municipal corporation. Hundreds of parcels were rented as long-term leases: lessees had the right to build there, and they owned those buildings, which they could then, in turn, put on the rental market. A three-level system was thus established in Manhattan, with the owners of the land, the owners of the buildings who were themselves lessees of the land, and the renters of the buildings. Land and property speculation developed, insuring that few of the ever-growing number of New Yorkers would own property. Between 1790 and

1814, moreover, the proportion of renters in the electoral body grew from half to three quarters.

During the Revolution, in the years of English and loyalist occupation, New York experienced two tragic fires. The first, on September 21, 1776 and six days after General Howe's English troops entered, led to the destruction of nearly 500 homes, a third of the city. The second, in August 1778, affected a neighborhood near the East River and destroyed some sixty buildings.

When peace was restored, reconstruction began. The city at the end of the century offered an astonishing spectacle. In 1794, a newly arrived Scottish immigrant commented that New York "made a very poor appearance from the water as the stores were all built of wood."[8] Enlightened observer that he was, La Rochefoucauld-Liancourt described it more favorably: "The old city had been built without any regular plan. Thus, in the nearby district that had to be rebuilt due to fire, all the streets are small and crooked. The sidewalks are very narrow or sometimes nonexistent and are further reduced by the cellar doors and steps of houses that take up the greater part of them and make it very inconvenient for walkers trying to use them. A few beautiful brick houses are found in the narrow streets, but a greater number of eyesores, built of wood, partly or entirely, small, low, many of them still bearing the mark of Dutch taste. The new part, near the North River and running parallel to its course, is infinitely more beautiful. The streets are generally straight, wide, intersecting at right angles, and the houses there are much better built. There may not be a more beautiful street than Broadway in any city in the world. It runs nearly a mile and must be made longer still. It is more than a hundred feet wide, and the same width everywhere. Most of the houses there are brick, and many of them are extremely beautiful. Its elevated position, its location near the North River, and the beauty of its size make it the most sought after area for the wealthiest residents."[9]

The war and New York's military role led to the construction of a new system of fortifications. The ease with

FIGURE 8
The New York fire (September 1776)
© Hachette Livre

which the English took over New York in 1776 exposed
the weaknesses of the old defense system. In 1789, Fort
George, located at the Fort Amsterdam site on the tip of
Manhattan, was razed with no protest. In its place the
Government House was built, designed to accommodate
the president of the United States during those years
when New York was the temporary capital of the young
nation. After the transfer of federal power to Philadelphia
in 1790, it served as the seat of the New York State
government until its removal to Albany in 1796. The end
of the island was transformed into a promenade; "known
as the Battery," it was very popular. The bourgeoisie
appeared there in the daytime, so pleasant was the place
and "beyond all compare with any other promenade
whatsoever." When night fell, prostitutes and their clients
took it over.[10] The Anglo-American tensions after 1800

that culminated with the 1812–15 war led to the construction of a new fort in Manhattan: the West Battery,
linked to the island by a wooden footbridge, and to the
additional construction of Forts Wood, William and Gib-
son, located on different islands in the bay.

Because of its growth, New York was forced to
strengthen its infrastructures. New docks were built in
1750, city lighting was improved, a new prison erected.
The Manhattan Company, created in 1799, put into operation a water system that had been planned before the
War of Independence. Most importantly, a huge number
of buildings were constructed, burned-down structures
restored, and new streets opened. New York counted
about fifty streets in the eighteenth century, more than a
hundred at the beginning of the Revolution, nearly 150
in 1800, and about 230 in 1820.

As in the past, some of these buildings served as places
of work and residence. Workshops or shops, warehouses
or houses, they had one or two stories at the most. Usually the facade opening onto the street was brick, while
the other walls were wood. Only the well-to-do New
Yorkers could afford building entirely in brick. Their roofs
were frequently tile or even slate, which replaced the
wooden shingles of the previous century.

Beginning in 1780, lower Manhattan began to be
divided into commercial streets—where stores and offices
were concentrated—and residential streets. After the
destruction of Fort George, Bowling Green became a fashionable spot. Rich New Yorkers settled there in modern
family homes that testified to a private sphere just beginning to take shape. "In the vicinity of the Battery, and for
some distance up Broadway," observed the Englishman
John Lambert in his 1808 travel notes, "they are nearly all
private houses, and occupied by the principal merchants
and gentry of New York."[11]

At best, less affluent and prominent New Yorkers lived
in houses like the ones that sprang up on the land belonging to Trinity Church. Others rented a room or a bed in a
boardinghouse, or with some individual anxious to
increase his income.

FIGURE 9
New York street scene during winter 1809
Baroness Hyde de Neuville. Museum of the City of New York

In 1811, the Common Council finalized a coherent development plan for New York. For thirty years, it had been surveying the lands lying north of the expanding city. Maps made by Casimir Goerck in 1785 and 1796 provided an orthogonal grid of streets dividing the municipal lands from east to west and from north to south. But in 1806, it was the whole island of Manhattan, and not just the city's domain, that the Common Council planned to survey. To avoid accusations of conflicts of interest, help was requested from the state legislature. On April 3, 1807, a statute entrusted to three commissioners— Gouverneur Morris, Simeon DeWitt, and John Rutherford—the responsibility and the "exclusive power to plan streets, roads and public places." Over the years that followed, the three commissioners and their secretary, John Randel, a surveyor, chose a rectangular plan that they submitted to the city in 1811.

The Commissioners' Plan took into consideration almost the entire thirteen miles that Manhattan measured from south to north, and not just the one or two already inhabited miles. The old city was left unchanged, but north of Houston Street on the east side, from Eighth Street to the central north, and from all of Fourteenth Street to the north, the lands were carved into rectangular islands marked off by twelve vertical avenues and 152 horizontal streets. Each block measured about 200 by 800 feet, and was itself divided into 50–70 lots, 25 by 100 feet. The commissioners planned for the construction of a reservoir for city water, a market, and a few squares, but no parks.

The 1811 plan marked a turning point in New York's history, and not only because it "striated" the "granite rock" of Manhattan "lengthwise" and "crosswise" and facilitated the numbering of the streets. "The avenue in the middle, Fifth Avenue," noted Le Corbusier in the 1930s, "serves as a spinal column for this gigantic sole. On one side, it is west, on the other east. The first street is at the south, on the ocean side, the last one is at the north, on the land side. Everything is ordered accordingly."[12] In fact, the pattern of development that the plan imposed testified to the changes the city had undergone since the mid-eighteenth century and the speculative ambitions that the commissioners encouraged. According to the surveyor John Randel, the great merit of the plan lay in the "ease it allows in buying, selling and making a profit from" real estate on Manhattan. It broke with the past with regard to the development of the road system. Until then, the opening of new streets had been a function of building projects; henceforth, the street pattern governed future operations. But this plan was not only a means for speculation. The grid imposed on Manhattan embodied the declared simplicity and equitable neutrality of the city's property policy. Its goal was to reconcile the contradictory principles of republican egalitarianism and speculative liberalism.

THE URBAN MELTING POT

In its own way, the 1811 plan testified to the breadth of social change that New York had experienced in less than two centuries. Until the 1640s, New Amsterdam's development was too halting for any real social organization to take root there. Aside from the successive directors of

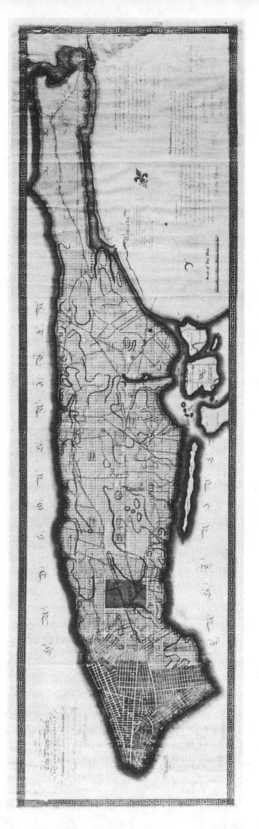

FIGURE 10

The Commissioners' Plan: The City of New York and Island of Manhattan, 1811
Museum of the City of New York

the New Netherland colony—Cornelius Jacobson May in 1624–25, Willem Verhulst in 1625–26, Peter Minuit from 1626 to 1631, Bastiaen Jansen Krol in 1632–33, Wouter Van Twiller from 1633 to 1637, and Willem Kieft from 1638 to 1645—the elite comprised only a small number of colonists. These included the director's legal adviser; the secretary of the colony, responsible for recording official acts; the council members whom the director could appoint or dismiss; and the pastor of the Dutch reformed church. Certain officials had vivid personalities and made their mark in the colony: Jean Mousier de la Montagnie, more popularly called Johannes La Montagne, a French Protestant who emigrated to the United Provinces and studied medicine in Leiden before visiting New Netherland in 1624 and settling in New Amsterdam in 1637; or the successive pastors of the Dutch reformed church, beginning in 1628 with Johannes Michaelius and Everardus Bogardus.

Thus New Amsterdam was no more than a village. Its population of 300 in 1630, growing to 500 fifteen years later, was employed by the Company—artisans, farmers, or sailors who had much in common, beginning with their life on the colonial frontier. In 1628, Reverend Michaelius judged them to be "for the most part, rather rough and unrestrained."[13]

Legal suits were common in New Amsterdam, both in the civil and the criminal courts. The disputes were often over unpaid debts, slander, or acts of violence. Some figures appeared regularly at court, or rather, at the tribunal, before the director general assisted by his adviser, who took the bench each Thursday. In the late 1630s, a certain Anthony Jansen, nicknamed "the Turk," was the talk of the local judiciary. The illegitimate son of a "Muhammedan" woman and a Dutch pirate who had been the admiral of the sultan's fleet before settling in the Moroccan port of Salé, Jansen, having only just arrived in New Amsterdam, figured as accuser or accused in numerous affairs. In 1639, when this fanatical litigant finally started attacking the Company itself and not just private individuals, he was immediately banished from the colony.

Beginning in the 1640s, economic growth was accom-

panied by social stratification, which became more pronounced after the 1664 conquest. For a long time, New
York was a small town where inhabitants knew each
other by sight and often ran into each other on the narrow streets. But geographical proximity is not the same as
social proximity. New York society was divided vertically
into what were then commonly called "the better sort,"
"the middling sort," and "the lower sort," according to a
hierarchy not always granted the absolute respect that
the elite would have advocated.

On the lowest rung were the slaves. New Netherland
was a slave colony from the late 1620s on, and in the
eighteenth century, the province of New York was the
English colony containing the most slaves outside of the
West Indies and the South. The first African slaves arrived
in New Amsterdam as early as 1626. Over the course of
the following decade, their number remained low,
because the Company had no clearly defined policy with
regard to slaves, even if slave ships sometimes came to
anchor in the port, such as the French privateer ship *La
Garce* in 1642.

Most of the slaves worked for the Company as laborers,
roadworkers assigned to building roads or erecting fortifications, or even farmhands. In 1639, Jacob Stoffelsen testified that he was "steadily employed in the Co's service as
overseer for the negroes belonging to the Company, the
said negroes in building Fort Amsterdam, which was completed in the year 1635, also in cutting timber and fire-
wood for the Large House as well as the guardroom, split-
ting palisades, clearing land, burning lime and helping to
bring in the grain in harvest time, together with many
other labors, which we have done with the Negroes."[14]
These men and women lived in an area called "the slaves'"
district, located to the north, near the present City Hall. In
the 1640s, other slaves belonged to individuals, or were
leased to them by the Company, along with the farms
where they worked.

After 1654, the loss of Brazil by the Dutch led the Company to change its slave policy. The slave trade thus served
as a partial remedy for its perpetual financial problems.
Curaçao, also governed, like New Netherland, by Stuyvesant,

became an important slave entrepôt, and New Amsterdam, which did not trade directly with Africa, was transformed into a slave market thanks to its connections with Curaçao and the sugar islands. Between 1654 and 1664, many slave ships belonging to the Company or to private shipowners came to New Amsterdam to unload their human cargo, often arriving from southeast Africa and Madagascar and bound for the Dutch colony or occasionally for the neighboring English colonies. Instructions from the Company dated April 11, 1661, informed Stuyvesant that "we have resolved not only that Slaves shall be kept in New Netherland, as we have heretofore ordered, but be moreover exported to the English and other Neighbors."[15] Henceforth they were imported in huge numbers. In 1655, 300 slaves disembarked from the *Witte Paert*, that is, 20 percent of the city's total population. On August 15, 1664, just two weeks before New Amsterdam fell, the *Gideon* arrived with a cargo of 290 surviving slaves out of the total of 300 who had embarked.

As the slave trade developed, owning slaves became commonplace in the city. Among the slave owners were a butcher, some innkeepers, bargemen, and even a wood turner, and their ranks increased as the number of available slaves grew. In the public sales, beaver pelts—or provisions inpelt equivalents—were bartered for slaves, greatly profiting Augustine Heermans, Cornelis Steenwyck, and later, Frederick Philipse, and other slave traders.

The proportion of slave labor in the population increased again in the early eighteenth century, under the aegis of the Royal African Company, a monopoly created in 1672. In 1665, New York had 120 slaves; it had 960 in 1712. From 1710 to 1730, one out of five New Yorkers was a slave, employed as a docker or in the port warehouses, a town house servant, or a farmhand on Staten Island, Long Island or in upstate Westchester. This strong presence of slaves, who came primarily from West Africa and landed first in the West Indies, greatly distinguished New York from Boston or Philadelphia, and made it more like Charleston, in Carolina, or Kingston, in Jamaica.

After 1730, economic troubles, artisans' hostility toward competition from slaves, the fear of possible revolts, and the rise in European immigration led to decreased reliance on male slave labor. The proportion of slaves in New York's population fell from 20 percent in 1730 to 7.4 percent in 1790. Unlike the situation in the past, these were not men but mostly women and children.

Some slaves, in particular servants and those employed in the craft industry, worked and lived in the homes of their masters, who usually owned two or three slaves. Men and women were not allowed to live together or to start families, but they managed to visit with each other and, despite restrictions, did their best to form social networks. Between 1677 and 1730, fearing a revolt because of the high number of the slaves, officials adopted several laws and judicial decisions meant to reinforce their authority.

Overall, these measures were effective, since the slaves very seldom revolted. In April 1712, a small number attempted an uprising, burning a few buildings, killing eight whites, and seriously injuring several others. The immediate suppression resulted in the execution of nineteen slaves and stronger restrictive measures. A second incident in 1741 was more mysterious. Dozens of black slaves were accused of plotting and starting several fires in Manhattan. Despite the lack of evidence, following a sensational trial, thirty slaves were condemned to death and executed, as well as four whites accused of aiding them, and seventy-two slaves were deported from the colony.

During the War of Independence, the slaves joined both sides, in exchange for promises of freedom. In fact, in 1781, the State of New York freed all the slaves serving in its units. After independence was achieved, an abolitionist movement arose, but freeing slaves was a slow business. Abolitionists of the New York Manumission Society obtained the prohibition of the slave trade in New York and the limitation to nine months of residence for out-of-state slaves. But Aaron Burr's proposal for immediate emancipation was quickly rejected. In 1799, a new law provided for the progressive emancipation of slaves: immediate for children, attained at the age of twenty-five for women, and at twenty-eight for men born before July 4, 1799. In 1817, another text provided for the emancipation of slaves starting from July 4, 1827, excluding those born between 1799 and 1827, who continued to fall under the 1799 law.

At the same time, a community of free African-Americans emerged. In 1790, they constituted less than a third of the 3,470 New York blacks, but made up 55 percent of the total ten years later, 83 percent in 1810, and 95 percent of the 10,886 blacks in New York in 1820. They quickly established their own churches, such as the African Methodist Episcopal Zion Church in the late eighteenth century, the Abyssinian Baptist Church in 1808, and the African Methodist Episcopal Wesleyan Church in Brooklyn in 1812. Mutual aid and insurance associations also multiplied, as well as African-American schools and literary societies.

One rung higher on the social ladder were the least respected white New Yorkers, those the texts of the time characterized as the "lower" or "inferior sort," or even the "rabble" or the "mob" in times of popular unrest. These were the humble folk of the port and the city, the indentured servants who had sold their labor to an employer for a period of four to seven years in exchange for the price of the transatlantic voyage—the apprentices, servants, unskilled laborers, and dockworkers, as well as the many sailors and soldiers stationed or stopping over in New York. With the slaves, they formed between a third and a half of the urban labor force. The port provided a livelihood for hundreds of sailors and dockers, while the city supported its street pavers, its water, wood and sand carriers, and its cartmen, not to mention the apprentices in the craft workshops and the numerous servants.

The line between this group and the skilled workers a step above them on the social ladder was not always clear. The cartmen, for example, whose bad reputation in New York in the years between 1650 and 1820 was well established, belonged to a guild and had to obtain municipal authorization in order to practice their trade. No doubt some of them were considered part of the "middling sort," the intermediate strata of New York society. Most of the artisans making up this group worked for themselves in the workshops that were rarely separate from their homes, and they represented almost half the city's labor force. They numbered about 4,000 in 1790, 10,000 in 1810, and 14,000 in 1820, representing the various building, clothing, furniture, decoration, shipbuilding, and printing trades.

Their political significance began to grow in the mid-eighteenth century. Greatly affected by the depression in the 1760s, they quickly formed the backbone of the resistance movements then developing against the British imperialist policy. The Sons of Liberty were, for the most part, artisans, as were the New Yorkers who won renown at Golden Hill in 1770.

In the days following the Revolution, they had considerable political clout. They first supported the Federalists and then, after 1796, the Republican Democrats, whose electoral victories they secured over the years. Most importantly, they defended a patriotic and egalitarian ideal of republican virtue. Thus, during the War of 1812, the artisans provided the city with about 100,000 hours of free work to build new fortifications. They arrived at the building sites in processions organized by trade and led by brass bands and banners. For example, "Free trade and Butchers' rights, from Brooklyn's fields to Harlem's heights," proclaimed the banner of the New York butchers.[16]

At the top of the social ladder clustered the elite, who possessed money, power, and learning. Ministers, doctors and colonial administrators were often respected, but rarely very powerful. They were scarce in New Amsterdam in 1645–64. Reverend Johannes Megapolensis, pastor of the reformed Dutch church of New Amsterdam from 1649 until his death in 1670, was one of rare influential figures from that group.

In fact, New Netherland was dominated by the strong personality of the director-general, Peter Stuyvesant. Son of a minister, Stuyvesant (1610–72) spent his whole career serving the Company. Originally an accountant's assistant, he was soon made a supercargo by the Company, charged with accompanying ship captains, serving as their business assistant as well as discreetly keeping an eye on them. This position of trust took him to Brazil in 1635 and then to Curaçao in 1638, where he became governor. Seriously wounded in 1644 when he tried to recapture the island of Saint-Martin from the Spaniards, he survived the amputation of his right leg and returned to the United Provinces. There he was fitted with the wooden leg that won him a place in popular engravings. Chosen as director-general of New Netherland in May 1645, his appointment was confirmed a year later, and he arrived in New Amsterdam in May 1647 to begin a mandate of seventeen years, the longest in the entire colonial history of New York.

Stuyvesant's English successors were less prominent figures. Personality was no doubt a factor, but so was the emergence of the local elite who, in 1765, included "First the Proprietors of the large Tracts of land," then "The Gentlemen of the Law," and finally, "The Merchants."[17] In reality, these three circles were only one, composed of the same families—Philipse, Beekman, Van Cortlandt, De Lancey, De Peyster, Bayard and others—throughout the colonial period.

Certain dynasties arose in the Dutch period, and their founders began modestly. The first Van Cortlandt had been a soldier for the Company before becoming a brewer and then a merchant. The first Livingston was an accountant. Vledrick Flypsen was a master carpenter; he married a rich widow with extraordinary commercial talents, Margaret Hardenbroeke De Vries, and, thanks to this fortunate union and his own talents, became a wealthy businessman. An examination of the lists of passengers aboard ships leaving for New Amsterdam between 1657 and 1664 reveals that out of 900 emigrants, one third were farmers, 28 percent soldiers and 25 percent artisans, contrary to the long-held view that most emigrants were members of the merchant class in the United Provinces. Flipsen was the son of an artisan, and Philip Schuyler, who settled in New Netherland in 1650 and quickly made a fortune, was the son of a baker.

The English conquest diversified the elite class. There continued to be many Dutch in this group. They quickly anglicized their names, turned the support of successive English governors to their profit, and made their fortunes by establishing successful trade relations with London. Many others were English, Scottish, French, or German in origin. The circle was very open: in 1768–69; 45 percent of the members of the newly founded New York Chamber of Commerce came from the colony's commercial and landed aristocracy, but 30 to 40 percent were new arrivals. Expanding commercial speculation and land investments, they all vitalized the political life of the colony, which was soon divided into aristocratic factions.

Circumstances prompted some of them to become interested in the law. If the men of law were looked down upon in the late seventeenth century, their image soon changed as needs increased. Law quickly became an acceptable and profitable career for a "gentleman." The New York bar was founded in 1748, and the profession counted among its ranks such distinguished figures as William Livingston, and, after the Revolution, Aaron Burr, Alexander Hamilton, and John Jay—not to mention the great lawyer James Kent, who endeavored to improve the training of those aspiring to the legal profession.

Landowners, merchants, and lawyers adopted aristocratic behavior, the first signs of which did not escape Francis Lovelace, who, in 1688, recognized in the wealthiest New Yorkers "the manners of court." In the 1750s, William Livingston compared the "Method of living" of his times to the frugality of his ancestors. His contemporary William Smith, the first historian of the province of New York, was also perceptive: "through our intercourse with Europeans, we follow the London fashions. . . . Our affluence during the late war, introduced a degree of luxury in tables, dress, and furniture, with which we were before unacquainted."[18]

United States independence from England and the departure of New Yorkers loyal to the British crown opened the way to a partial reshaping of the urban elite. Many loyalists' possessions were seized and resold, among them those of the rich and famous James De Lancey. Most importantly, in the decades that followed the Revolution, the ties existing between land and commerce were broken. The elite landowners withdrew from business while a ruling class emerged, composed of merchants, bankers, and businessmen. Some of them belonged to the great families of the colonial era, such as the Bayards, the LeRoys, the Roosevelts, or the Lawrences, who had withstood the revolutionary turmoil better than the landed gentry.

Others came from Europe, or often from New England. Archibald Gracie left Scotland for the shores of the Hudson in 1784. By the following year, he had made the wise decision to marry the sister of three wealthy New York merchants—Moses, Nehemiah, and Henry Rogers. After a few years in Virginia, where he conducted business, he settled in New York. From 1793 until his death in 1829, he was one of New York's major figures in port commerce. Shipowner, merchant, administrator for banks and insurance companies, vice president of the Chamber of Commerce, he owned a beautiful summer home on the shores of the East River, Gracie Mansion, which became the official residence of the mayor of New York.

John Jacob Astor was another example of the social fluidity of the New York elite. Born in Germany in 1763, this adventurous spirit launched himself into the fur trade in the early 1780s. Arriving in New York in 1784, he set out to build a real-estate empire. He acquired land and buildings in Manhattan and threw himself into real-estate speculation. By 1840, he was the richest living American.

Thus New York's social stratification reflected very pronounced economic inequalities. At the end of the seventeenth century, the poorest third of the New York population possessed only 3 percent of the wealth, as opposed to 40 percent belonging to the richest 10 percent. No doubt inequalities were less pronounced there than in the European capitals, but they already existed in the 1660s and increased steadily throughout the eighteenth century. Development in the craft industries and manufacturing accompanied a growth in poverty after 1760 and especially after 1790. The male population was greatly affected, the family unit weakened. As for single women—unmarried, widowed or abandoned by their husbands—their situation was hardly enviable. Economic life remained dominated by men, and society by a republican ideology that regarded moral virtue as sacred and considered women to be notoriously less endowed with it than men.

The elite's response to the rise in poverty was charity, but the traditional system proved no longer adequate. In the eighteenth century, poverty was a problem that fell under the auspices of the aldermen and church wardens. Thus, about thirty people were supported in 1700, about forty in 1725, and about sixty in 1735, not including those who benefited from private generosity. In 1736, the city established an almshouse, flanked some forty years later by a reformatory. But in the early nineteenth century, the phenomenon changed scale: municipal assistance involved more than 8,000 individuals in 1813, and more than 16,000 in 1815! The machinery broke down.

At the same time, the New York middle classes' perception of poverty changed. Until then, poverty had been a matter of divine providence, not personal failing. Henceforth, emphasis fell on the moral weaknesses of the poor and their individual responsibility. Thus, the Society for the Prevention of Pauperism was founded in 1817, and its members embarked on a critical inquiry into the morals of the poorest.

BABEL ON THE HUDSON?

The inauguration ceremonies for the Erie Canal in November 1825 hardly reflected the diversity of New York's population. Nevertheless, this diversity is one of the commonplaces most often repeated by visitors and observers in the seventeenth century. "On the island of Manhate, and its environs, there may well be four to five hundred men of different sects and nations" and "eighteen different languages," noted Father Jogues in 1643.[19] In this respect, it seems, the Dutch and then English town contrasted strongly with the colonies of New England, Chesapeake Bay, the South, and even the West Indies.

The city was incontestably diverse from the beginning because of the very nature of the Company's project. Until the 1640s, the majority of New Amsterdam's population were Dutch in name only. The first inhabitants were mostly French-speaking Protestant Walloons, who could neither speak nor understand Dutch, as the Reverend Johannes Michaelius noted bitterly in 1628. The rise in the proportion of Dutch had to wait until the expansion of the Rensselaerswyck area and especially the colony's development between 1640 and 1664. During this period, nearly one immigrant out of five came from the German states bordering the United Provinces, such as the duchy of Cleves, the free cities of Bremen and Hamburg, the East Frisian islands, Westphalia, or the Rhine regions. Almost an equal proportion came from the Scandinavian countries, including the then Danish Schleswig-Holstein.

Among these immigrants, the most famous was the son of a minister from the Faroe Islands who settled in New Netherland in 1639, Jonas Bronck. He gave his name to the river that bordered his lands and that became the "Bronck's River." Less than one in ten immigrants came from France, mostly from Normandy, Picardy, and Saintonge. Some of these French, like the merchant Jacques Cousseau from La Rochelle, first emigrated to the United Provinces or into the Palatinate before crossing the Atlantic. A small majority of immigrants came from the United Provinces, and among them, those from Holland were the minority, since nearly six out of ten Netherlanders came from Gelderland, Utrecht, Zeeland, Brabant, Limburg or the northern provinces of Friesland, Drenthe, Overijssel and Groningen.

In addition to these arrivals from Europe were the African slaves, a few Amerindians, and a small group of Jews, the first twenty-three of whom disembarked in New Amsterdam in September 1654 after the fall of Dutch Brazil. These Spanish and Portuguese Marranos first took refuge in the United Provinces to escape persecution, before settling in Brazil. Peter Stuyvesant and Reverend Johannes Megapolensis did not disguise their anti-Semitism, but the West India Company, anxious to attract immigrants to New Netherland and to show consideration for Jewish merchants in Amsterdam, forced them to welcome these refugees to New Netherland, where they established the Shearith Israel congregation.

During the English period, New York welcomed French Protestants—about 200 families fleeing persecution and the Revocation of the Edict of Nantes. The majority were from Saintonge, Poitou, and Normandy, and had gone into exile in London before emigrating to New York. In the 1690s, a few of them were wealthy merchants, like Gabriel Laboyteaux, Benjamin Faneuil, or Etienne de Lancy, who became Stephen De Lancey shortly after his arrival in New York, and founded a powerful dynasty. Many were poor, such as the cobbler Etienne Doucinet or the laborer Jean Doublet. A group with close political and economic ties, they established a church in 1688, entrusted to a minister from Ariège, Pierre Peiret.

Their integration into society as a whole became evident in the 1690s, when several Huguenots married outside the group. However, this tendency was checked by Peiret, who renewed their interest in spirituality. Peiret was the presumed author of *Trésor des consolations divines et humaines*, published in French in New York in 1696. The Huguenots also had the edifying example of Elie Neau from Saintonge. Settling in the West Indies in 1679 and then in New York in 1690, Neau was captured by a French privateer in 1692, condemned to the galleys, and imprisoned in the Château d'If. Until he was released in 1698, his letters from prison testified to a flawless faith and a degree of mysticism unprecedented in the history of French Protestantism.

But after 1700, New York's Huguenot congregation rapidly declined, owing to the death of Peiret, the difficulty of replacing him, and Neau's conversion to Anglicanism upon his return to New York. In the decades that followed, other internal conflicts further weakened the "French Church." Henceforth, affluent members like DeLancey or the silversmith Simeon Soumainque preferred Trinity Church. Dwindling, the congregation disbanded in 1776, having tried in vain for thirteen years to find a pastor. Upon its reopening in 1796, it quickly placed itself under the authority of the Protestant Episcopal Church, and in 1804, took the name of Eglise du Saint Esprit.

Later, a second wave of immigrants arrived from the British Isles. In 1677, nearly 80 percent of New York's inhabitants were of Dutch origin, 18 percent English, and about two percent French Protestants and Jews. Twenty years later, six white New Yorkers out of ten were Dutch, three out of ten English, and one out of ten French. But the greatest waves of British immigrants arrived in the eighteenth century, and in 1790, three quarters of the some 33,000 New Yorkers were originally British (42 percent English, 24 percent Irish, eight percent Scotch and two percent Welsh).

This diversity helped to produce tensions that sometimes erupted. In the early 1680s, New Yorkers had a customs collector arrested and sent back to England, guilty in their eyes of continuing to do his job when Governor Andros had forgotten to renew authorization for his unpopular levies. A few years later, the first colonial assembly, unenthusiastically created by the Duke of York, adopted a "Charter of Freedoms and Privileges Granted by His Royal Highness to the Inhabitants of New York and its Dependencies," which subjected the tax to the consent of the assembly. The Duke of York, who had become King James II, hastened to nullify this charter in 1685, and three years later, to suppress the assembly and even the colony of New York, henceforth entrusted to Governor Andros as part of the great Dominion of New England.

In the spring of 1689, the news of the Glorious Revolution and the arrival on the English throne of William of Orange unleashed a violent revolt in New York. Targeting the colonial authorities appointed by James II, it was led by Jacob Leisler, a former soldier for the West India Company, of German origin, who had become a merchant after a profitable marriage in 1663, only to see his fortunes reversed in the 1670s. Leisler was among those colonists who did not want to adapt to a new English regime. In their eyes, the Glorious Revolution provided an opportunity to end twenty-five years of frustration and to demonstrate their rejection of the sociopolitical order New York had known since the conquest. Backing Leisler were many artisans and common folk, often of Dutch origin. Against him were the wealthiest Dutch merchants, the very ones who had chosen to support the new masters of the colony and had reaped the benefits. Leisler and his supporters managed to retain control of New York for nearly a year, until William III nominated a new governor for the colony, Henry Sloughter. Then the tables quickly turned. Leisler was arrested in March 1690, accused of rebellion and of high treason, tried in unfair court proceedings, condemned to death, and hanged on May 17, 1691.

The Leisler episode left its mark on the city's and the colony's memory. Henceforth, New York was the capital of a royal province administered by a governor and granted an elected assembly. But antagonisms surfaced again when Leisler's former supporters and adversaries angrily confronted each other in 1701, and they were one of the basic factors underlying the political life of the times. Over the long term, the rebellion's failure marked the colony's takeover by a coalition of the new Anglo-Franco-Dutch business elite, and the beginning of an Anglo-Americanization process that made ethnic tensions secondary to political and socioeconomic factors.

This Anglo-Americanization was manifested notably by the development of a legal system that replaced the Dutch procedures in force until then. Most importantly, the tensions that led to the revolutionary episode and then to the course of city politics between 1790 and 1820 demonstrate how New York had become an American city, rather homogeneous and distinctly uncosmopolitan. It was no surprise, then, that the opening ceremonies for the Erie Canal left out the theme of ethnic diversity, so prized a century and a half earlier.

THE FORMATION OF URBAN CULTURES

On the other hand, the Erie Canal ceremonies testified to the richness and the democratic and republican vitality of New York public culture in the early 1820s. Artisans' guilds, various associations, officials from all levels, and of course the citizenry marched together in the procession, as they had previously on the occasion of Lafayette's visit to New York in 1824, the announcement of peace with Great Britain in 1815, or for the ratification of the Constitution, and George Washington's inauguration in 1789.

This civic model grew out of a series of changes that affected New York beginning in 1730 and that began to

turn it into an intellectual center. Until then, New Yorkers proved rather indifferent to matters of the mind.
Before the 1690s, New York had no printers, and urban
culture was primarily oral and very materialistic. Its true
center was the inn. Taverns played an important role
from the Dutch period on, and in 1653, one of them even
became the official seat of the first municipality in New
Amsterdam. "Nearly the just fourth of the city of New
Amsterdam consists of brandy shops, tobacco or beer
houses," remarked a disapproving Peter Stuyvesant upon
his arrival in New Amsterdam.[20] But these taverns where
inhabitants met, smoked, ate, and played billiards (the
first tables appeared in the 1730s) were also the places
where they discussed politics or did business. Convivial-
ity and utilitarianism got along well there.

New Yorkers' clear inclination toward well-lubricated
sociability was matched by the modest intensity of their
religious feelings. The city asserted itself as a privileged
place for pluralism, very different from Puritan Boston or
Quaker Philadelphia. Of course until 1664, the Dutch
Reformed Church benefited from a theoretical monopoly over the public expression of faith, but in fact, the
colony proved itself to be tolerant with regard to private
practices. "No religion is publicly exercised but the
Calvinist," remarked Father Jogues in 1643. "And orders
are to admit none but Calvinists, but this is not
observed: for besides the Calvinists, there are in the
colony Catholics, English Puritans, Lutherans, Anabap-
tists here called M[en]n[on]istes, etc."[21]

The English conquest again reinforced this diversity. In
1687, Governor Dongan could continue Father Jogues'
inventory: New York counted Dutch Calvinists, Dutch
Lutherans, Anglicans, a few Catholics, orthodox Quakers
who were "Women especially," "Singing Quakers, Ranting
Quakers, Sabbatarians, Antisabbatarians, some Anabap-
tists, some Independents, some Jews; in short of all sorts
of opinions there are some, and the most part of none at
all."[22] The Baptists and the Presbyterians were organized
in 1716, the Jews built their first synagogue in 1729, the
Moravians were established in Manhattan in 1751, and
the German Reformed Church in 1758, not to mention

the deists and the nonbelievers, discreet but very much present in colonial New York.

Diversity does not mean equality. Catholicism aroused great hostility beginning in the 1690s, and a 1700 provincial law even prohibited Catholic priests access to the province. The little Catholic community, with only about 200 members, had to wait until after the Revolution to acquire a church, Saint Peter's, dedicated in 1786. On the other hand, because the Anglicans benefited from the authorities' strong support, all the inhabitants of the province, regardless of their religious convictions, were taxed in 1697 to finance the construction of Trinity Church.

Nor is diversity synonymous with intensity. Already in 1648, Pastor Backerus judged his flock to be "ignorant in regard to the true religion, and very much given to drink."[23] The theme of New Yorkers' indifference to religious questions quickly became a commonplace. Even the religious revival that caught fire in the colonies in the mid-eighteenth century hardly affected New York. The famous English preacher George Whitefield attracted many thousands of listeners during his visits in 1739 and 1740, but this was mere curiosity and had no further repercussions.

One of the reasons for this was may have been the development of new cultural forms. On the model of the Edinburgh of Adam Smith and David Hume, New York acquired institutions devoted to sharing intellectual ambitions, and concerned with the social and political dimensions. In the 1720s and 1730s, the publishing industry and the press helped to shape a public urban culture. Certainly New York was not as prolific as Philadelphia, but the presses of the New York publishers, James Parker or Hugh Gaine for instance, printed many books, magazines, and especially newspapers. The *New York Gazette*, founded in 1725 by the colony's official printer, William Bradford, expressed views close to those of the royal governors. The awakening of public opinion may explain the founding of the *New York Weekly Journal* by John Zenger in 1733, a newspaper much more prone to criticism. Zenger was brought to court by the colonial authorities in 1735. The ruling in his favor in this famous case—the first in a history of complex relations between the press and political power in New York—reinforced the principle of free expression in the colony. The bookstore business flourished as well, thanks especially to the lack of copyright legislation. New York boasted some of the most extensively stocked bookstores in the colonies, like that of Garrat Noel, on Dock Street, or James Rivington's influential London Bookshop on Hanover Street.

Mid-century also saw the simultaneous founding of King's College, which became Columbia College after the Revolution, and the New York Society Library in 1754. The Chamber of Commerce was created in 1768. After the Revolution, associations and organizations multiplied, strengthening the fabric of urban culture, such as the New-York Historical Society, founded in 1804. In 1815, DeWitt Clinton was able to declare that the return of peace enabled the municipality "by patronizing the arts and sciences and encouraging the cultivation of the human mind, to elevate still more the character of this great community and to erect imperishable monuments of public utility."[24]

Nevertheless, the emergence of this civic model should not obscure other facets of New York cultural life. In comparison with Boston, the future Athens of America, and Philadelphia, the city of brotherly love, New York appeared to observers of the time to be a city where the pleasures of the mind were hardly cultivated at all. New Yorkers were regarded as interested only in money. "Tho' the province of New York abounds certainly more in riches than any other of the other northern colonies," bitterly noted Cadwallader Colden in 1740, a Scot who had arrived in New York twenty years earlier and one of the few inhabitants interested in scientific and philosophic questions, "yet there has been less care to propagate knowledge or learning. The only principle of life propagated among the young people is to get money, and men are esteemed according to what they are worth." A few years later, in 1757, the lawyer and historian William Smith mentioned a "long shameful neglect of all the arts and sciences."[25]

In fact, New York was not a literary and artistic center

at that time. Until the Revolution, there were few writers there, apart from Colden, who published the important *History of the Five Indian Nations* (1727) as well as many works on physics and botany, and the two lawyers, also historians and journalists, William Livingston and William Smith, the latter of whom wrote the first history of the province of New York, published in London in 1757. The beginnings of literary life that appeared in the early nineteenth century remained limited to a very small number of gentlemen who became writers, like Washington Irving. His *History of New York by Diedrich Knickerbocker*, published in 1809, brilliantly marked the city's entry into American literature. Signs of artistic life were weaker. In the absence of local artistic talent, rich New Yorkers went to Boston to have their portraits painted by Copley; the New York Academy of the Fine Arts, founded in 1802 and becoming the American Academy of Fine Arts in 1817, was primarily occupied with providing its subscribing members copies of sculptures from the Louvre.

In the end, these literary and artistic beginnings were much less significant than the development of a civic culture. From the mid-eighteenth century on, New Yorkers increasingly took possession of public space. There were vigorous discussions in the hundreds of taverns the city counted on the eve of the Revolution. Samuel Fraunces's establishment, soon known as the Fraunces Tavern, became one of the hot spots during the revolutionary decades. The Sons of Liberty met there to discuss the Stamp Act or the non-importation movement, and Washington bade farewell to his officers there in December 1783. Most of the inns drew a working class clientele of artisans and laborers, while others were simple dockside eating houses where soldiers and seafaring men and women poured in. But the city's business affairs were often discussed within their walls, as well as in the cafés that made their appearance in the mid-eighteenth century. The Merchants' Coffee House hosted the newly created Chamber of Commerce in 1768 and the Society of the Cincinnati in 1786. The Tontine Coffee House, opened in the early 1790s, became the gathering place for the New York Insurance Company, and the Bull's Head

FIGURE 11
Tontine Coffee House by Francis Guy (on left, about 1791)
The New-York Historical Society

Tavern, in the Bowery, witnessed butchers and cattle drovers establishing the price of cattle.

New York's pulse sounded in its taverns and cafés, but the civic culture that developed there did not remain prisoner to that smoky, drunken atmosphere. New Yorkers knew enough to go out into the streets when circumstances required, for confrontations with the English, for the approval of the Constitution, the peace of 1815, Lafayette's visit, and the inauguration of the Erie Canal. Only the entire city offered a large enough stage for republican New York.

II
QUEEN OF THE
NEW WORLD
1820–1890

FIGURE 12
General View of New York in the nineteenth century
© Hachette Livre

3

THE VENICE OF THE ATLANTIC

"I have never seen the bay of Naples, I can therefore make no comparison, but my imagination is incapable of conceiving any thing of the kind more beautiful than the harbour of New York. Various and lovely are the objects which meet the eye on every side, but the naming them would only be to give a list of words, without conveying the faintest idea of the scene. I doubt if ever the pencil of Turner could do it justice, bright and glorious as it rose upon us. We seemed to enter the harbour of New York upon waves of liquid gold, and as we darted past the green isles which rise from its bosom, like guardian centinels of the fair city, the setting sun stretched his horizontal beams farther and farther at each moment, as if to point out to us some new glory in the landscape. New York, indeed, appeared to us, even when we saw it by a soberer light, a lovely and a noble city. . . . Its advantages of position are, perhaps, unequalled any where. Situated on an island, which I think it will one day cover, it rises, like Venice, from the sea, and like that fairest of cities in the days of her glory, receives into its lap tribute of all the riches of the earth."[1]

Such enthusiasm from the scathing pen of the very English Mrs. Trollope, in whose eyes nothing American generally found favor, attested to the fascination the metropolis on the shores of the Hudson held for its visitors throughout the nineteenth century. The city was the largest, the richest, the most impressive in the Americas. Hyperbole was the rule; an exalted feeling of perpetual change and unlimited growth prevailed. New York was the "queen of the Atlantic coast," the "London of America," the "Liverpool of the New World," the "empire city."

THE PATHS TO GLORY

As in the past, the key to this greatness was economic. "Commerce is a centripetal force," noted the economist Michel Chevalier in 1834, and "along the whole Atlantic coast there is only one mart, New York."[2] Its dominance was reinforced by the territorial expansion of the United States. The infrastructures soon followed. Beginning in the first decades of the century, many turnpikes, the Seneca, the Catskill, or the Great Western, facilitated contact by horse, stagecoach, or carriage between the metropolis, its hinterland, and the other cities along the Atlantic coast.

Beginning in the 1820s, New York benefited from the expansion of river commerce. The Erie Canal proved to be a commercial and financial success, quickly imitated. In 1823, the Champlain Canal was opened between the lake of the same name and the Hudson; ten years later, the Delaware and Raritan Canal linked New York and Philadelphia. The United States retained 1,200 miles of canals in 1830 and 3,000 in 1840. The canals between Lake Erie and the Ohio (1832), the Miami (1845), and the Wabash (1856) rivers allowed the metropolis to capture a portion of the Ohio trade, to the detriment of New Orleans. Beginning in 1850, external freight exceeded internal freight on New York's Erie Canal. Thanks to all these canals, navigated primarily by barges pulled by horses or mules, and then by small steamers, New York strengthened its hold over the hinterlands and became a distribution center for the West and the South.

Navigation by steamship was also a New York affair. Robert Fulton navigated his *Clermont* on the waters of the Hudson on August 17, 1807. Soon steamships built by Fulton and his partner Robert Livingston crisscrossed the New York bay in every direction, by virtue of a generous monopoly granted by the Albany legislators. The competition had to be content with opening lines to New Jersey, Pennsylvania, or Connecticut, or with operating illegally. In 1824, the United States Supreme Court put an end to the Fulton and Livingston monopoly in a famous ruling, *Gibbons vs. Ogden*, that granted only the United States Congress, and not the individual states, the right to regulate interstate commerce.

The consequences of this judicial decision were immediate. Many companies sent out their steamers to capture the New York market, and these commercial rivalries sometimes led the captains to neglect their passengers' safety in order to make better time than their competitors. One of them, a young captain named Cornelius Vanderbilt, who had been for some years illegally plying between New Jersey and New York, began to amass a fortune, later based on railroads. Other owners, no less ambitious, established ties with New England and tried to reduce the travel time between Boston and New York, using a combination of steamer and railway.

In May 1831, one of these steamers transported Alexis de Tocqueville from Newport—where the packet ship from Le Havre had been forced to seek refuge due to bad weather—to New York. "It is impossible to get an idea of the interior of this immense machine," he wrote his mother. "Suffice it to say that it contains three large salons, two for men, one for women, where four hundred, five hundred and often eight hundred people eat and sleep comfortably."[3]

New York did not neglect the railway. New Yorkers undoubtedly lagged behind Boston, Philadelphia, and Baltimore, who had been spurred on by their desire to compete with the Erie Canal. But the New Yorkers reacted promptly to the potential threats to their supremacy posed by the line from Baltimore to the Ohio valley, built between 1827 and 1852, and the line from Boston to Albany, opened in the 1840s. The Bostonians' efforts to "cut off or absorb the fountains of our prosperity," denounced in 1842 by John Delafield, president of the future New York & Albany Railroad Company, did not worry New York officials for long.[4]

Railroads linked New York to Philadelphia by the mid-1830s, to Boston a few years later, and soon after that to the Great Lakes. An early railway network, the New York Central, was started by an Albany merchant named Erastus Corning in 1853. It united eight small lines that had opened between Albany and Buffalo beginning in 1830, and had long been limited to transporting passengers, thus protecting freight transport on the Erie Canal. As for the Erie Railroad network, it departed from Piermont, an improbable terminus thirty-three miles north of New York in the Hudson Valley, and ran parallel to the Pennsylvania border across the entire state until it arrived at Dunkirk, on the shores of Lake Erie. From there, both these lines headedwest, toward Detroit, Toledo, and Chicago, while ties to more southern networks expanded, linking Baltimore to Saint Louis via Cincinnati, or Philadelphia to Chicago and Cincinnati via Pittsburgh.

The link with Albany was secured in the early 1850s by the Hudson River Railroad, which ran along the eastern banks of the river, while the New York & Harlem Railroad, further inland from the river, extended north of the city into the Bronx and Westchester County. Beginning in 1866, a bridge crossing the Hudson at Albany allowed passengers and freight to avoid the inconveniences of ferry transfers. The Erie Railroad, for its part, preferred to construct an extension to Jersey City.

Thus by the mid-1850s, New York City had successfully managed its railway revolution. "The metropolis will ere long stand in as close business relations with every town in the United States, as, fifty years ago, it did with its own uptown wards," applauded Isaac Kendall in 1865. "In this general growth of the continent, New York will stand as the great heart of the country."[5]

In fact, the concentration of railroad lines that led to New York did serve to strengthen the city's hold on the continent through the 1860s and 1870s. Cornelius Vanderbilt gradually took control of the lines between New York and Albany, and then of the New York Central line that linked the Hudson Valley to Buffalo. In 1866 and 1867, he failed in his efforts to take over the Erie line, facing an alliance of three speculators who had invested heavily in this company—Daniel Drew, Jim Fisk, and Jay Gould, whose nickname was "the Mephistopheles of Wall Street." Gould alone remained to challenge Vanderbilt in 1869, and did his best to build a competing railroad empire, but failed because of risky gold speculations. As owner of all the lines that entered New York, Vanderbilt was able to launch the construction of the city's first true railway terminal, Grand Central Station, located on Forty-Second Street—the southern limit beyond which steam engines were forbidden from running, beginning in 1856.

In the same period, the transportation revolution overwhelmed transatlantic routes. The first line of regular packets, the Black Ball Line, soon had to face competition on the Atlantic. In 1822, the New York merchants Preserved Fish and Joseph Grinnell founded the Blue Swallow Tail, and their competitors, the firm of Byrnes, Trimble & Co., the Red Star Line. The same year, two lines between London and New York opened, while the son-in-law of Admiral de Grasse, Francis Depau, established the first regular link with Le Havre, and was soon competing with the line owned by his rivals, Leroy, Bayard, and Co.

Other companies appeared in the 1830s and 1840s, like the Dramatic Line of shipowner Edward K. Collins, whose ships were given such names as *Shakespeare* or *Sheridan*. The result of all these changes was easy to see: four packets in 1818, fifty-two in 1845, departures from New York, Liverpool, Le Havre and London multiplying, with three departures per week on the New York–Liverpool line.

Beginning in the 1840s, the coming of the steamship led to the gradual decline of the sail packets. In 1860, 90 percent of the tonnage in the New York harbor was still transported by sailing ships, but this proportion fell to half in 1880, and to a fifth in 1890. Steamships soon took over the transport of mail and passengers, leaving the sailing ships to transport only heavy goods after 1860. After the Black Ball Line disappeared in 1878, the steamship lines multiplied, weaving regular routes between New York and Liverpool, Bremen, Hamburg, Le Havre, and Marseille, with fleets bearing the famous names of Cunard, Collins, Inman, White Star, Guion, Norddeutscher Lloyd, HAPAG, or the General Transatlantic Company.

THE EMPORIUM OF THE AMERICAS

New York's "unparalleled growth," noted Michel Chevalier in 1834, "is not the work of lawyers and military men; the merit belongs chiefly to the industry, the capital, the intelligence, and the enterprise of that, numerically speaking, insignificant minority of Wall Street and Pearl Street." It is easy to measure their significance, he added: simply "consider what New York would be without them."[6]

Importing was an old occupation for New York, whose share rose from one third of total American importations in 1820 to two thirds just before the Civil War, and then maintained itself at about this level until the end of the century. New York's reach continued to expand. Boston remained the chief American port for commerce with India, but New York maintained direct ties with Madras and Calcutta. Certain New York firms, like Griswold & Co., Howland & Aspinwall, Olyphant & Co., built their fortunes on commerce with Canton.

The list of objects, goods, and products unloaded on the Hudson and East River docks was a long one. New York merchants, aware of the demand, were fond of European textiles, the chief import item until the Civil War. Thus they dressed America in cotton and woolen cloth from England, in English, Irish, and German linen, in silk from Lyon, and various luxury fabrics from Paris. Others concentrated instead on metal goods, from the fine cutlery of Birmingham and Sheffield to the semi-finished metals of Liverpool, to the rails, pipes, and then steel of Bristol. From Holland, the Iberian Peninsula, the West Indies, and especially France, came impressive quantities of alcohol and wine. Cases of Cognac brandy, Champagne, and Bordeaux sat side by side with wines from Oporto or Jerez, and gin from Amsterdam.

Besides the pottery, porcelain, and precious gems with which the jewelers Tiffany & Young bedecked rich New

FIGURE 13

The New York port in 1828: South Street seen from Maiden Lane
Metropolitan Museum of Art, The Edward W.C. Arnold Collection
of New York Prints, Maps and Pictures, Bequest of Edward W. C.
Arnold, 1954 (54.90.18)

Yorkers, the port of New York received coal from Liverpool (until Pennsylvania took over), Cuban sugar (which replaced sugar from Jamaica and other British sugar islands after 1815), Brazilian coffee, hides from the Rio de la Plata and the Orinoco, silver from Mexico, guano from Peru, cigars from Cuba, and tea from Canton.

As industrial expansion accelerated in the 1870s, importation of manufactured articles declined. Henceforth, raw materials passed through the New York docks on their way to the factories: wool or silk fibers, cow, calf, goat or kid hides, and rubber. Considerable quantities of half-finished products headed for the chemical and steelmaking industries; and finally, raw produce like sugar, coffee, and, to a lesser extent, tea.

New York's hold on American export trade was less apparent, but it was also growing. The metropolis controlled almost a quarter of the nation's exportation and reexportation in 1860, a much greater proportion during the Civil War, and then about 40 percent in 1890, despite a relative decline. Until the 1860s, New York exported cotton, flour, and smoked meats, destined for West Indian markets and to feed ships' crews on all the seas of the world. It shipped flaxseed to Ireland, as well as the potash used to make soaps and detergents.

The quality of New York flour, disputed in the past, improved in the 1820s when standards of quality were strictly applied. In a few years, the opening of the Erie Canal made northwestern New York State a rich grain-producing area whose flour passed through the docks of Manhattan. Rochester, a simple village founded in 1812, numbered 1,500 inhabitants in 1821, and 20,000 in 1840. Thanks to the canal, the Genesee Valley became New York's granary, and Rochester the American flour-milling capital. New York is "the depot for the production of an immense region of the country," noted John Adams Dix in 1827.[7] Its rivals Baltimore and Philadelphia, which exported even more flour than it did in 1820, were definitively outdistanced.

The principal exportation product was cotton. The thousands of bales that passed through the Hudson docks arrived from the islands off the coast of Georgia, the Georgia and Carolina inlands, and the coast of the Gulf of Mexico. New York merchants sought cotton sources in Charleston, Savannah, Mobile, and New Orleans, where they often established permanent offices. Some of them, like the fabulously wealthy Jeremiah Thompson, became shipowners and in the early 1820s established sail packet lines between New York and the cotton ports.

Beginning in the 1860s, New York exported grains to Great Britain and, to a lesser extent, France, as well as livestock and meat. The huge Brooklyn silos stored millions of tons of wheat and corn from the Midwest. Near the Hudson, on Eleventh Avenue between Sixtieth and

Sixty-Third Street, thousands of head of beef cattle occupied the New York Central Railroad cattle yard. In the late 1880s, cotton, dairy products, tobacco, and kerosene departed from New York, as well as manufactured articles, a sign that the American economy had moved on to an industrial regime.

BROADWAY, PEARL STREET, AND THE BUSINESS REVOLUTION

The generalist merchant of the colonial period gradually gave way to firms and tradesmen specializing in one activity, one type of product, or one function. In 1820–40, merchants made a fortune in auction sales of imported products. A few firms dominated, like those of John and Philip Hone, or John Haggerty and David Austin. Nearly half of the port's total imports passed through their hands in the 1820s, and still a fifth by the 1830s.

Specialized importers succeeded them, like Anson Phelps, who built his fortune on shipments of iron and copper that he imported from Europe. Some concentrated on importing textiles, others on wine, cutlery, dishes, coffee, or sugar. Many wholesalers bought products from importers, which they, in turn, resold to New York tradesmen and to merchants from the South, East, or West who came to New York once a year to replenish their stocks. These visitors often took rooms above the shops on Pearl Street, exactly where the wholesalers carefully housed their clerks, thus attracting clients to their warehouses. Beginning in the 1870s, the tide gradually turned: henceforth, New York wholesalers sent their catalogues and their sales representatives to inland retailers.

Other merchants preferred the export business, and acted as brokers or agents between American producers of grain or cotton and British importers. Thanks to improved communications and the creation of specialized commodity markets in New York—for grains in 1850, for cotton in 1868—the largest and most skillful of these merchants were no longer satisfied with the simple role of intermediary. Following the example of David Dows, a major grain merchant, they established specialized trading firms that

FIGURE 14
View of Broadway in 1834
© Roger Viollet

relied on the brokerage companies and the commodity-markets commission.

This business revolution began within the narrow perimeters of the streets of lower Manhattan. "South Street," in 1852, "is occupied by the principal shipping houses, and the offices of most of the foreign packet lines. The dry goods jobbing and importing business, formerly confined to Pearl Street, has extended to William, Broad, Pine, Cedar, Liberty, etc."[8] Along these streets rose the brick buildings, three to five stories high, that housed New York commerce. Merchandise was stored in the upper floors, while offices on the ground floor accommodated the ledger clerks, the accountant, the cashier, the right-hand man, and the partners themselves.

Another revolution unfolded a few hundred blocks away—the retail business. Stores and shops began to specialize in the 1820s. Storefronts and shop windows, often in the neoclassical style, gave up their colorless reserve to attract attention and display to customers what was sold there. A shop, lectured the journalist Freeman Hunt in his *Hunt's Merchants' Magazine*, had to be elegant and well-organized, with a salesclerk friendly and knowledgeable about his merchandise. Even though all shops did not answer Hunt's criteria, Broadway became the center of commerce.

"The mania for converting Broadway into a street of shops is greater than ever," deplored the aristocratic Philip Hone in 1850. In fact, all sorts of stores were to be found there. "Throughout there are nothing but shops with gaudy displays, garish and tasteless, where the prices are written in figures a foot long," remarked Louis Simonin. "Gigantic signs call out to the passer-by from all sides; a few of them, painted on transparent cloth hung on ropes, span the entire breadth of the street, thrown from an upper story window to the one across from it."[9] But Broadway was also home to the largest and most sophisticated stores in New York. Fashionable women strolled along it to shop, to see and to be seen, and all of New York's luxury hotels established themselves close to lower Manhattan's thoroughfare.

The first large department stores appeared next to the independent shops. The most famous belonged to Alexander Turney Stewart, an Irishman who opened a dry-goods shop on Broadway in the 1820s. Twenty years later, he had become a clothing merchant and wholesaler, and by 1846, he had grown rich enough to open his "Marble Palace of fabrics and fashions," a four-story building on the corner of Broadway and Chambers Street that was striking to New Yorkers and visitors alike. In the early 1850s, *Putnam's* magazine proclaimed the spot to be unrivaled worldwide.

Nevertheless, a few years later, Stewart had built an even more impressive "Steel Palace" along a whole stretch of Broadway between Ninth and Tenth Streets. "An army of store clerks are measuring and wrapping up silky cloth and a thousand feminine trinkets from morning till night," noted Louis Simonin.[10] In fact, if Stewart's "palaces" constituted the most visible aspect of his enterprise, they accounted for less than a fifth of his turnover, which was nearly fifty million dollars in 1870. They constituted, literally and figuratively, the showcase for the wholesale business that Stewart ran on a national scale and that was the principal source of his fortune.

The great department store's formula gained a following. Soon, Stewart had to face competition from many stores, often small retailers who managed to grow. In 1858, Rowland Hussey Macy, a recent New Yorker who had tried his hand at many occupations without much success before arriving in the metropolis, opened a modest specialty store—gloves, handkerchiefs, ribbons—on Sixth Avenue between Thirteen and Fourteenth Streets. Macy's founder put into practice four simple but, at that time, revolutionary principles: direct cash purchase from manufacturers and importers, sale at the same price to everyone (the one-price policy), the lowest prices and aggressive advertising, if necessary. The formula worked, and Macy's gradually expanded on its original site. The store occupied as many as eleven different buildings in 1872, before being reorganized more rationally into distinct departments. The owner also proceeded to carefully decorate and make improvements, unprecedented at that time: a restaurant for ladies was opened in 1878; two years later, the Sixth Avenue facade was completely redone, and electricity was installed. For its thirtieth anniversary in 1888, Macy's moved to a new location on the corner of Broadway and Thirty-Fourth Street. The spot seemed remote, but the judicious nature of this choice became evident in the 1890s.

Nonetheless, most of the large stores were concentrated around Broadway between Fourteenth and Twenty-Third Streets. That was where Lord and Taylor opened in 1872, in what was perhaps the first steel-framework building in New York, as well as B. Altman, Best, Stern Brothers, and John A. Hearn and Sons. Specializing in women's clothing, this section of Broadway, near the wealthy residences on Fifth Avenue, was soon nicknamed "The Ladies' Mile." Few stores dared to choose other locations, besides Macy's and Bloomingdale's, which opened its doors on Third Avenue at Fifty-Sixth Street in 1872, a less posh neighborhood than Broadway's, with its "palaces" and other "commercial cathedrals."

THE PORT OF NEW YORK

In the early 1820s, port improvements remained perfunctory. "The time has not yet come for the formation of massive permanent quays in the harbor of New York," noted James Fenimore Cooper in 1824. "Wood is still too cheap and labor too dear, for so heavy an investment of capital." The wharves were simple wooden frameworks filled with loose stone and covered with planks and earth. "The wharves of New York form a succession of little basins, which are sometimes large enough to admit thirty or forty sail, though often much smaller. These irregular docks have obtained the name of 'slips.'"[11]

The frenetic activity at the port soon necessitated changes. "Along the entire length of the quays," observed the Spanish scholar Ramón de la Sagra in 1835, "a forest of masts rises belonging to vessels from all nations and to the steamships used for exchange between the different states of the Union. On the river to the north, in the bay and the eastern branch, magnificent steamboats are continually passing each other as they depart and arrive at all hours of the day and night, laden with passengers, merchandise and raw materials."[12]

In the early 1840s, a New York engineer named Browne noted the difficulties resulting from the presence of so many ships. Some sixty wharves then lined the East River, and a good fifty lined the Hudson—with no overall plan to govern the organization of the port. The result: Certain parts "are often in so crowded a condition, that many vessels necessarily have to anchor off in the stream, and there discharge their freights with lighters or barges, or to wait for a week or ten days before they can secure a proper berth for unloading, and then, oftentimes, the best they can obtain is an outside one, which obliges them to discharge their cargoes over the decks of two or more vessels."[13]

The port looked no different a quarter of a century later. In 1864, a fascinated Duvergier du Hauranne described "the docks and the harbor, the prodigious movement among the islands and along the shore, the continually swirling smoke of those odd steamships which are like floating houses topped by an engine that is moving its long rods up and down like nervous, agitated arms. They come and go, cross in front of each other, bellowing stridently all the while, and it is a miracle that they do not collide with each other every day."[14]

To relieve this congestion, the port was expanded along the East River and especially on the Hudson. In his *Leaves of Grass*, Walt Whitman could then, with good reason, sing of "mast-hemm'd Manhattan." On the Hudson, piers and quays extended as far north as Eleventh Street by 1860. There was another wave of development after the Civil War, and by the end of the century, the port reached Seventieth Street. On the East River, growth was slower, but the port gradually took over the marshes, and then the drained lands, located north of Corlear's Hook.

The port also expanded along the other shore of the East River: Brooklyn became an important port after the construction of two huge docks, the Atlantic and the Erie, and the 1867 opening of the U.S. Navy Yard. On the New Jersey side, Samuel Cunard's decision to have his transatlantic steamers berth at Jersey City marked the beginning of the development of the Hudson's western shore.

All this development changed the ecological balance of the Hudson estuary and the Long Island strait. Some of the flora and fauna formerly found there disappeared. By about 1880, the oysters that connoisseurs enjoyed in the many oyster cellars on Canal Street or Broadway no longer came from the New York or Long Island waters as they had in the past, but from the Chesapeake Bay, whose beds had been better preserved. In 1888, the endless appropriation of land along the East River and the Hudson also led to the adoption of a federal law that charged the U.S. Army Corps of Engineers with establishing the limits of authorized expansion.

At the same time, the structures and operations of the port evolved. Approaching New York became less dangerous with the 1828 construction of two lighthouses on Navesink Heights, in New Jersey, complementing the first

FIGURE 15
Dynamiting the Hell Gate reefs
© Roger Viollet

lighthouse erected at Sandy Hook in 1764 and backed up
in 1823 by a beacon ship. Shoals were systematically
marked and reported on navigational maps, and the
major channels marked with beacons.

In the 1850s, and then again in the 1870s and 1880s
with more convincing results, the reefs that made up Hell
Gate—at the confluence of the East River and Long Island
Sound, and one of the most dangerous and dreaded spots
in the New York harbor waters—became the object of
impressive dynamiting campaigns. The pilots of the New
York port, who did not have a good reputation, saw their
monopoly abolished in the late 1830s, to the great profit
of their private competitors.

The mooring conditions in the port itself remained
mediocre for a long time. The modest pillared piers of the
colonial era were replaced by the wooden framework ones

described by James Fenimore Cooper. But these deteriorated quickly, especially the parts that were not permanently submerged. Mid-century, the authorities took it upon themselves to make improvements. In 1855, a commission issued recommendations for maintaining the piers and docks, and in 1857, the construction of new piers became subject to municipal authorization.

1870 marks the real turning point in the harbor's history, with the creation of the city's Department of Docks. Its mission was to supervise the land, the area, and the building of the port, and to put an end to the chaos that ruled along a good portion of the waterfront, astounding its observers. The *New York Times* spoke of the "rotten structures" that were "the abode of rats and the hiding places of river-thieves," while the Frenchwoman Olympe Audouard noted "the lack of beautiful quays: what bears this name is only a long road, revoltingly filthy, bordered by horrible wooden huts."[15]

The new Department of Docks had to alter the appearance and systematize the operations of the port. It was placed under the prestigious authority of the former commander-in-chief of the Union armies and unsuccessful candidate in the 1864 presidential elections, General George Brinton McClellan, a man of experience who had had many opportunities during his military career to build roads and railways.

After a competition calling for plans for the future port, and public hearings, the solution that McClellan himself recommended was accepted: a masonry wall and, at regular intervals, docks and piers of wood and masonry, surrounding Manhattan for more than twenty-seven miles, as far north as Fifty-First Street on the East River and Sixty-First Street on the Hudson. Work on the first of these piers, called Pier 1 and located on the Hudson near Battery Park, was begun in 1872. But McClellan's project progressed slowly due to technical and financial difficulties. The general resigned, and one of his successors, the engineer George Sears Greene, head of the Department of Docks from 1875 to 1897, assumed responsibility for modernizing the port. Under his leadership, the masonry wall, the piers, and the docks were built from Grand Street on the East

River, and to Eleventh Street on the Hudson. After 1883, the project reached Thirty-Fourth Street on the East River and Sixty-first Street on the Hudson. It was finally completed just before the United States entered World War I.

THE CONTINENT'S BANKER

The growth of the port led to the growth of New York's financial district, soon known by the name of the lower Manhattan street where, set back a bit from the docks, money matters were handled: Wall Street. External trade and the continent's economy functioned largely on credit, and New York became the place for negotiating the necessary financial arrangements within institutions specializing in the businesses of banking, finance, speculation, insurance, inheritance management, and financial information.

After their modest beginnings following the Revolutionary War, the commercial banks experienced impressive growth. They numbered twenty-five in 1845, eighty-two in 1860, 506 in 1883. Some of them were private, while others were state-chartered corporations. All of them engaged in discounting and rediscounting letters of exchange, amassing deposits, and making loans. Their strength derived in part from a favorable political and legislative environment. A guarantee fund for the notes issued by the banks was created in 1829, and in 1863, a federal law, the National Currency Act, reorganized the American monetary system by officially placing New York at the top of its financial pyramid. But the growth of New York's banks was due especially to the fact that other American banks found it convenient, and soon indispensable, to keep annual deposits there that were considered part of their own reserves.

With the proliferation of commercial banks came the development of related services like credit-verification offices, which helped to minimize risks. The first company of this type, Lewis Tappan's Mercantile Agency, which verified borrowers' solvency thanks to a tight network of local informers, appeared in 1841. The firm was bought out in the mid-1850s by one of its competitors,

FIGURE 16
The financial district about 1840
© Hachette Livre

B. Douglass and Company, which was taken over itself in 1858 by R. G. Dun and Company. Henceforth, this firm shared the market with its rival J. M. Bradstreet.

New York had many commercial banks interested in the financial markets and public loans as well as the stocks and bonds of private companies. Until the Civil War, the banks primarily played the role of intermediary and consultant between holders of capital, mostly the English, and American borrowers. Many were tied to their British counterparts, Baring, Wilson, Wildes, or Wiggins. Thus, Nathaniel Prime, Samuel Ward, and James Gore King, the partners of the largest commercial bank in New York between 1826 and 1848, had close connections to the House of Baring, whereas August Belmont was the New York agent for the Rothschilds. In the 1850s, the rapid growth in the construction of the railways increased the role of these commercial banks, as they often specialized in railway loans and stocks, following the example of Winslow, Lanier & Co., founded in 1849.

New York commercial banks changed scale beginning in the 1860s. Banks were needed for placing the federal loans issued after the Civil War for the industrial growth that followed the restoration of peace. This was the moment when the late nineteenth century's greatest American banker, John Pierpont Morgan, began his career. The son of Junius Spencer Morgan, a New England businessman who settled in London in the mid-1850s, the young Morgan began working for the New York counterpart to his father's firm at the age of twenty. In the first years of the Civil War, he opened his own company. In 1864, he became a partner in the firm of Dabney, Morgan & Co., which specialized in railroad investments and the distribution of loans issued by foreign governments.

In the early 1870s, Morgan formed a partnership with the firm of Drexel & Co. of Philadelphia. Under his leadership, Drexel, Morgan & Co. soon became one of New York's largest commercial banks. Morgan participated in the liquidation of the Civil War debt and in the investment of many American and foreign loans. Then in the 1880s, he played an active advisory role for railroad companies such as the New York Central and the Pennsylvania.

At the same time, immigrants were creating commercial banks. With the exception of the Lazard Brothers, who opened offices in New York in 1880—nearly forty years after three Jewish immigrants from France, Alexandre, Simon, and Lazare Lazard, founded a dry-goods firm in New Orleans—most of these newcomers were German Jews. Joseph Seligman, for example, left Bavaria for Pennsylvania at the end of the 1830s. After several years of peddling, he settled in New York and got started in the clothing industry. During the Civil War, he won an important uniform contract for the Union soldiers, and then helped invest 200 million dollars worth of war loans. In 1864, the Seligman Brothers firm was established, and it soon had branches in New Orleans, San Francisco, Paris, London, and Frankfurt, where it specialized in investing public and private American loans in Europe. Abraham Kuhn and Solomon Loeb began as grocers in the Midwest, and then became clothing manufacturers in New York before founding a bank specializing in railroad title subscriptions in

1867, under the impetus of Jacob Schiff, a major partner after 1880.

As the century progressed, these commercial banks became more and more involved in the development of the Stock Exchange, located at 40 Wall Street. Officially established under the name of the New York Stock Exchange and Board on March 8, 1817, it began modestly, with only twenty members in 1817 and thirty-nine in 1820. It owed its origin to federal loans issued during the War of 1812, which revitalized a New York market that had first appeared briefly in 1792. After 1820, a nascent national stock market developed, thanks especially to the seven million dollars in loans that the building of the Erie Canal required.

Even though competing stock exchanges existed in Boston and Philadelphia, New York, with its abundant money, significant volume of transactions, and ceaseless speculation, became the logical center for the securities market. The flow of capital into the financial markets was facilitated by improved new techniques, like call loans: the speculator borrowed money from a bank by promising to pay it back immediately upon the bank's demand. As a guarantee, he used the stocks he acquired with the borrowed sums, which came from bank reserves made up of deposits from the rest of the country. Beginning in the 1850s, Wall Street's success rested upon the railways, and at the end of the century, upon the country's industrial growth, because investors cheerfully speculated on railroad, mining, or oil stocks. In 1886, shares exchanged on a single day at the stock market reached the one-million mark for the first time.

At the same time, all the activities needed to support these financial operations were developing. The initial publication in 1882 of the *Wall Street Journal* testified to the importance of specialized financial information. By this date, Wall Street already housed many offices of business lawyers, like Blatchford, Seward & Griswold (1854) or Shearman & Sterling (1873), who provided financiers and soon corporations with legal advice and arrangements.

Bankers and stockbrokers were not the only ones to make New York's financial district famous. Many successful trust companies for managing private inheritances were established. Insurance companies, provided in 1820 with a Board of Underwriters to help them establish premium rates and minimize the risks incurred, often successfully competed with banks in the search for capital and the follow-up of investments. Marine insurance also developed, boosted by the growth of the port and the healthy state of the American merchant marine. The Atlantic, a joint-stock company converted into a mutual insurance company in the 1840s, became New York's largest maritime insurer under the leadership of its president, Walter Restored Jones. But after the Civil War, the situation changed, due to the decline in the merchant marine. Henceforth, the powerful Lloyd's and other British insurers competed too heavily with New York insurers, whose activities were limited to cargo. Soon marine insurance in New York was reduced to only the Atlantic Mutual Insurance Company.

Fire insurance also appeared at the end of the eighteenth century. It developed locally, but the companies struggled to gain a national clientele. Furthermore, they almost all collapsed following the great fire of December 16 and 17, 1835, which led to some fifteen million dollars' worth of losses for the insurers. The ones that succeeded them had to face another blaze, almost as dramatic, ten years later. In fact, fire insurance companies lacked firm financial footing, and the 1849 law that made it easier to create them tended to make them weaker. Business failures multiplied, and in 1859, the State of New York had to intervene to regulate that sector of business. Eight years later, the New York Board of Fire Underwriters was created in order to better control the companies and strengthen fire-prevention measures among those insured.

Life insurance alone was a great success. Companies proliferated: Mutual Life in 1842, New York Life in 1849, Equitable Life in 1859, Metropolitan Life in 1868. Immediately following the Civil War, they set out to conquer America and Europe, thanks especially to the refinement of so-called industrial insurance: designed for workers, this was based on weekly payment of modest dues col-

lected house-to-house by the company's agent. Metropolitan Life made this its specialty, which accounted for
its spectacular growth.

By the mid-century, the impact of all these financial
institutions was so great that the monthly magazine *Putnam* remarked, "The banks of New York are becoming
every day more important in an architectural point of
view," not hesitating to comment ironically upon "their
classical costumes after the most approved Yankee-Greek
mode."[16] In fact, neoclassical buildings proliferated in
the 1830s and 1840s, in particular after the 1835 fire that
ravaged lower Manhattan's financial district. The first
office building was constructed in the 1840s by Richard
Upjohn, at the prompting of the wardens of Trinity
Church, inaugurating with its five stories an architectural
model destined for success. Soon the sixteen granite
columns adorning the new Merchants' Exchange on Wall
Street, unveiled in 1842, symbolized the growing presence of finance in the metropolis.

METROPOLITAN INDUSTRIALIZATION

For the most part, New Yorkers were not employed either
in commerce or in financial occupations. "New York is
not merely a commercial city," noted the mid-century
businessman James Robertson. "She is largely engaged in
manufactures of various kinds,—indeed more so than
any other city in America."[17]

In fact, the manufacturing sector's role grew rapidly as
a result of New York's commercial dominance, low transport costs, and the growth of the local market. Beginning
in the 1830s and 1840s, industrial reorganization affected
not only New York but also its entire periphery. Despite
the inevitable inertia, an industrial belt soon developed
and attracted the mechanized industries that required
large amounts of space.

Hoboken, Jersey City, Newark, and Paterson, in New
Jersey, Bridgeport and Danbury in Connecticut, and
Brooklyn and Yonkers in New York offered less expensive
land and better hydraulic resources than Manhattan for
textile mills, sugar refineries, ironworks, and tanneries. In

1847, William Colgate, an Englishman who had immi-
grated to the United States in 1795 because of his father's
declared Jacobinism and had opened a business in lower
Manhattan in 1806, transferred his soap-, candle-, and
starch-making factory to Jersey City. In 1873, Isaac Merritt
Singer, who made sewing machines and whose factory
and foundry had been located in two buildings on Mott
Street and Delancey Street since 1858, left Manhattan for
a factory constructed on a ten-acre property in Elizabeth-
port, New Jersey, where the enterprise could produce
more than a thousand machines a day. About 1880,
Newark's industrial enterprises employed nearly 30,000
workers, and New Jersey's foundries, sugar refineries and
slaughterhouses employed many thousands more.

In Brooklyn, a city of 50,000 workers, the first factories
were constructed in the 1780s. Close to the wharf and the
ferry, they served as breweries, craft-industry workshops,
and slaughterhouses. Beginning in the 1840s, the growth
of the port transformed the shores of the East River—from
Red Hook in the south to Newtown Creek in the north—
into a zone of warehouses, silos, sugar and kerosene
refineries, tanneries, ironworks, and shipyards. Williamsburg was the home of Frederick C. Havemeyer's sugar refinery, the city's largest, as well as Charles Pratt's kerosene
refinery, Astral Oil Works, which made this convenient
whale-oil substitute used for lighting, and Continental
Ironworks, a huge plant that produced the armor plates for
the Union's first battleships. Bushwick, another independent village that Brooklyn soon absorbed, specialized in
making beer, and was home to a large brewery established
by Samuel Liebmann in 1855, and renamed Rheingold
Breweries in 1880 in honor of its most famous brand.

Manhattan had other assets that explained its own industrial geography. In addition to a major local market and an
easily summoned labor force, it offered advantages with
regard to the circulation of information. It is not surprising
that New York primarily retained its printing, publishing,
garment, tobacco, furniture, and musical-instrument-
making industries. In 1870, the proportion of the labor force
in these various sectors that worked in New York City made
up more than four fifths of the regional total, whereas a

FIGURE 17
The Novelty Ironworks Factories about 1850
Metropolitan Museum of Art, The Edward W.C. Arnold Collection of
New York Prints, Maps and Pictures, Bequest of Edward W. C. Arnold,
1954 (54.90.588)

majority of leather, textile, or iron workers were employed in factories within the industrial belt.

Lower Manhattan housed the premier New York industries, those that reaped the benefits of being close to the financial district. In the Third Ward, near the East River, garment makers, printers, and publishers set up shop, making this "the metropolis's great workshop" by the 1840s. The publisher Harper Brothers, the lithographer Currier & Ives, and the American Bank Note Company, a printer of notes, stamps, and stock certificates, stood side by side with dozens of small metallurgy, plumbing, or heating businesses.

Shipbuilding, the only heavy industry remaining in Manhattan, was localized along the shores of the East River as it had been in the past, but the shipyards moved north of Corlear's Hook in the 1830s to the district known as the Dry Docks. That was where the epoch's most famous shipbuilders were to be found—Henry Eckford, Isaac and William Webb, Christian Bergh, and Jacob Westervelt—whose clippers, schooners, brigs, and steamers earned the East River yards their reputation. Their shipyards neighbored Manhattan's last iron factories, which provided them with boilers, engines, and, later, on the propellers for steamers. The largest of them, Novelty Ironworks, founded in the early 1830s, extended for more than 300 yards along the riverfront between Twelfth and Fourteenth Street, and employed nearly 1,200 workers by mid-century. Besides Novelty, other iron foundries like Allaire, Morgan, Cornell, or Delameter Works, tanneries, and all the subcontracting trades related to shipbuilding, gave the Dry Docks district a very industrialized aspect. On the other side of Manhattan, on the shores of the Hudson, were found those enterprises involving wood and stone, as well as coal sheds.

Outside of the ironworks and shipyards, buildings equipped with steam engines or hydraulic turbines—mechanized workshops—were rare: sawmills, distilleries, printers, or breweries. Primarily New York included a host of very small operations—custom tailor shops and shoemakers or clothing workshops tucked away in garrets or tenement rooms—that represented four fifths of all workers in the 1840s.

In the mid-nineteenth century, the mens' clothing industry became the city's largest employer. Prior to 1820, it was nearly nonexistent, because clothes were often made at home. But it grew rapidly, thanks to the expansion of the market to farmers and inhabitants of the Midwest and California. To respond to this growing demand, more clothes had to be produced at a lower price. In the 1840s and 1850s, the favored solution was the large firm that employed a few permanent workers in its shops and resorted mainly to a less costly labor force that worked at home. Lewis & Hanford, for example, employed seventy-five in-house cutters and nearly 4,000 seamstresses who worked at home. Brooks Brothers—a mens' clothing firm founded in 1818 by Henry Sands Brooks and taken over by his five sons (who adopted the corporate name that made them famous) when he died in 1833—employed seventy-eight cutters and 1,500 seamstresses. After 1850, the continual quest for economy and flexibility resulted in the development of subcontracting and sweatshops that better answered those requirements.

Like the garment industry, New York manufacturers became less and less dependent on foreign trade. In the 1820s, industry was still largely dependent on maritime trade, which explained the importance of the flour mills, sugar refineries, distilleries, and shipyards. But within a few decades, the development of the local market and domestic demand enhanced the growth of sectors not directly tied to the harbor. In 1860, nearly eight out of ten workers were employed in the garment sector, in the printing, publishing, and building trades, in small iron-works, or in other occupations not directly related to foreign trade.

At the same time, the New York landscape changed. Geographic concentration and architectural specialization went hand in hand, especially after the Civil War. Industrial buildings proliferated, responding to the demand, and also because they constituted better investments for their owners. In the 1860s, the area located between Canal Street to the south and Houston Street to the north became the center of New York industry. Along Broadway and on adjacent streets, like Spring, Prince, or Broome Streets, rose cast-iron buildings with ornate neoclassical facades. Their five or six stories were rented to various commercial and industrial firms that installed their warehouses and production workshops there. Soon cast-iron buildings were one of Manhattan's characteristic architectural features.

THE COLOSSUS OF THE NEW TIMES

The inauguration of the Statue of Liberty on October 28, 1886 was a major event. In the presence of the president of the United States and former governor of New York, Grover Cleveland, with six hundred invited guests and thousands of spectators, Bedloe Island, in the heart of New

FIGURE 18
Nineteenth-century print showing the construction of
the Statue of Liberty's head
© Leonard de Selva/CORBIS

York Bay, received the work of the sculptor Auguste
Bartholdi, the huge statue offered by the French to the
American people at the initiative of the jurist and historian
Édouard de Laboulaye. In order to help raise money in the
United States to complete its massive pedestal, Emma
Lazarus had composed her poem, "The New Colossus," a

few years earlier, celebrating New York's destiny to welcome immigrants by the millions:

> Not like the brazen giant of Greek fame,
> With conquering limbs astride from land to land;
> Here at our sea-washed, sunset gate shall stand
> A mighty woman with a torch, whose flame
> Is the imprisoned lightning, and her name
> Mother of Exiles. From her beacon-hand
> Glows world-wide welcome; her mild eyes command
> The air-bridged harbor that twin cities frame.
> "Keep, ancient lands, your storied pomp!" cries she
> With silent lips. "Give me your tired, your poor,
> Your huddled masses yearning to breathe free,
> The wretched refuse of your teeming shore.
> Send these, the homeless, tempest-tost to me,
> I lift my lamp beside the golden door!"[18]

The poem would not be engraved on a bronze plaque
and affixed to the base of the statue until 1903. For the
moment, Liberty's high torch not only proclaimed the
generosity of American hospitality to the world, it also
illuminated the spectacle of New York's economic power,
the vision of its commercial, financial, and industrial
ascendancy over the North American continent and an
ever growing metropolitan area. The statue turned its
back to the city to better view the open sea, symbolizing
New York's ambition to compete with London for domination over the international economy. Henceforth, the
pulse of that economy would, to some extent, follow the
rhythm of Manhattan's and Brooklyn's docks, offices,
stores, and workshops.

4

THE EMPIRE CITY

New York was transformed by its economic omnipotence. Taken together, Brooklyn and New York counted about 220,000 inhabitants in 1830, one million in 1860, and 2.5 million in 1890! New York became a metropolis. Henceforth, everything was different. An unsympathetic Mark Twain discovered there "a splendid desert—a domed and steepled solitude, where a stranger is lonely in the midst of a million of his race." More moderate and also more of a New Yorker, Asa Greene saw it as "a very great city; a very populous city; a very expensive city; a very scarce-of-hotels city; a remarkably religious city; a sadly over-run-with-law-and-physic city; a surprisingly newspaperial city; a rather queerly governed city; an uncommon badly watered city; a very considerable of a rum city; a very full-of-fires city; a pretty tolerably well-hoaxed city: and moreover, a city moderately abounding in foul streets, rogues, dandies, mobs and several other things."[1]

A NEW SCALE

"A very great city," indeed—a city with capacities for expansion that are endlessly fascinating. In 1836, the former mayor Philip Hone, an observant chronicler, made ironic note of "the old downtown burgomasters" (of which he was one!) "marching reluctantly north to pitch their tents in places which, in their time, were orchards, corn-fields or morasses a pretty smart distance from town."[2]

The conquest of Manhattan was rapid: in seventy years, New York extended its hold on the island farther than it had over the course of the first two centuries of its existence. "Before the revolution of a century," boldly prophesied DeWitt Clinton in 1824, "the whole island of Manhattan, covered with habitations and replenished with a dense population, will constitute one vast city."[3]

In 1825, the urbanized area did not extend beyond Canal Street, less than three miles north of the tip of Manhattan; it soon reached Houston Street, and in the early 1840s, Fifth Avenue ran to Twentieth Street. In 1860, the city, now with its 814,000 inhabitants, extended as far as Forty-second Street, with its sights on Fiftieth Street, where, in 1858, the first stones were ceremoniously laid for the future Saint Patrick's Cathedral, the pride of New York Catholics. On the East Side of Manhattan, Ninetieth Street was reached by 1880, One Hundred and Thirty-fifth Street by 1890. On the West Side, development was slower until the 1890s, but the city steadily overtook the whole island. In 1900, DeWitt Clinton's prediction had come true. Manhattan was entirely plotted out.

But by then, it had been a long time since New York had simply been Manhattan. By mid-century, New York was "the Queen of the Western World, with New Jersey on the one side and Brooklyn on the other. The three form but one city in fact though differing in name like London and Westminster."[4] Matthew Dripps's 1860 map embodied this new perception of the metropolis: besides Manhattan, it included Brooklyn, Hoboken, Hudson City, and Jersey City.

The need for, and the arbitrary nature of, limits to the metropolitan area were highlighted by the authors of a report on the *Social Statistics of Cities* at the time of the 1880 federal census. "It seems proper, in treating of the vast population occupying the cities of New York, Brooklyn, Jersey City, Newark and Hoboken, to consider them not only as constituting five different municipalities, but as one great metropolitan community." "It is true" they add, "that this mode of reasoning might easily be carried

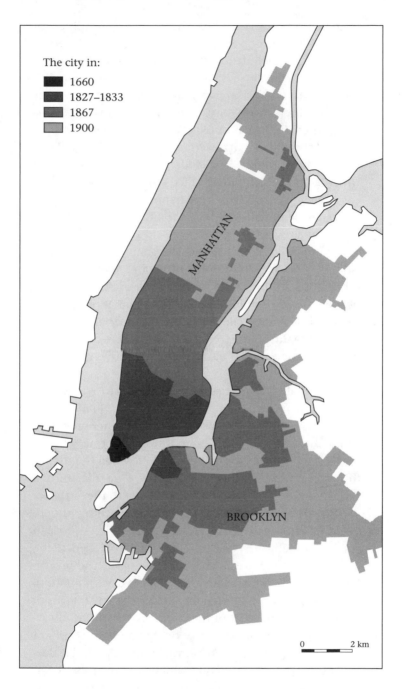

MAP 4
The growth of New York in the nineteenth century

to the extreme of absurdity. There is no controlling reason why Flushing, New Rochelle, Yonkers and Paterson
might not be included in the same community. Indeed,
the villages and towns strung along the railways for fifty
miles from New York are very largely made up of persons
doing business in the city, or occupied in manufactures
which there find their market. Wherever the line may be
drawn it must be an arbitrary one, and it has been
thought most proper to include only those larger towns
which are most intimately allied with New York as their
commercial center, and, as it happens, which transport
their raw material and their products from and to it
largely by wagons."[5]

On the west bank of the Hudson, Jersey City and
Hoboken became half residential and half industrial
suburbs, served by a fleet of ferries. Jersey City's population increased tenfold between 1840 and 1860 to reach
29,000 inhabitants. Close by, Newark, specializing especially in the shoe industry, was home to more than 70,000
people on the eve of the Civil War, four times more than
in 1840.

Indisputably, the most impressive growth was Brooklyn's, "New York's dormitory," according to Charles Dickens. Around 1815, its landowners, among them the merchant Hezekiah Beers Pierrepont, transformed themselves into property developers. They divided their lands
into small parcels and, in less than a decade, turned
Brooklyn Heights—the area that overlooked the ferry pier
on the East River—into a fashionable neighborhood.
What was once a little village became a leading American
residential suburb. Wealthy New Yorkers settled there,
attracted by the bucolic charm of the place, the breath-
taking view of Manhattan, and the perfect combination,
if we are to believe Pierrepont, of "all the advantages of
the country with most of the conveniences of the city."[6]

At the same time, the ferry district and the shores of
the East River experienced heavy commercial and industrial development. Brooklyn, which was incorporated as
a city in 1834, adopted a city plan four years later. As
with Manhattan, the principle of a grid appealed to the
Brooklyn commissioners, but their plan included various

orientations and thoroughfares that traced diagonals beginning from the pier.

Brooklyn's development led to the gradual urbanization of neighboring villages, Williamsburg in particular, which was absorbed by its hungry neighbor in 1855. Farther north, Stephen Halsey, a fur trader, conceived of a plan for a residential neighborhood that he christened Astoria in 1839. Despite the reference to the fabulously wealthy John Jacob Astor, Astoria did not develop until the early 1870s, when Henry Steinway, the piano maker, set up his business and housed his workers there.

The expansion of New York and Brooklyn made urban transportation a crucial issue. By mid-century, it had become difficult to cross the city on foot. For the wealthiest inhabitants, who moved about in their own carriages, the distance was hardly a problem, but the situation was very different for hundreds of thousands of other city dwellers. Many solutions were implemented successively or simultaneously.

The first suburban train line, the New York & Harlem Railroad, was opened in 1832. Originally drawn by a combination of animal and steam power, the New York & Harlem gradually ascended Fourth Avenue north, first to Fourteenth Street, and then to Eighty-fifth Street and the village of Yorkville, and finally to the village of Harlem a few years later, at One Hundred and Tenth Street. By the end of the 1830s, nearly a million people already used the line each year to go to work in the city. The number was three times that on the eve of the Civil War, as Harlem and Yorkville grew proportionately.

In New York itself, the first horse-drawn omnibuses went into operation in the 1820s on Manhattan's main thoroughfare, Broadway. Their success compelled the municipality to grant permits to interested carriers and earned New York the nickname of "the city of omnibuses." About eighty such vehicles circulated in 1833, 255 in 1846, and 700 in the 1850s. The omnibus had its drawbacks: it was slow, relatively expensive, and each car could only carry a dozen passengers. In 1850, the aldermen noted sadly that "during certain periods of the day and evening, and always during inclement weather, passengers are packed into these

vehicles, without regard to comfort or even decency, sometimes, and many are utterly unable to secure seats, even
after waiting for hours."[7]

Over the course of the 1850s, the omnibuses were
replaced by horse-drawn streetcars, which were faster and
less expensive. Their rails soon covered Manhattan's
avenues and some of its streets. In 1860, they transported
about 45 million people. Not to be outdone, Brooklyn's
network developed to the south and northeast, beginning from the ferry pier.

But the horse-drawn streetcars were not enough for the
daily circulation of the populace. Too many New Yorkers
did not have the means to use them, and those who did
could not escape the jostling in the cars and the congestion in the streets. City dwellers were exasperated, and in
the 1860s, the first plans for rapid transit appeared.

In 1868, Alfred Beach, inventor, editor of *Scientific
American* and son of the owner of the *New York Sun*, Moses
Yale Beach, obtained permission to make two tunnels
under Broadway. Officially, it was a matter of perfecting a
system for transmitting the mail pneumatically, an idea
very much in vogue at the time. In reality, Beach wanted
to build a pneumatic underground railway, but he kept
his project secret, for fear of provoking the streetcar
lobby. In 1870, a prototype was tested. It was extraordinarily successful: 400,000 New Yorkers used it in the first
year. But Beach's attempt was short-lived, because he
could not find the necessary capital to develop the operation on a large scale. He abandoned it for good in 1874.

On the other hand, the plan for an elevated railway
was a success. Soon christened the "el" by New Yorkers
(for "elevated railway"), run by steam and then electric
power, it became one of the landmarks of the New York
urban landscape. Manhattan soon counted three elevated
lines over Second, Third and Ninth Avenues. Brooklyn
had three lines as well that opened in the 1880s.

New York was "in nests of water-bays" as Whitman
wrote, and since the seventeenth century, a network of ferries existed between Manhattan and Long Island, Staten
Island, and New Jersey. About 1850, a ferry weighed
anchor every five minutes for Brooklyn, and every ten

FIGURE 19
The elevated railway (the el)
© Roger Viollet

minutes for Jersey City. The only bridges that linked Manhattan to the mainland were found in the north, over the narrow Harlem River.

Following the Civil War, a plan was launched for a bridge over the East River, unthinkable before that time. John Augustus Roebling, its promoter, was an engineer of German origin who had emigrated to Pennsylvania in the early 1830s. He had perfected the wire cable and had constructed several suspension bridges over the Niagara gorges and the Ohio River. Work began in 1867, but Roebling died two years later, a victim of an accident on the construction site. His son, Washington Roebling, succeeded him and led the project to its completion, despite many technical difficulties. In 1872, he too was the victim of an accident and was confined to his home. His was a case of aeroembolism, or the bends, and resulted from an attempt to sink wooden caissons under one of the towers of the bridge under construction. Subsequently, he followed the progress of the work through a telescope,

FIGURE 20
New York, NY—Brooklyn Bridge: the cable anchorage under
construction. Engraving. © Bettmann/CORBIS

and transmitted his instructions through an intermediary, his wife Emily Warren Roebling.

A total of sixteen years of work were required before the 1883 opening of the new bridge, which became one of the city's attractions. "Even seen from afar, this bridge astounds you like one of those architectural nightmares given by Piranesi in his weird etchings," wrote Paul Bourget. "You see great ships passing beneath it, and this indisputable evidence of its height confuses the mind. But walk over it, feel the quivering of the monstrous trellis of iron and steel interwoven for a length of sixteen hundred feet at a height of one hundred and thirty-five feet above water; see the trains that pass over it in both directions, and the steam boats passing beneath your very body, while carriages come and go, and foot passen-

gers hasten along, an eager crowd, and you will feel that
the engineer is the great artist of our epoch, and you will
own that these people have a right to plume themselves
on their audacity, on the 'go-ahead' which has never
flinched."[8]

A CONGESTED CITY

Not even the Brooklyn Bridge, nor the city's altered scale,
nor the different means of transportation resolved the
problems of overpopulation and infrastructure deficien-
cies that plagued New York. Its newspapers and its inhabitants were unanimous in denouncing—sometimes vehe-
mently—the faults of the empire city: it was dirty, poorly
lit, and badly paved; it was "half finished," exclaimed one
visitor in 1849. Duvergier de Hauranne, on a walking tour
there fifteen years later, found New York "mean and repel-
lent" and denounced "the broken pavement, the muddy
streets, the parks full of weeds and briars, the horse-drawn
omnibuses—clumsy wagons that roll on iron tracks, the
irregularly placed houses, mottled with enormous posters,
have the neglected ugliness of an open-air bazaar."[9]

The congestion in the streets had become a commonplace in the newspapers by the 1830s. Asa Greene gave this
advice for crossing Broadway: "You must button your coat
tight about you, see that your shoes are secure at the heels,
settle your hat firmly on your head, look up street and
down street, at the self-same moment, to see what carts
and carriages are upon you, and then run for your life."[10]

Traffic congestion was not the only problem. The
roads, like the sidewalks—or what served as sidewalks—
were in a sorry state, often cluttered with garbage of all
kinds that made pedestrian travel perilous. As late as 1890,
the Frenchman Albert Delaporte explained that "the
municipal government" left "the city streets in a
deplorable state" because "New Yorkers' only means of
transport" were "the elevated railway" and "the 'cars'" or
tramways that circulate night and day;" New York streets
were "paved without paving stones . . . , with pebbles of
various sizes driven into the ground in a totally incoher-
ent fashion." "It is only at street crossings, out of kindness

FIGURE 21
New York in the snow, mid-nineteenth century
© Hachette Livre

to pedestrians" that "a few flag stones" are provided "to allow crossing without too much pain for sensitive feet or too much mess if there are horse droppings."[11]

These difficulties, a result of the ceaseless flow and activity of newcomers into an area that was not growing proportionately, were reflected again in housing. The population density per square mile was high in Manhattan in the 1830s, and only increased over the course of the decades that followed. New York was no longer on the same scale as any other American city, including Brooklyn.

Indeed, after 1820, real-estate supply proved less and less equal to demand. In Manhattan, property developers and builders primarily constructed two- or three-story houses in the districts then opening north of the colonial city. These lodgings were sometimes meant for the most affluent New Yorkers, such as the houses on Washington Square or Lafayette Place, whose Corinthian columns won the admiration of the New York elite. But most of them were more modest and meant for mid-level New York society. A veritable speculative rush was unleashed in the mid-1830s by these so-called "modern" houses, supposedly embodying the domestic virtues and the independent spirit of the middle classes of the time.

Housing for the poor did not interest developers. Returns on such investments were too limited, especially in comparison with what the "modern buildings" offered. Thus, most immigrants and workers remained in lower Manhattan neighborhoods, crammed into makeshift housing, often the former homes of merchants or artisans, hastily divided and reconverted into rental properties, called "rookeries." Hygiene was abysmal, but the owners drew considerable profits from them.

Economic crisis struck in May 1837. The American economy was plunged into a depression that lasted until 1843, ruining speculators and halting construction in the new districts. Real-estate supply collapsed while the city continued to grow. Thus all the elements of a severe housing crisis came together: "Thousands and tens of thousands are compelled to exist from day to day under the constant, crushing pressure of . . . terrible sufferings resulting directly from the miserable houses in which they live," reported the *Morning Courier* in 1847.[12]

When the economy picked up again, the reconverted houses of the preceding decades were replaced by the first buildings meant especially for the very poor. These first tenements—the word, an old one, had been applied to all kinds of housing until this time, but now it entered permanently into the New York imagination—were built according to the clearly understood interests of their owners. In the absence of any regulations, the buildings, five or more stories high, were erected on the 25-by-100-foot lots provided for in the 1811 city plan. Each story housed several dwellings, dark, poorly ventilated, without running water, the rooms sometimes arranged in a row, like the compartments of a train car, earning the building the nickname of "railroad tenement." It was not unusual for the cellars to serve as living quarters for the very poorest residents.

In working-class districts with their mix of housing, workshops, warehouses, factories, and slaughterhouses, the tenements aggravated the overpopulation problems. Gotham Court, one of New York's largest and most infamous tenements, was built on Cherry Street in 1850. Its six floors were meant to house 140 families, and soon accommodated a hundred more. These harshly criticized tenements were succeeded by a new generation of working-class housing in the late 1870s, called "dumbbell tenements." Their floor plan respected the Tenement House Act of 1879, which required a window for each room for ventilation purposes.

More than 20,000 buildings of this kind were constructed between 1879 and 1901. They stood six or seven stories high, each floor divided into four dwellings of less than 100 square feet each—that is, about 400 people per building and 4,000 per block. Ventilation was theoretically ensured by a narrow air shaft separating each tenement building from the neighboring one. Suffice it to say that living conditions for the poorest New Yorkers had only relatively improved. By the late 1880s, some districts reached record population densities per acre. In 1899, the statistician Adna Weber noted that "with a population of 523.6 inhabitants per acre, the Tenth Ward is probably the densest district in the Western world, Josefstadt in Prague having 485.4, the *quartier* Bonne-Nouvelle in *arrondissement* Bourse in Paris 434.19, and Bethnal Green North in London 365.3. The Eleventh and Thirteenth Wards are also very densely populated. They are the really congested districts of New York, and yet their population had continued to increase since 1860."[13]

On streets or in buildings, this urban congestion demonstrated the difficulties of adapting municipal services to the needs of New Yorkers. By the 1820s, nearly everything falling into this domain remained to be invented, because the idea of forceful municipal action was foreign to the eighteenth- and early nineteenth-century city. Over the course of the following decades, the Common Council began to grapple with the problem. In 1844, New York's aldermen replaced the night watch, which had become obsolete, with a municipal police force, organized according to the model of the London police; nine years later, and despite very strong opposition, the police were given uniforms—blue coat, gray pants, blue cap—meant to reinforce their authority. But these representatives of the law often owed their positions to the patronage system of municipal political life, and hardly earned unanimous approval.

Tensions surfaced when the Republicans, in control in Albany, created a metropolitan police district in 1857, under state control and combining New York and Brooklyn, and thus provoked the anger of the Democratic mayor Fernando Wood. Violent riots set metropolitan and municipal police against each other. Gradually however, the municipality worked to strengthen the authority of the New York police and to consider seniority and professional experience, and not just party affiliations, when it came to promotions and appointments.

Fire fighting followed a similar course. In the mid-century, fire departments remained staffed by volunteers, but their membership evolved: henceforth, artisans and gentlemen rarely participated, whereas the working class developed a masculine camaraderie within their companies. But a stubborn rivalry among the companies often undermined their effectiveness, especially since the lack of any coordination made fighting fires as uncertain as it was spectacular. The system's shortcomings were demonstrated by the "Great Fire" of December 1835, which ravaged the area of Pearl Street and Hanover Street, destroying nearly 700 buildings, and by the fire of July 1845, which reduced the Bowling Green neighborhood to ashes. After 1860, the trend was toward professionalism, on the model of the police: a permanent corps of firefighters, organized in a quasi-military fashion, replaced the volunteer companies and operated within the framework of the metropolitan district created in 1865.

In the area of public health and sanitation as well, the idea of public intervention long remained inconceivable.

The cholera epidemic that struck New York in the summer of 1832 appeared to be divine punishment, Providence's great design. The city's inhabitants fled, the Methodists organized public prayers, and the usefulness of proclaiming a day of official fasting was seriously debated. The few limited measures of hygiene then implemented were quickly forgotten as soon as the disease disappeared.

It was in the late 1830s that public-health problems began to preoccupy the authorities. In 1835, New Yorkers, consulted by their municipal council, decided to create a water system to replace the public and private wells, the rainwater cisterns, and the primitive pipelines constructed in a few streets by the Manhattan Company in 1799. On July 4, 1842, New York celebrated: Thanks to a thirty-five-mile aqueduct and two reservoirs, one a receiving structure located between 79th and 86th Streets and Sixth and Seventh Avenues, the other a massive distributing water tower built at the intersection of Fifth Avenue and Forty-Second Street, the water from the upstate Croton River was now available to New Yorkers. Henceforth, fountains could be constructed in the city. Soon, the wealthiest New Yorkers treated themselves to the latest in luxury plumbing. Domestic use of water increased, and New York grew so quickly that the system had to be enlarged in the early 1860s, and then, ten years later, the Croton network had to be extended to include other rivers.

The aqueduct's inauguration coincided with the first concerted efforts to improve public health. In 1845, a detailed report on *The Health Conditions of the Working Class Population of New York*, the work of John Griscom, a physician and municipal health inspector, put health and poverty in perspective. It took years for the vision of public health that Griscom proposed to be recognized—at least until the publication in 1866 of a report on *The Health Conditions of the City* prepared by the Council of Hygiene and Public Health of the very respectable Citizens Association. Supported with examples, the report warned against the dangers of overpopulation and criticized the industrial use of land in working-class districts as well as the inadequacies of the drainage and sewer systems. Paying new attention to scientific expertise, it defined the many health issues to be addressed by the Metropolitan Board of Health, created that same year.

In practice, the hygienic ideal was never more than partially realized. In 1849, a municipal service responsible for sewers was established, but at that time New York had only seventy miles of pipelines, and only about double that in 1857, for nearly 500 miles of streets. The situation really improved only in the 1870s and 1880s, at the instigation of the Metropolitan Board of Health. Garbage collection and street cleaning continued to provide topics for chroniclers and foreign critics. New York "is an enormous pigsty," complained Philip Hone. This was quite literally true: until the Civil War, there were numerous pigs in New York streets, where they played the role of urban street cleaners, astonishing Charles Dickens on his walks along Broadway in 1842.

Health promoters occasionally met with more success. They were able to spread the idea that poverty was not a sign of moral deficiency, but of an unfavorable environment. During yet another cholera epidemic, in August 1866, George Templeton Strong judged it "shameful that men, women and children should be permitted to live in such holes as thousands of them occupy this night in this city."[14] Some initiatives succeeded: public baths were built in New York in the 1850s, and even, twenty years later, floating baths (large wooden structures) on the Hudson and the East River.

Most importantly, the mid-century witnessed the development of a movement that favored the creation of green spaces, grievously lacking in the city designed by the 1811 plan. The idea was not new, and it did not originate in New York. It was first embodied in the landscaped cemeteries created in many cities after 1830, modeled on the Mount Auburn cemetery in Boston. The landscaped cemetery of Green-Wood opened in Brooklyn in 1838 on the wooded heights of Gowanus, looked out over New York Bay, and offered its many visitors a place to contemplate and meditate in contact with nature carefully cultivated by human hands.

This was not enough to compensate for the lack of parks at a time when the Manhattan shoreline was becoming less and less accessible to its inhabitants. In 1851, on the advice of a group of wealthy merchants, the mayor Ambrose Kingsland recommended that a park be created "in a style worthy of the city." Three years were spent resolving controversies, debating, and maneuvering to choose the site. "Give us a park, be it central, sidelong, here, there, anywhere, . . . a real park, a large park," came the exasperated cry from the *Commercial Advertiser* in summer 1853. Others proposed to substitute the plan for a huge park with a series of small ones, scattered throughout the city. "That would certainly be less aristocratic," commented John Griscom, "more democratic, and far more conducive to public health." In the end, the center of the island was preferred to the shores of the East River, and the idea of a "central park" was approved by the legislators. But it took many years to expropriate the property and compensate the site's owners, and to begin work.[15]

The project accepted in spring 1858, following a public competition, was the joint work of a young English architect, Calvert Vaux, and the former journalist and gentleman farmer turned superintendent of the park in the making and landscape architect Frederick Law Olmsted. Both of them were anxious to design a landscaped park that would be, to quote Olmsted, "an oasis" or "an arcadia, in the desert of brick and mortar" that was New York.[16] The new park was to offer its visitors a pastoral vision at odds with the urban setting, in order to combat its pernicious effects through the contemplation of "natural landscapes," supposedly elevating the visitors' souls and contributing to the preservation of social order.

Opened progressively as the work on it advanced, Central Park responded at first to Olmsted's bucolic expectations. Its use became more democratic after 1870, to the extent that immigrants and workers ventured there in growing numbers. By 1890, Central Park had become the great park that its advocates had called for four decades earlier. Furthermore, it gained a following: in the late 1850s, Brooklyn launched a similar project, Prospect Park, which Olmsted and Vaux were asked to complete after the Civil War. Many other American cities imitated New York and Brooklyn's example and hired Olmsted to create new rural parks.

THE IMMIGRANTS

The Central Park of the 1880s, where a very diverse population mixed, reflected the rise in immigration since 1830. From this perspective as well, New York was changing. At the end of the 1820s, James Fenimore Cooper could still declare that the city "is composed of inhabitants from all the countries of Christendom," but that, "beyond a doubt a very large majority, perhaps nine tenths, are natives of the United States."[17] In 1840, a third of New Yorkers were born in foreign countries, in 1855, more than half, and between 1860 and 1890, still forty percent. In Brooklyn, the proportion of foreigners was slightly lower, but it reached 47 percent by 1855, before remaining between 30 and 40 percent over the three decades that followed.

New York was by far the most important United States port of entry for European immigrants. Around ten million of them disembarked on the Hudson and East River quays between 1820 and 1890, two thirds of these after 1860. Departing from Le Havre, Bremen, Hamburg and Liverpool, less often from Cork, Galway, Marseilles, London, Greenock, or Glasgow, the majority of them had left their countries for economic reasons. Driven away by the decline of rural industries, the demise of local crafts, and the growing commercialization of agriculture, they were drawn across the Atlantic by the hope of a better life. Others, less numerous, emigrated to escape religious or political persecution. A very great majority of these European immigrants intended to continue their journey farther inland on the continent. But by necessity or by choice, a significant proportion of them settled in New York. For all of them, the arrival in the New York harbor marked the end of an adventurous Atlantic crossing under difficult conditions that did not improve until after the Civil War.

Until the mid-1850s, the ships loaded with immigrants berthed at the Manhattan quays or in Long Island

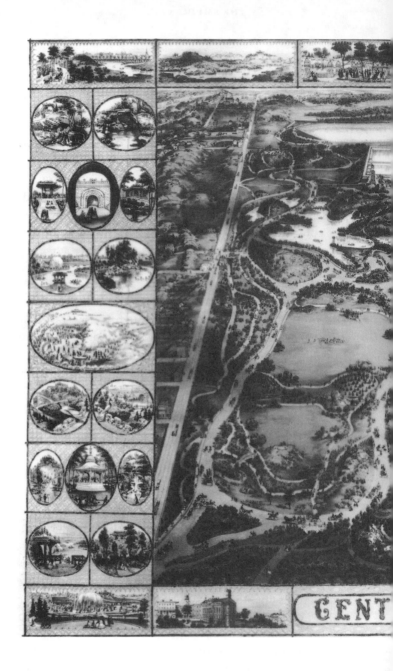

CENT

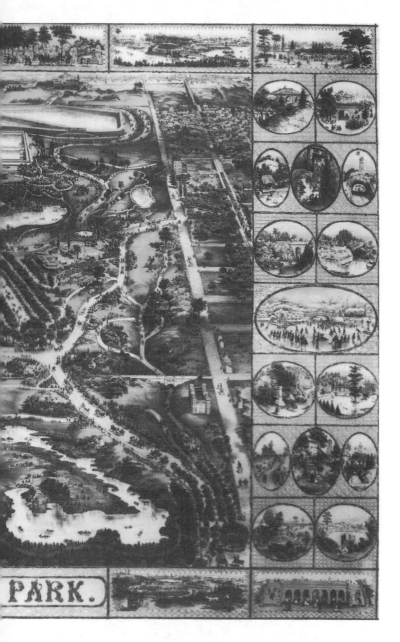

FIGURE 22
Central Park in 1863
The New-York Historical Society

or New Jersey ports, such as Perth Amboy. Hardly disembarked, the new arrivals fell prey to unscrupulous compatriots or Americans, ready to take advantage of their ignorance of the city and the new country. A German immigrant from the Trier region, Angela Heck, the wife of a tailor, recounted her arrival in New York in May 1854: "Everyone left the ship, for there were no more people who were sick on board. Then our trunks were taken to shore on a steamboat, and we also came on a steamboat. There was a young man there from Hefnig near Echternach who was there to meet his countrymen, a real rascal. He then led all of us who were in the ship to a German boardinghouse in New York. There we ate three meals and slept one night. Then everyone had to pay seven francs. My husband had to pay fourteen francs for the two of us, since they had put all the trunks in the cellar and no one could get them back before he paid."[18]

The keepers of the second-rate boardinghouses along the docks and Greenwich Street did a good business, charging high prices for the rooms they rented to new arrivals and often holding their bags as collateral. Faced with growing abuses, the authorities finally responded. In 1847, a law gave them the theoretical means to better protect immigrants by establishing a Board of Commissioners of Emigration. Made up of six individuals appointed by the governor, the mayors of New York and Brooklyn and the presidents of the two major mutual-aid associations—the German and Irish Emigrant Societies—the new authority had the power to inspect ships and help immigrants. The following year, another law regulated the operations of boardinghouses and rooming houses.

In 1855, a landing and welcome center was created for similar reasons. It was located just off the tip of Manhattan, in the old West Battery fort that had become Castle Garden in 1824. Demilitarized, the spot became a fashionable place to welcome celebrities, such as Lafayette or the singer Jenny Lind, the "Swedish nightingale." There, from 1855 to 1890, arriving immigrants could find train or boat tickets, and useful advice about continuing their journey or getting oriented in New York. Wilhelm Bürkert, a young man from Württemberg who disembarked there in September 1875, recounts that "innkeepers came to offer their services," and he himself took lodgings with a compatriot.[19] But abuses did not disappear altogether.

Throughout these years, the vast majority of immigrants came from the German states and from Ireland. From 1850 to 1875, eight out of ten foreigners in New York, and more than seven out of ten in Brooklyn, were born in Ireland or in a German state. In 1890, this proportion still exceeded 60 percent on both sides of the East River. Other immigrants came especially from England, Wales, Scotland, France, and Canada until the late 1870s, and then, in growing numbers, from Italy and the Russian and Austro-Hungarian Empires. There were about 5,000 French in 1850, for example, and twice that number in 1880. Until 1875, they formed the fifth largest group of foreigners in New York, behind the Irish, German, English, and Scotch.

By the late 1840s, New York was largely a German-Irish city, actually the largest Irish and German city outside of Ireland and Germany. In 1860, more than 200,000 New Yorkers hailed from Ireland, and nearly 120,000 more from the German states; in 1890, those numbers were 190,000 and 210,000 respectively, not counting the tens of thousands of others who lived in Brooklyn.

But national labels are sometimes deceptive and mask the importance of regional affiliations among immigrants. Many "Irish" identified themselves instead by their native counties and were members of one of the numerous county associations—Sligo, Kerry, Cork, Connaught, Longford, and many others—that were created in New York.

Likewise, the "Germans" came before 1871 from the thirty-nine states making up the German Confederation, and after 1871 from the many components of the German Empire. In the 1840s and 1850s, they came from western or southern German states—Bavaria, Württemberg, the two Hesses, the grand duchy of Baden or Rhenish Prussia—all heavily populated regions, rich in an age-old tradition of mobility and migrations, and affected by the impact of economic development on farming and craft industries.

FIGURE 23
Passengers in steerage: German immigrants at Le Havre,
waiting to get under way © Hachette Livre

After 1860, the regional origins of German immigrants changed: the proportion of Bavarians decreased, and that of the Prussians, now coming from Prussia and not the Rhineland, doubled. Henceforth, Saxon, Berlin and Westphalian dialects replaced Swabian and Upper Rhenish on Manhattan and Brooklyn streets.

The extent of this European immigration contrasted with the reduction of the place of African-Americans in the city. In absolute numbers, there were twice as many blacks in New York and six times as many in Brooklyn in 1890 as in 1820, but this increase was far below that of the white population. Consequently the proportion of blacks plummeted: one out of ten New Yorkers was black in 1820, three out of one hundred in 1850, one or two out of one hundred in 1890. In the second half of the nineteenth century, New York was becoming an increasingly white city.

NEW YORK IN SLICES

It was also becoming a deeply segmented city. Growth and power widened the social divisions. New York, Philip

FIGURE 24
Irish immigrants en route to New York
© Hachette Livre

Hone lamented, had "arrived at the state of society to be found in large cities of Europe": the "daily and hourly contrast" between the "two extremes of costly luxury in living, expensive establishments and improvident waste," and "squalid misery and hopeless destitution."[20] It was not by chance that, in 1849, the journalist George Foster published a work entitled *New York in Slices*, a series of vignettes on contemporary society that won immediate success. The metropolis easily lent itself to such exercises in dissection—it really did seem to constitute a collection of parts rather than a whole.

One of the principal "slices," the working class, was undergoing huge changes. With the industrial boom in the 1820s, the demise of the artisanal world begun in the eighteenth century accelerated. The growth of production, subdivision, and the development of subcontracting destroyed the already weakened ties between master artisans and journeymen. The situation varied from one occupation to another, of course. Workers in the garment industry, furniture making, or the shoe trade often worked at home or in sweatshops. In printing, a majority were employed in the mechanized workrooms of the big newspapers and publishing houses, and a minority at engraving and job printing. Construction workers were faced with the development of subcontracting, while those in the shipyards or the food industries saw their occupations hardly evolve at all.

This working-class world was not solely masculine. In many respects, the situation of female workers was more precarious than that of many male workers. The range of jobs they could hold was more limited, their salaries were lower, and they fell prey more often to unemployment. Some worked in central workshops or factories, where they had to face industry regimen, but where the pay was better and the work more regular. A majority of them, especially in the clothing and shoe industries, worked at home, which disrupted the organization and functioning of the family unit.

For the vast majority of former craftsmen turned tradesmen and industrial workers, industrialization prompted an ideological and moral crisis, at the same time as it degraded their living and working conditions. Skilled artisans recognized that they had become industry's labor force against their will. The new New York working class was born—and not painlessly—from the ashes of the "republic of artisans," defeated by triumphant free enterprise.

Hardly had this new class appeared before it was undermined by the effects of immigration. Beginning in the 1840s, the world of New York workers was rebuilt on foundations far removed from its republican and artisan origins. The 30,000 workers of 1840 grew to 220,000 in 1880, and the vast majority of them were immigrants. Born in Ireland or the German states, they easily dominated in most occupations. At mid-century, domestic help, dressmakers, and laundresses were generally Irish, as well as laborers, dockers, and masons. Tailors, shoemakers, bakers, carpenters, and cigar makers, on the other hand, were German. All in all, eight out of ten workers were born in foreign countries. As for native Americans, they were concentrated in a few occupations and made up one third of the carpenters, carters, machine operators, shipyard workers, and printers.

A new middle class also appeared. It was made up in part of artisans and master craftsmen who had been able to negotiate the changes that had taken place since the 1780s and who found themselves at the head of small or midsize enterprises. Their role was no longer that of production, but of management and direction. Furniture makers like Charles Baudouine or Henry Weil, called "cabinetmakers" in the New York directories from the 1850s, were actually entrepreneurs who employed many workers. Similarly, the "tailors" J. C. Booth or H. L. Foster were businessmen more often found in their offices than in their workshops.

In these decades, New York also witnessed the proliferation of a new world: office workers, clerks, cashiers, copyists, accountants, sales assistants, and small shopkeepers peopled, by the thousands, the offices of trade companies, banks, insurance firms, businesses, and stores. A great majority of this population was male, including those employed in sales: in 1850, Freeman Hunt's *Merchants' Magazine* reproduced an article from a New Orleans newspaper that compared the situation in Philadelphia, where one found mostly women sales clerks, to the situation in New York, where the salesman was king.[21] In 1890, this situation began to change, driven by the large stores. New York then counted nearly 10,000 female sales clerks and a few thousand new women employees in the city's offices. But there were still more salesmen than saleswomen, and office employment especially remained largely dominated by men.

Urban growth also disrupted New York's upper class. Not that it became democratic: a mere five percent of New Yorkers possessed half their city's wealth in 1828, and two thirds of it in 1845. But with the help of economic and demographic expansion, the number of rich people increased, going from some 8,000 individuals in 1828 to about 15,000 in 1845. In the 1840s, New York counted one hundred people with actual fortunes estimated at over one million dollars. John Jacob Astor's fortune probably approached eighteen million dollars. New or inherited, most of this wealth came from trade, even if it had diversified into finance, real estate, and insurance. Only a few millionaires were involved in industrial investment—in the New England textiles mills, for example.

Until the Civil War, the prominent figures came from the great colonial families or emerged due to post-revolutionary changes. Many merchants and businessmen from New England played an important role in New York's economy, and their names sound like a litany of New York's major trading firms. Preserved Fish and his cousin Joseph Grinnell, who started a white whale-oil business in 1815 and established their own line of sailing ships, the Blue Swallow Tail, came from the whaling town of New Bedford. Seth Low and his son Abiel, who made their fortune in the China trade thanks to the excellence of their "greyhounds of the seas," such as the clipper ship *Houqua*, arrived from Salem in the late 1820s. The Gardiners came from Norwich, the Griswolds from Old Lyme, the Goodhues from Salem. Anson Phelps, who became a metal importer, was born in Connecticut, and Rowland H. Macy was originally from Nantucket. Descendants of the colonial elite and New England businessmen formed two separate groups, but they mixed enough to constitute a high society that combined dynamism, prudence, and a concern for respectability—the "old New York" depicted in the novels and short stories of Edith Wharton, herself the daughter of a Jones and a Rhinelander.

After the Civil War, large fortunes multiplied. Thirty years later, New Yorkers constituted 1,368 of the 4,047 millionaires in the United States. Most of them had made their fortunes in the railroads, manufacturing, or finance, and their investments were less diversified than the preceding generation's.

In becoming revitalized, New York's upper class also splintered. The pre-war merchant families, like the Grinnells, the Goodhues, and the Howlands faded into the background. New fortunes appeared: the Drews, Fisks, Goulds, Vanderbilts, and others like Edward H. Harriman in the railroads, J. P. Morgan and August Belmont in finance, John D. Rockefeller or Andrew Carnegie in industry. Unlike at the beginning of the century when the old colonial elite had absorbed wealthy merchants from New England and elsewhere, the "old New York" of 1870 closed itself off with a bitterness stamped with the proud memory of its former position, and scornfully rejected those it considered social climbers.

This division in the upper class between old fortunes and new wealth was not the only example of its fragmentation. The Protestant elite expressed its hostility toward Catholics and Jews by forming tightly closed circles. Jewish bankers and businessmen, for example, who were often of German origin, could blame the growing anti-Semitism at the end of the century for their estrangement from Protestant American high society and the German immigrant elite, most of whom were Christian.

MANIFESTATIONS OF DEMOCRACY

Such sharp contrasts between the different "slices" of New York throughout the nineteenth century could not help but produce tensions and conflicts. They occurred within the context of the profound changes in political life after 1820. The challenge to the principles of deference that previously ruled, and Andrew Jackson's 1828 election to the White House, attest to the relative democratization the country was then experiencing.

In fact, urban growth coincided with the granting of voting rights to all white men born in the United States or naturalized as citizens. The electorate grew from 18,000 men in 1825 to 43,000 in 1835. These constituents were not content with simply choosing members of the municipal council as in the past. Beginning in 1821, they elected their mayor through indirect vote, by means of their elected municipal council. After 1834, the election was by direct vote: 30,000 voters came out to elect their first magistrate in 1834, 60,000 in 1854, 82,000 in 1865, 200,000 in 1880, and 273,000 in 1888.

Of course the public sphere was not open to all, since women and non-naturalized immigrants were excluded from it. As for African-Americans, they were subjected to discriminatory treatment. The New York State Constitution of 1821 abolished poll-tax restrictions for white American males, but for blacks, it established the requirement of possessing real-estate property valued at a minimum of 250 dollars—thus limiting the number of black voters to 16 in 1826, and to 68 in 1835.

Despite these limitations, the relative democratization of the public sphere offered a significant proportion of New Yorkers the possibility of resolving the social conflicts that divided them. During the 1829 elections, a radical movement, the Working Men's Party, assembled mechanics, craftsmen, journeymen, and apprentices who were unhappy with the economic changes that were marginalizing them. The Working Men won nearly one third of the votes, but they split up a few months later, their various factions regained by the Jacksonian Democrats.

Following this political setback, workers and artisans tried to achieve their demands by creating the General Trades' Union of the City of New York. They launched many strikes in 1833, and especially in 1836. Excluded by these very male organizations, women workers also tried to organize in the mid-1840s, forming the Ladies' Industrial Association. But all these attempts were stymied by employers' resistance, the crisis of 1837, and the massive influx of immigrants into the New York workers' market. Thus craftsmen and workers returned to the political fray. Most of them rejoined the ranks of the Democrats, where they made up the left wing, with a minority preferring the Whigs or the xenophobic parties then making their appearance.

Even limited as it was, the democratization of the electorate rendered former modes of government obsolete. A model based on deference, rank, and rule by the elite was replaced by a more democratic, and thus segmented, system. Henceforth, the New York political arena witnessed groups with very divergent interests confronting each other and finding themselves compelled to hear each other out. The power of the elite diminished. But that did not mean that patricians abandoned the political arena; most of the New York mayors were upper-class merchants and lawyers, such as Philip Hone, the sugar producer

William F. Havemeyer, and attorneys Robert H. Morris and Caleb Woodhull. By controlling the executive power and the office of the mayor, which was granted more and more responsibility, the patricians ensured themselves the upper hand in areas that affected the entire city. Until the mid-1880s, they also continued to control New York's two main partisan machines, the Democratic Party and the Whig Party, which became the Republican Party in the 1850s.

On the other hand, through a form of power sharing, these same patricians, nicknamed the Swallowtails after the Civil War, became less involved in the Common Council, the seat of legislative power. The Council saw its powers decline, because henceforth it only dealt with the business of the various districts, not the whole city. But it fulfilled a vital function in becoming the authority that took the interests of New York's new voters into account. In the 1830s, they were represented there by artisans, workers, and men who decided to make politics their occupation. These new council members did not have the patricians' social and financial resources at their disposal. To make up for this disadvantage, they set up organizations in their own districts to insure their victories in municipal elections—even if the organizations were defined in terms of the two major political parties of the time, the Democrats and the Whigs.

The development of this more democratic, more partisan, and more organized system manifested itself in an extraordinarily lively political atmosphere during the 1830s and 1840s. The municipal democracy's pulse followed the rhythm of public gatherings where Whigs and Democrats presented their platforms, decried their opponents and made yet more promises. The City Hall Park welcomed frequent gatherings, and the streets of Manhattan served for partisan demonstrations.

The famous events of the evening of October 30, 1835 testify to the vitality of public life at the time: during a gathering of the Democratic Party to choose candidates for the upcoming elections, the party bosses, afraid of being in the minority, put out the lights in the room in order to end the meeting. Immediately, hundreds of participants pulled candles out of their pockets and, thanks to Loco-Foco brand matches, relit the chamber. The meeting could continue, the conservative leaders were ousted, and their adversaries, who considered themselves defenders of "pure democracy," earned the nickname of Loco-Focos.[22]

The results of local elections were nearly always very close, the two main parties running neck and neck. No vote could be neglected. In April 1834, Cornelius Lawrence, a Jacksonian Democrat, was elected mayor with 181 more votes than his opponent, Gulian Verplanck. The Whigs then entertained the hope of carrying the general elections in the following autumn, and they mobilized their troops just like their Democratic adversaries. "The Opposition thought itself able to contest the possession of the State and relied upon carrying the city," noted Michel Chevalier who was in New York at the time. In the end, the Democrats won. "But now the cannon of the Opposition is silent, and that of Tammany Hall only is heard," while "the streets of New York, which do not indeed require it, receive no additional light, except from the Jackson processions, which parade them nightly by torch-light."[23]

After 1840, the influx of Irish and German immigrants gradually altered the composition of the electorate. In the mid-1850s, nearly half the New York voters were naturalized immigrants. This proportion continued to grow, and henceforth the key to success became their support. Now Democrats and Whigs did not hold the same trump cards. Although they both hedged on the issue in the early 1840s, the Whigs were closer to the nativists, who managed to get one of their own elected as mayor of New York in 1844, the publisher James Harper. As for the Democrats, they decided to court the immigrant vote to establish their rule.

From then on, a new system theoretically fell into place. New York possessed a Democratic majority dependent on the naturalized immigrant vote and assured of victory when they were united; a Whig minority; and then Independents and Republicans, who could only hope to win by taking advantage of possible dissension in their opponents' ranks.

There was much reason for discord, having to do with Tammany Hall, the political machine the Democratic Party relied upon to dominate New York. Originally composed of artisans and businessmen, the St. Tammany Society, founded in the late 1780s, became New York's branch of the Democratic Party half a century later. The men of Tammany clearly perceived the new conditions of municipal politics and their consequences. Their famous leader William Tweed noted that in New York "the population is too hopelessly split up into races and factions to govern it under universal suffrage, except by the bribery of patronage or corruption."[24]

It took Tammany about thirty years for the most visible corruption to give way to simple patronage. In New York in the 1850s and 1860s, temptation was very strong and easily satisfied. Thanks to extortion, under-the-counter payoffs, cheating on the municipal markets, and dubious property and real-estate speculation, the Democratic city council members in the early 1850s were soon dubbed "the Forty Thieves." William Tweed, an entrepreneur and chief of a prestigious fire company with a tiger for its symbol, became the symbol of Tammany. Elected alderman for the Seventh Ward, he used this post as his apprenticeship in New York politics. Over the course of the next ten years, he pursued his career within Tammany Hall, and in April 1863, he became its head, or "grand sachem" in the lingo of the organization.

"Boss Tweed" then built a system based on bribery and corruption. Holding strategic posts simultaneously, such as commissioner of public works and of refuse collection, he was assured control of thousands of jobs that he could redistribute to his friends and to those he owed favors. He and his friends, "Tweed's ring," became masters in the art of converting their influence into cash and diverting city finances to profit themselves, pocketing 200 million dollars in a few years while the municipal debt skyrocketed. Having become a millionaire, the "Tammany Tiger" took up residence in a magnificent home on Fifth Avenue and lived in luxury. But Tweed had gone too far, and in 1871, his excesses, denounced by a series of articles in the *New York Times* and in savage caricatures by Thomas Nast, led to his downfall, arrest, and sentencing. Even though he managed to escape and reach Spain, he was handed over by Spanish authorities and died in a New York prison in 1878.

In the 1870s and 1880s, his successor tried to keep patronage within limits acceptable to New Yorkers, and especially to improve the machine's operations in the districts. "Honest" John Kelly, the first Irish-American and first Catholic to lead Tammany Hall, began to build a hierarchy that depended upon "district captains," responsible for answering the demands of neighborhood voters, providing them with help and assistance, finding them work, and, of course, securing their votes on election day.

Because they controlled so many jobs, the men of Tammany had the means to practice patronage politics, but they proved more discreet than Tweed when it came to corruption. Sensational declarations like George Washington Plunkitt's were rare. Plunkitt, the colorful former butcher turned building contractor and "district captain," proposed a subtle distinction between "honest graft" and "dishonest graft." Public and private interests merged, according to him, and it was fine for professional politicians, coming from modest working-class backgrounds, to get rich by taking advantage of their networks and their power, as long as they did not do so at the city's expense.[25]

In reality, Tammany was never all-powerful. "Honest" John Kelly had to compromise with the Swallowtail Democrats—Tilden, Seymour, and O'Connor—who controlled a share of the nominations. He also had to fend off Swallowtail Republicans and Independents whose only chances of winning votes consisted of crying corruption and wrapping themselves in the flag of reform. In fact, they gained control of City Hall in 1872, following the Tweed debacle, and again in 1878, when Edward Cooper was elected mayor with the votes of Republicans and anti-Tammany Democrats. But their lack of professionalism and structure, and their minority position in normal times, prevented them from claiming any staying power. The cynical Plunkitt dubbed them "morning glories" on the grounds that they wilted soon after they opened.

During the 1850s and 1860s, some reformers tried to limit the powers of the municipality by convincing New York State to create specialized commissions, considered to be less politicized and more administrative. In 1870, Tweed obtained a new charter from Albany that abolished these commissions and returned to the New York municipality its former domains. Subsequently, the reformers concentrated their efforts on improving municipal operations. Thus in 1883, they succeeded in pushing through reforms in the recruitment and management of municipal civil servants in Brooklyn and New York that limited the impact of the Tammany patronage system and reinforced municipal bureaucracy.

Such initiatives did not undermine a political system anchored in New York demography, but attested to the delicate balances, power struggles, and interests that divided the metropolis.

THE CANAL AND THE BRIDGE

Little more than half a century separated the opening of the Erie Canal and the inauguration of the Brooklyn Bridge, but the metropolis of 1883 hardly resembled the city that had celebrated the new canal in 1825. No doubt the great bridge flung across the East River symbolized the spatial growth of New York and its recent expansion, just as the canal testified to the city's continental ambitions. "Babylon had her hanging gardens, Egypt her pyramids, Athens her Acropolis, Rome her coliseum—so Brooklyn has her bridge," proudly proclaimed a sign that was hung in a store window.[26]

Times had changed, and the project's completion did not prompt a civic celebration. On May 24, the mayor of Brooklyn, Seth Low, the town councillors, war veterans, and local personalities marched in procession from Brooklyn's city hall to the bridge entrance, accompanied by a military escort. At the same time, the President of the United States, Chester Arthur, the governor of New York State, Grover Cleveland, the mayor of New York City, Franklin Edson, and their respective retinues—a total of twenty-four horse-drawn carriages escorted by 600 soldiers from the Seventh Regiment in summer uniforms, helmet, white pants, gray jacket—left the Fifth Avenue Hotel headed toward the New York entrance of the bridge.

Then the presidential procession crossed the great work on foot, saluted by cannons from navy ships anchored in the East River. On the other shore, they were received by the Brooklyn group and assembled at the official grand-stand to listen to the military band and successive speeches given by the president of the bridge's board of trustees, William C. Kingsley, the mayors of both cities, Congressman Abram Hewitt, and the pastor Richard Storrs. The figures present then gathered at various receptions held in their honor, and the celebration concluded with a huge fireworks display. That same evening, precisely at midnight, the bridge was opened to the public.

Throughout the day, many New Yorkers witnessed the ceremony, but they did not take part in it directly, so fearful were the authorities of incidents. As night fell, the East River quays did not empty out. Hundreds of small boats were anchored nearby. Soon the fireworks, launched from the height of the new bridge, lit a striking scene: Manhattan and Brooklyn united by a powerful link of steel, the huge and anonymous crowd, the illuminated yachts, boats, and ferries. The city of 1825 had become a gigantic metropolis that was claiming its modernity. The torch-bearing citizen who joined the parade to celebrate the Erie Canal was henceforth the spectator watching the lights of the city.

5

MANNAHATTA

The sometimes painful apprenticeship in diversity and democracy announced profound cultural transformations. "Mannahatta," the metropolis dear to Walt Whitman, its self-proclaimed bard—"city of orgies, walks and joys," "proud and passionate city—mettlesome, mad, extravagant city,"—thus entered into American culture, stimulating the imagination, arousing curiosity, eliciting mistrust and incomprehension.[1]

This general fascination with New York reflected its economic power, but it was also nurtured by what an English visitor, Lady Emmeline Stuart-Wortley, called "the cosmopolitanism of her citizens . . . , the heterogeneous compounds, and the kaleidoscopical varieties presented at every turn."[2] Thus multiple cultures developed and crystallized, uniting, opposing, or dividing New Yorkers according to their social origin, place of birth, sex, or skin color. New York became bourgeois and working class, American and cosmopolitan, destitute and opulent, masculine and feminine.

A KALEIDOSCOPE OF CULTURES

Until the late 1870s, the horizon line of Brooklyn and Manhattan was dominated by "the forest of spires" of religious buildings that "indicate as plainly as the forest of masts at her wharves her thrift and greatness," and demonstrated the local influence of a culture of morality, piety, respectability and self control.[3] Methodists, Baptists, Presbyterians, Congregationalists, Episcopalians—these Protestant churches proliferated along the two banks of the East River beginning in the 1820s, accompanying urban development and attempting to respond to the spiritual and social expectations of thousands of middle-class New Yorkers.

The 230 or more Protestant churches that New York boasted in 1850 were the product of the religious revival, that widespread evangelical movement that hit the metropolis, like all of the Northeast, during the first half of the century. Manhattan and Brooklyn experienced their moments of intense religious fervor: in 1829–30, Charles Grandison Finney, one of the most eloquent figures of the religious revival, came to preach the merits of temperance, the necessity of virtue, and the grandeur of faith, and found himself behind the pulpit of the Second Presbyterian Church of New York a few years later.

But undoubtedly the essential changes stemmed less from these exceptional moments than from the middle class's slow absorption of the evangelical values that shaped behavior. Among thousands of New Yorkers, these values were conveyed by the importance accorded to home and family, the ultimate measure of this new moral respectability. For housing, they preferred the thousands of two to four-story brick homes, lined up in rows and built for them in Manhattan, Brooklyn, or Williamsburg—James Fenimore Cooper called them "second-rate, genteel houses." In 1835, for example, the ones on Vandam Street, a little street in Greenwich Village, housed the tailor Edgar Harriott and the merchants Ichabod Hoit, James Brooks, and Henry Elsworth, all men "of moderate circumstances" who could put into practice the domestic ideal of the times.[4]

Home was no longer the place where work and family life mixed, as it had been in the past. On the contrary, it was a private space clearly distinct from the outside world. If such men enjoyed receiving friends and acquaintances, they did so respecting the advice and the rules

FIGURE 25
Trinity Church © Roger Viollet

repeated for them in the many etiquette handbooks published and sold in New York. The new bourgeois etiquette made the parlor the center of the house, a screen between the outer world and the family domain, the public and the private. New York wives ruled magisterially over these parlors. Their mission was to see that their children and spouses scrupulously respected the moral precepts and good manners with which they had inculcated them. True chiefs of staff, they had to oversee the efficient and discreet operations of the complex mechanism that was domestic organization. They also had to practice the new rules of middle-class hospitality themselves when they went visiting or received guests, gave dinners, or answered an invitation. Becoming the mistress of a home was an art as well as an ideal to which middle-class New York wives aspired, learning the social subtleties of the calling card with one of the corners folded or of greetings returned, or ignored.

Middle-class New York women were not content with simply acquiring these good manners, and these moral and domestic values, for themselves. They tried their best to spread them and promote them. That was the role of the various associations, Tocqueville noted. They existed in New York as elsewhere, "religious, moral, serious, futile, very general and very limited, immensely large and very minute."[5] Societies were formed to promote temperance, help the poor, abolish slavery, eliminate prostitution, protect children, improve education, or encourage a taste for reading, the practice of debate, religious sentiment.

New York was the headquarters for such associations. From its office on Nassau Street and then on Astor Place, the American Bible Society, founded in 1816, distributed millions of Bibles. The American Tract Society, created in 1825, inundated the country with various books, brochures, and pamphlets calling for a religious awakening. The city also housed the National Temperance Union, which tried to coordinate the actions of thousand of local societies in the fight against alcoholism, and the American Anti-Slavery Society, spearhead of the abolitionist movement.

For these societies, New York was an ideal recruitment center. Middle-class New Yorkers threw themselves into active volunteerism with a passion. They organized Sunday schools, financed orphanages, created societies for mothers, and defended the principles of popular moral reform. The New York Missionary Society (1827) and the Association for Improving the Condition of the Poor (1843–44) divided Manhattan into several hundred districts where they launched their volunteers, charged with educating minds, elevating souls and, as a last resort, offering charity. The New-York City Temperance Society, founded in 1829, counted 50,000 members in 1835 and 167,000 in 1842.

Education was another concern of these volunteers.

Unlike the private and boarding schools meant for wealthy children, the Free School Society, founded in 1805, was dedicated to providing elementary instruction for children in its charity schools, where strict discipline ruled, inspired by the Englishman Joseph Lancaster's model. Evangelicals also organized Sunday schools that were fairly successful. The education system was reorganized in the early 1840s. In each district, an education committee was responsible for managing the various aspects of the school system, under the supervision of a central council. In principle, the new system was supposed to be open to all. In practice, it remained very marked by evangelical Protestantism, to the great displeasure of New York Catholics, who, under the leadership of the city's bishop (and later archbishop), John Hughes, built an impressive network of parochial schools over the next two decades.

Beginning in the mid-century, evangelical concerns increasingly gave way to the requirements of respectability. In the 1830s, in the struggle against prostitution, the New-York Society of Public Morals, the New-York Female Moral Reform Society, and the New York Female Benevolent Society directed efforts toward saving the souls of prostitutes, not toward eradicating prostitution itself. Half a century later, those opposed to prostitution no longer concerned themselves with prostitutes' salvation, but attacked them rhetorically, politically, and sometimes even physically. In the 1870s, Anthony Comstock, the most famous member of the new New York Society for the Suppression of Vice, increasingly intervened and literally pounded on doors in the New York brothels. Ten years later, his example was imitated by mayors Grace and Hewitt, who ordered police raids and revoked opening permits for saloons they considered suspect. Henceforth, defending New York's morality gained priority over reforming women lost to the wicked life.

However dominant it was, this Protestant Victorian culture had to come to terms with different lifestyles and thinking that were just as powerful. The wealthiest New Yorkers shared certain cultural concerns with the middle class, but they often took them to such extremes that their meaning changed. Thus the upper middle class of that time, labeled aristocrats by their detractors, attended religious services, but their simple presence made the churches they frequented fashionable spots, sought out both by ambitious pastors and the faithful flocks concerned with seeing and being seen. The New York smart set crowded into the oldest and richest church in New York, Trinity—nicknamed "the cathedral of America" after its 1846 neo-Gothic reconstruction by the architect Richard Upjohn—and Grace Church, where, noted the caustic Philip Hone, "the word of God costs the people of quality who pray in this splendid temple about three dollars each Sunday."[6]

After 1847, many New Yorkers crossed the East River each Sunday and joined the residents of Brooklyn Heights to hear the waves of eloquence that Henry Ward Beecher, the pastor of the Plymouth Church, poured forth. Son of the famous evangelical preacher, Lyman Beecher, and brother of Harriet Beecher Stowe, the author of *Uncle Tom's Cabin*, and Catherine Beecher, feminist and reformer, Beecher was one of the city's most respected and influential voices for three decades. But his reputation was tarnished by scandal in 1874 because of an accusation of adultery, even though he was subsequently acquitted in court.

The lifestyle of the wealthiest New Yorkers demonstrated a deep concern for social prominence, sometimes matched with a flagrant desire for ostentation. Unlike the middle classes who clung to the virtues of frugality and restraint, in the 1830s and 1840s, and especially after the Civil War, the upper class had no qualms about living a life of luxury easily matching European aristocracy. In the 1840s, William, the son of John Jacob Astor, resided in a huge brick mansion on Lafayette Place, directly across from a lovely row of nine homes with neoclassical columns. These housed, among others, the fabulously wealthy David Gardiner (whose daughter Julia married the President of the United States, John Tyler, in 1844) and the grandfather of Franklin Roosevelt, Franklin Delano. Washington Square, Brooklyn Heights, and soon afterward Fifth Avenue abounded in lavish homes—such as Cornelius Vanderbilt's mansion on Washington Place or the residences of the Astors and the millionaire

FIGURE 26
Cornelius Vanderbilt residence
© Hachette Livre

Alexander T. Stewart on Fifth Avenue, at Thirty-third and Thirty-fourth Streets.

The appearance of the huge fortunes made in the railroads, industry, and financing beginning in the 1860s accelerated these tendencies and confirmed the "natural and demonstrable, not accidental or artificial" supremacy of Fifth Avenue.[7] William Henry Vanderbilt, son of the Commodore, settled into a private mansion at Fifty-first Street in 1882, his two daughters settled into another one on the corner of Fifty-second Street, and his two sons, William Kissam and Cornelius, had equally luxurious homes built by their architects, Richard Morris Hunt and George Post, at Fifty-second and Fifty-seventh Streets.

Other millionaires preferred the charms of Madison Avenue. In the 1880s, Charles Tiffany had the architect Stanford White build him a veritable castle in the German Renaissance style. Henry Villard entrusted to Charles McKim the construction of an impressive grouping of three Italian Renaissance–inspired palaces. In that same period there appeared on the west side of Central Park the first apartment buildings luxurious enough to attract the upper middle class. The Dakota, built between Seventy-second and Seventy-third Streets in 1882 by the architect Henry Hardenbergh, was the most accomplished example of these.

These wealthy New Yorkers, increasingly richer and more numerous as the century advanced, lived the life of an upper class with aristocratic pretensions. They married among themselves and constituted solidly bound family networks. They belonged to very exclusive clubs and circles, like the Saint Nicolas Society (1835), restricted to the descendants of the great colonial families, the Union (1836), which counted less than 400 members, or the Century, opened in 1847 to less than one hundred of the select. They owned beautiful properties in the New York area. "Imagine the most beautifully carved shorelines, hills covered with lawns and trees in blossom descending toward the sea," wrote Tocqueville in 1831, "and best of all, an incredible multitude of country houses, as grand as exquisite apartments but so carefully executed." In the summer, these privileged few willingly fled the heat of the city to take the waters at Saratoga, a town of spas and other pleasures in central New York State; in 1864 Duvergier de Hauranne saw it as the "Vichy of America," where "you stroll about until you tire of it."[8]

After the Civil War, high society launched the reputation of the seaside resort of Newport, Rhode Island, where families like the Vanderbilts, Belmonts, and Goelets owned veritable summer palaces. Some of them, like John C. Stevens, were responsible for founding the New York Yacht Club in 1844, and had the yacht *America* built, which triumphantly defied its English rivals in 1851. Others, at the instigation of the financier Leonard Jerome, revived the thoroughbred races in the New York area by creating the American Jockey Club in 1866; its first president was August Belmont.

Dinners in the city, receptions, balls, country holidays on Long Island or in Hoboken, private concerts, all this social life gave the New York season its style. Elegant New Yorkers had the chance to display finery so lavish it sometimes even astonished those familiar with the Saint James court or the imperial Tuileries. This elite society made painstaking efforts to preserve its exclusive character and limit access to newcomers. Henceforth, the New York social set appeared in the pages of a directory, and in 1872, Caroline Schermerhorn Astor and her social advisor, Ward McAllister, founded the Committee of the Patriarchs, responsible for determining who was acceptable company and who was not. Such pretensions were further reinforced by the marriages of several New York heiresses to English aristocrats, following the example set by the daughter of Leonard Jerome, who, in 1873, become Lady Randolph Churchill.

Such displays of wealth prompted some mockery. In the eyes of certain spokespersons for the middle class, the ostentatious expenditures of the very rich undermined the moral values of Protestant America. Other preferred to make fun of their lifestyles and their dilemmas. In 1857, William Butler Allen published a satire in the weekly magazine, *Harper's*, entitled "Nothing to Wear," mocking the difficulties encountered by rich New Yorkers when it came to dressing. This gave birth to a minor but infinitely varied genre, with the adventures of the dandy Fitz Frivol in *Nothing to Do*, followed by *Nothing to Eat* and *Nothing to Say*! These barbs confirmed the middle classes' inability to control the ostentation of the top tenth of society—whose members called themselves the "Upper Ten."

Actually, a vast majority of New Yorkers—those who made up the working classes—resisted the moralizing efforts of the middle class no less fiercely. The working-class world that emerged in the 1820s and 1830s from the ruins of the old artisanal order proudly claimed its own traditions, values, and social practices. The workers practiced a vigorous male ethic in which a sense of honor, a taste for violence, and a desire for independence was mixed with a concern for solidarity and a love for celebrating.

Like the middle-class culture, this one also had its own territory, institutions, and rituals. The Bowery, the plebeian equivalent of elegant Broadway, was its center. In its cabarets, theaters, brothels, bowling alleys and billiard rooms, inside and outside its dance halls, dives, oyster bars, and menageries, workers mingled with card-trick players, swindlers, streetwalkers, crooks of all kinds, and bourgeoisie in search of forbidden pleasures. In the 1830s, the young Walt Whitman could applaud actors in the Bowery Theater such as Edwin Booth, father of Lincoln's assassin, and Edwin Forrest, the darling of the times, in plays by Shakespeare or blockbusters like *The Last Days of Pompeii*. The theater halls were always full of workers who came to be entertained. In 1831, they threatened to smash the theater and drive the British actor Joshua Anderson off stage under an avalanche of rotten fruit, because they suspected him of harboring disdain for the New York theater scene.

A number of these workers were single and lived in boardinghouses in lower Manhattan, not the kinds of homes idealized by the middle class. Hardly in search of privacy, they turned to the volunteer fire companies for the spirit of camaraderie, and to the cabarets for human warmth, where, the temperance leagues scoffed, they wagered a share of their salaries on cockfights or prize fights. Because they were white Americans and their working conditions were constantly changing, they often looked for scapegoats and tolerated neither immigrants nor blacks.

In July 1834, workers and artisans took on the abolitionists, such as the brothers Arthur and Lewis Tappan, and the blacks. Many clashes in these years set organized bands of American workers, like the Spartan Association, against Irish immigrants. Fistfighting was a way of giving weight to their claims of independence, just as the surprise attacks that some of them launched against the tenants of the brothels and the prostitutes of lower Manhattan reinforced their feelings of masculine supremacy.

One of the main differences between the culture of these male workers and that of women workers and wives, daughters, and mothers of workers lies here. The conditions in which these women lived did not allow them to distinguish between home and the outside world, so essential to middle-class moralists of the time. Like working-class men, working-class women were also often forced out of their tiny, ill-equipped living quarters. But unlike the men, they were responsible for the domestic economy of their families; they had to find, or make their children find, water, food, and fuel. These tasks prompted them to form neighborhood networks of support, exchange, solidarity, and sociability, resuming—and adapting to the large metropolis—older traditions of cooperation and mutual aid.

Other women, for the most part single, found a certain kind of independence in New York, not without risks and constraints, but exhilarating. Dressmakers and saleswomen, the "belles" of the Bowery knew how to enjoy themselves and put on the great airs that one observer of the time, George Foster, characterized as "Boweryism." They did not hesitate to accompany their "B'hoys" on steamships or sleds, on picnics in Hoboken, booing the latest play, or dancing in one of the many dance halls of New York nightlife. Goaded by necessity, these working-class women sometimes became streetwalkers and helped to swell the significant numbers engaged in New York prostitution.

The arrival of hundreds of thousands of European immigrants disrupted this working-class culture. In the past, foreign workers had constituted too small a minority to challenge the cultural dominance of the white American working class. The only exceptions were the black domestics and laborers that made up a large portion of the approximately 15,000 African-Americans in New York. After 1840, however, a majority of the metropolis's workers were of foreign origin, and Bowery regulars had to come to terms with the new order of things.

Irish, German, English, Scottish, or French, the immigrants were not without roots. They had not made a clean break with their past by crossing the Atlantic, and no doubt retained the cultural baggage they had brought with them much longer than the personal effects spilling out of their trunks. Most of them settled into the working districts of lower Manhattan, close to the wharves, shipyards, and especially the shops where many found work. Since they liked living close to their compatriots, lower Manhattan in the 1840s witnessed the emergence of groups of immigrants sharing the same European origins. Whereas American workers tended to live in neighborhoods close to the Hudson, many Irish settled in the Sixth Ward, in the center of Manhattan, while German-speaking immigrants preferred the Lower East Side, soon nicknamed Klein-deutschland, or Little Germany.

In reality, these clusters did not attain the scale of neigh-borhoods; in all the wards of New York, including lower Manhattan, there were immigrants of diverse origins as well as native Americans. But within these heterogeneous neighborhoods, small concentrations of immigrants origi-nally from the same village or region proliferated. The addi-tion of these clusters gave each neighborhood its particular character.

Within these working-class streets, immigrants created their own institutions, which were remarkably similar from one group to another. In fact, their needs were iden-tical: a religious practice, mutual support and assistance, leisure-time activities. The Catholicism of most of the Irish, French, Bavarians, and Rhenish explained the prolif-eration of parishes—only two until 1825, and thirty-two in 1865. Henceforth, Catholicism was the majority religion in the metropolis. To respond to this growth, Rome created an archdiocese in New York in 1850, and established sepa-rate dioceses in Newark and Brooklyn three years later.

Quite logically, the Irish, who constituted the greatest number, dominated the Catholic hierarchy and most of the parishes. After John Dubois, a French priest exiled dur-ing the French Revolution who ended his career as Bishop of New York (1826–42), came an Irishman, John Hughes, who was named the first archbishop of New York and ener-getically managed the spiritual destinies of Catholics in the metropolis until his death in 1864. His successor was an Irishman from Brooklyn, John McCloskey, who became the first American cardinal in 1875. In 1865, twenty-three of the thirty-two New York parishes were Irish, and eight were German, like Saint-Nicolas or the Most Holy Redeemer. One was French, Saint-Vincent-de-Paul, estab-lished in 1841, first on Canal Street and then on Twenty-third Street. The appearance of Italian parishes in the last third of the century did not undermine Irish dominance.

Immigrants created many associations. Early in the century, the English placed themselves under the patronage of Saint George, the Scottish under Saint Andrew, and the Irish under Saint Patrick. New York was also home to a German Society, a French Benevolent Society, and a Hebrew Mutual Benefit Society. As gathering places for newcomers, they all offered information and advice about finding employment. The growth in immigration beginning in the 1820s and 1830s led to their diversification over the half century that followed. Regional societies assembled immigrants from Mecklenburg or Sligo County. Political or nationalist societies were established, such as the two Irish republican organizations—Fenians and Clan na Gael—that fought against British domination and launched unfortunate military expeditions against Canada from New York in 1866 and 1870. Following the Paris Revolution of February 1848, the Democratic Society of French Republicans was founded.

Immigrants also formed mutual-aid societies, masonic lodges, fire companies, rifle clubs, and militia companies. In about 1850, New York counted a great many Irish militias, Bavarian, Scottish, or Italian companies, and a French company, the Lafayette Guard, created in 1847. In 1849, according to Lady Stuart-Wortley, there were about one hundred of these companies, that is about 6,000 militiamen, and at least 10,000 members of rifle societies. All of them paraded with martial conviction down the streets of New York and did the honors at national celebrations or occasions involving the arrival of a prestigious compatriot.

Immigrants liked to get together. The Scottish met in New York's Caledonian Club, the Germans belonged to various gymnastic clubs, singing societies, and theater groups, such as the Arion Gesangverein or the Deutscher Liederkranz. They established numerous ethnic newspapers, many of which vanished as quickly as they appeared. The Irish *Truth Teller* was published from 1825 to 1855, before being absorbed by the *Irish American*, founded in 1849; the Germans read the *New Yorker Staats-Zeitung* or one of the many other New York newspapers and magazines printed in the German language; the French-speaking population read the *Courrier des États-Unis*, established in 1826.

But the immigrants' influence on urban culture was especially noticeable in the city streets. Within Little Germany, in lower Manhattan, life was "almost the same as in the Old Country," claimed Karl Griesinger at the end of the 1850s.[9] There was no need to know how to speak English there, and on Sundays, the neighborhood streets overflowed with immigrants going to mass, settling into the pubs to empty mugs of beer, attending shows, or listening to choral groups singing folk songs. Thus it was quite easy for immigrants to withstand the ambient xenophobia and the influence of the evangelical American bourgeoisie.

BRIDGES AND GAPS

This diversification of New York's cultural life did not proceed without tensions. Until mid-century, New Yorkers shared common bonds despite the very real gulfs between them. They ran into each other at market, crossed paths as they made their rounds. New York offered abundant opportunities and places for gathering. Its inhabitants joined to celebrate the anniversary of the Declaration of Independence on July 4, and organized civic holidays and parades in which many participated, with the notable exception of women, held to a passive role, and blacks, victims of a pervasive racism. In the 1830s and 1840s, these parades were open to immigrant societies, who could thus demonstrate their loyalty to their city and country of residence.

New Yorkers shared certain distractions as well. The city's theaters welcomed quite a heterogeneous public, even if it hardly mixed. "Till the curtain fell, I saw not one quarter of the queer things around me," noted the Englishwoman Frances Trollope after a performance at the Chatham Theater. "Then I observed in the first row of a dress-box a lady performing the most maternal office possible; several gentlemen without their coats and a general air of contempt for the decencies of life, certainly more than usually revolting." In the Park Theater, across from the City Hall, workers and artisans crowded into the pit,

FIGURE 27
The Park Theater, 1822 by John Searle
The New-York Historical Society

the bourgeoisie into the three levels of boxes, and the laborers, prostitutes, and blacks into the gallery. This spectacle, which astonished and shocked European visitors, changed in the mid-1830s to the extent that the Park, newly renovated, became more bourgeois. The young Whitman, used to the New York stage, saw it as "the more stylish and select theatre" in New York, while the Bowery

Theater was "pack'd from ceiling to pit with its audience of alert, well dress'd, full-blooded young and middle-aged men, the best average of American-born mechanics," who came to applaud Booth or Forrest.[10]

But this diverging of the cultures was slow to evolve. Other attractions, like the American Museum, welcomed a mixed crowd. Its founder, Phineas Taylor Barnum, was the prototype of those poor and ambitious young men who came to New York to seek their fortunes. After working as a grocery-store clerk and then keeper of a boardinghouse, Barnum launched his career in 1835 at the age of twenty-five in traveling shows for fairs. He began his new profession by presenting to New York and New England audiences a black woman who, he claimed, was 160 years old and had been George Washington's nurse. Barnum returned to New York as a success in 1841, acquired the Scudder's Museum on Broadway, and renamed it the American Museum. In 1864, Duvergier de Hauranne did not suppress his irony: "The temple of art in New York is the Barnum Museum, where Icelandic giants, Patagonian women, dwarves, sea serpents, albinos, and heaven only knows what else are being shown, and where the open-mouthed visitors are being taught the great art of mystification."[11] But the place's true merit lay in its mix of genres, at once curiosity shop, fairground show, and melodrama theater. There visitors discovered Charles Stratton, a midget known as "General Tom Thumb," as well as ornithological and geological collections that had no equal in New York at the time. The success of the American Museum never lapsed for twenty-five years.

Nevertheless, this quarter century witnessed a profound change. Not without suffering, not without violence, the many cultures of the metropolis revealed themselves to be increasingly incapable of accepting one another.

The growing number of conflicts and riots were an indication of this increasing intolerance. In spring 1849, the first violent episode took place at the Astor Place Theater, which had opened two years earlier at the instigation of wealthy bourgeoisie who considered the Park too common. The Astor Place Theater was a center of refine-

FIGURE 28
Barnum American Museum (left), on Broadway
© Hachette Livre

ment almost entirely reserved for its subscribers, who
were all people of quality. Etiquette required the men to
wear coats and white gloves. For working-class New Yorkers, who frequented the Bowery theaters, the Astor Place
Theater immediately became a detested symbol of snob-
bery and the bourgeois desire to take over what had formerly been shared by many.

In May 1849, the New York appearance of the English
tragedian William Macready, who was to perform at the
Astor Place Theater, touched off a crisis. For many years,
Macready had been in open conflict with his American
rival Edwin Forrest, the darling of the New York working
class. The two men had different visions of their craft. Forrest subscribed to the democratic tradition of American
theater at that time, and Macready defended the idea of

FIGURE 29
The Astor Place riot (1849) by Currier & Ives
The New-York Historical Society

an art beyond the ordinary. On May 7, Macready's first performance in *Macbeth*, one of Forrest's great roles—he was performing it that same evening in the Broadway Theater—set off an uproar. Forrest supporters, who had besieged the galleries, greeted the English actor's entrance "with a shower of missiles, rotten eggs and other unsavory objects, with shouts and yells of the most abusive epithets," noted Philip Hone in his journal.[12] Three days later, a second performance took place under heavy protection, but the theater was surrounded by thousands of workers, who tried to invade it. The troops opened fire, killing twenty-two and injuring more than a hundred.

Following the riot, the city was deeply divided. The New York correspondent for a Philadelphia newspaper reported that the whole affair "leaves behind a feeling to which this community has hitherto been a stranger—an opposition of classes—the rich and poor . . . a feeling that there is now in our country, in New York City, what every good patriot hitherto has considered it his duty to deny—a high and a low class."[13] The idea that in New York all social classes could gather at the theater was dead.

Other certitudes suffered a few years later. In 1857, conflicts between New York City's Democratic mayor Fernando Wood and New York State's Republican governor led to three violent riots that occurred within a few weeks of each other. In June, the mayor's municipal police and the governor's newly created metropolitan police came to blows at the city hall when the metropolitan force tried to arrest the mayor. Fifteen days later, Wood's supporters celebrated July 4 in their own way: the Dead Rabbits, an Irish gang from Mulberry Street who supported the mayor, attacked the metropolitan police in the Bowery, and then took on their traditional rivals, the Bowery Boys. In a few hours, the streets of the Lower East Side were transformed into a battlefield where hundreds fought each other, leaving a dozen men dead. The *Tribune* ran headlines on the barricades erected in the streets and the "civil war" in the Sixth Ward—nicknamed the "Bloody Ould Sixth." The metropolitan police had to call out two regiments of militia to restore order, temporarily, on the evening of July 5. A few days later, the Seventeenth Ward, the German neighborhood, erupted, prompting more police violence.

Still, these troubles were minor compared with the cataclysms of summer 1863, in the midst of the Civil War—five days of the worst violence that New York had ever experienced. On July 13, the federal government's decision to draft troops by drawing lots provoked a riot. Artisans, industrial workers, laborers, and fringe elements took to the streets, first attacking the draft office and buildings that symbolized federal power. They blocked the tramways, pulled up the rails, attacked the police, and erected barricades. But the affair rapidly took a different turn. The rejection of the draft went hand in hand with the rioters' hostility toward the Republican Party, their hatred of the blacks, and their sense of a true class struggle.

On July 14, 15, and 16, the rioters attacked individuals and institutions known for supporting the Republicans. The offices of Horace Greeley's newspaper, the *Tribune*, were set on fire. A murderous hunt for blacks resulted in lynchings and maimings. Over the course of this second phase of violence, the rioters were mostly Irish Catholics, industrial workers, or manual laborers, whereas the protest against the draft had originally involved Germans and Americans as well. It took the intervention of five federal regiments hastily called back from the Gettysburg battlefield for order to be reestablished with cannon fire. But this serious crisis in the New York social order left more than a hundred dead.

Seven years later, the streets of New York were the scene of new uprisings. This time they resulted from the Irish Protestants' desire to celebrate—with a parade—William III's victory over James II in the Battle of the Boyne (1690). On July 12, 1870, the Orangemen were assaulted by the Irish Catholics. Despite police intervention, there were eight casualties. The following year, the Orangemen tried once again to parade with strong police and military protection, but things deteriorated when the troops opened fire on the hostile crowd that gathered along the route. This time, there were sixty-five deaths.

Another sign of the growing rifts in the metropolis appeared in a completely different domain: the creation of cultural institutions. These institutions no longer attempted to respond to the expectations of the whole city, but rather to a particular group of individuals or interests. For the promoters of the Metropolitan Museum (1870) and the Metropolitan Opera (1883), who were part of New York's new economic elite, these institutions served very much as a convenient means for affirming their social status and their desire for cultural exclusivity, both in relation to the New York working class and to "Old New York," which refused to associate with them. William Vanderbilt and his friends financed the construction of the Metropolitan Opera because, despite their fortunes, they could not obtain boxes at the very patrician Academy of Music.

As with the theater, it was no longer a question of mixed audiences for the concert. The desire for refinement and social cohesion prevailed over democratic impulses. Along the way, it was necessary to educate the listeners and rectify their bad musical or theatrical manners as quickly as possible. Theodore Thomas, New York's most famous conductor in the 1890s, did not spare any efforts during concerts. At the head of the New York or the Brooklyn Philharmonic, he struggled against the chatterboxes, the boisterous, the absentminded, the latecomers, and the lovers of superfluous encores. At every occasion, including open-air summer concerts held in Central Park, Thomas endeavored, in his own words, "to form a refined musical taste among the people by the intelligent selection of music; to give . . . only standard works, both of the new and old masters, and to be thus conservative and not given to experimenting with the new musical sensations of the hour."[14] Respectability, classicism, education—so many essential principles for the Victorian bourgeoisie of New York.

The same marching orders awaited other types of entertainment, formerly considered a little risqué. In the 1880s, Tony Pastor opened a vaudeville hall near Union Square, in the same building as Tammany Hall. Unlike the saloons and the concert-cafés, Pastor's show was aimed at a respectable audience attracted by the great variety of acts—songs, recitations, declamations, juggling, magic— that followed one after another for two hours. Vaudeville claimed to be both entertaining and acceptable, stripped of all its vulgarity. It had to win the approval of middle-class women who wanted to bring their families there without fear of encountering anything compromising or indelicate.

THE BRAIN OF AMERICA?

Some New Yorkers wanted to see their city become the intellectual and cultural capital of the United States, if it could not be the political capital. "In civilization, every powerful nation must have one intellectual centre, as every individual must have a brain, whose motions and conceptions govern the entire system," noted the journalist George Foster in 1849. "In the United States, New York is that centre and that brain."[15]

Wishful thinking was the response of many European visitors, attuned to New York's materialism. "It seems that an excess of civilization and well-being has suffocated their intelligence and feeling for beauty," noted Duvergier de Hauranne, to the point that "utilitarian positivism reigns here as an absolute master."[16] Nevertheless from another perspective, efforts to make New York an intellectual center and to develop a civic culture were clearly multiplying. In 1824, the Atheneum opened as both a library and a place for debates and talks. But the project was short-lived. The Atheneum was little more than a well-frequented club when Gustave de Beaumont and Alexis de Tocqueville went there to read the newspapers during their stays in New York, and it closed its doors in 1839. The cultural model that it embodied, based on learned societies made up of enlightened amateurs and wealthy dilettantes, had become obsolete.

In the 1840s, the idea that writing or painting could be made into a profession became increasingly acceptable. Until then, amateurism was a rule and a moral obligation. The writers of the so-called Knickerbocker school—Washington Irving, James Fenimore Cooper, William Cullen Bryant—considered themselves gentlemen. "Let the avocation of literature be a recreation of an opposite character of one's business or profession," proclaimed Bryant in 1825.[17] The Bread and Cheese Club, founded by Cooper in 1822 and surviving for a few years, gathered together writers, but also artists, lawyers, merchants, and doctors—all men of good company interested in matters of the mind.

Reacting against this view of literature's place in society, a circle appeared in 1840 that aspired to make writing a profession. This depended upon the countless newspapers, magazines, and publishing houses that called New York home. Thanks to technical innovations, the new rolling presses of the 1830s could now print 2,000, then 4,000, and then 20,000 pages per hour.

A popular press, called the "penny press," thus developed. The sensational headlines of Benjamin Day's *Sun*, or James Gordon Bennett's *Herald*, aimed at a readership curious for news about the metropolis. The Jewett affair in 1836 made big headlines for several weeks. The murder of the young and beautiful Helen Jewett in a Thomas Street brothel and the trial of her presumed assassin, Richard Robinson, divided New York, to the great profit of the two newspapers that clashed over the suspect's guilt. When, at the end of the trial, Robinson was acquitted, James Gordon Bennett and the *Herald*, who had championed him, celebrated unabashedly.

Beside these decidedly sensationalistic newspapers appeared more restrained competitors, often more closely linked to a political current. Horace Greeley made the *Tribune*, which he founded in 1841, into an important daily paper for the Whigs, and then the Republicans, at the same time as it served as one of the most influential supporters of the abolitionist movement and social reforms. On the other side of the East River, the *Brooklyn Eagle*, for whom Walt Whitman was, at one time, editor-in-chief, supported the Democrats, even while attempting to appear as the newspaper for all Brooklynites. The *New York Times* appeared in 1851, connected with Republican circles, but it did not yet exert as much influence as the *Tribune*.

Literary and political journals developed alongside the serious newspapers. The *Democratic Review*, edited by John L. O'Sullivan, published Poe and Thoreau, Bancroft and Longfellow. It embodied the aspirations of cultural nationalism shared by the "young America" generation of Melville and Whitman. At the same time, in addition to Greeley and O'Sullivan, William Cullen Bryant, the owner of the *Evening Post*, and Charles Francis Briggs and George William Curtis, of the monthly *Putnam's*, became prominent intellectual figures.

These years in which a literary democracy bloomed were fleeting. Melville and Whitman, the avant-garde of the movement in the 1850s, soon broke with the circle that preferred literary hacks to writers. Curtis, who became the political pen of the weekly *Harper's*, Edwin Lawrence

Godkin, his colleague at the *Nation* magazine, and a number of their fellow journalists were either partisans of a radical laissez-faire approach or cautiously supported moderate social reform. Disgusted with the corruption in municipal political life, frightened by the riots that shook the city and by the rise of socialism, captivated by the idea that culture represented a refinement antithetical to ordinary life, they all turned their backs on the democratic aspirations of the preceding decades.

This adoption of middle-class views extended far beyond the sphere of political commentary or social analysis and constituted the dominant trend in literary culture in the 1880s. Under the leadership of its high priest, William Crary Brownell, a former journalist for the *World* and the *Nation*, who became the chief literary advisor for Scribner's, the publisher, it was celebrated in the columns of *Century*, *Scribner's*, and other magazines with hundreds of thousands of readers. New York witnessed the triumph of Victorian culture.

In contrast, the reputation of the academy was very modest. In the mid-century, Columbia College (then on Madison Avenue) was "an obscure fact," according to the diary of one of its own trustees, George Templeton Strong. Its two rival institutions, City College (founded in 1847) and New York University (established in 1831 and located on Washington Square), were no less unassuming. Until the end of the 1870s, they attracted few students or professors. In 1876, John W. Burgess, who had studied with the illustrious Theodor Mommsen at the University of Berlin, agreed to leave the rustic charms of Amherst College in Massachusetts for a chair in history, political science, and international law at Columbia. There he found "a small old-fashioned college" with a library that was open less than two hours a day.[18]

But the universities soon evolved. Impelled by one of its trustees, the businessman Samuel Ruggles, and thanks to the support of two key editorialists of the time, Curtis and Godkin, Columbia's president, Frederick Barnard, created a School of Political Sciences in 1880, at the suggestion of Burgess. Modeled on the Free School of Political Sciences established in Paris a few years earlier, its aim was to educate the political and administrative elite, not academics. Its appearance, following the creation of a School of Law (1858) and a School of Engineering (1864), prefigured Columbia's transformation into a great university.

Columbia's growing specialization also illustrated a new tendency in New York intellectual life, characterized by the emergence of all kinds of cultural and professional associations. The list is long, the diversity revealing, and the names indicative of their national ambition: American Ethnological Society (1842), New York Academy of Medicine (1847), American Geographical Society (1851), American Society of Civil Engineers (1852), American Institute of Architects (1857), American Numismatic Society (1858), New York Academy of Sciences (1876; formerly the Lyceum of Natural History, 1817), American Society of Mechanical Engineers (1880), American Institute of Electrical Engineers (1884), and many others.

THE CITY OF THE IMAGINATION

As the metropolis entered the imagination of New Yorkers, it also entered the imaginations of Americans and foreigners. Until the growth of Chicago, it was the only city that embodied the ambiguities of a culture torn between a rural tradition and an urban bias.

For some, New York was the symbol of the corruption that threatened the stability of American society. "Cloacina of all the depravities of human nature," according to Thomas Jefferson's kind formula, New York imperiled the vocation, values, and virtues of rural America.[19] Everything about the city's growth during the century's first decades was grounds for fear. "There is not yet any great capital in America, but there are already very large towns," noted Tocqueville with regard to New York and Philadelphia. "The lowest classes in these vast cities are a rabble more dangerous even than that of European towns." It was more dangerous, of course, for the "future of the Democratic Republics of the New World," because of the social menace represented by the "freed Negroes" and "the crowd of Europeans" who lived there. "In towns, it is impossible to prevent men assembling, getting excited together, and forming sudden passionate resolves," wrote Tocqueville again.[20]

New York symbolized the dangers of the big city. Prostitution was so widespread there that in the 1830s, George Templeton Strong, never at a loss for a neologism, mentioned in his diary the existence of a "whorearchy" in New York.[21] The growing number of New York slums led to the emergence of a true "urban question." The Five Points neighborhood—located in lower Manhattan north of City Hall, and named after the notorious intersection of Anthony (now Worth), Cross (later Park), and Orange (now Baxter) Streets—became a catchword for antiurban complaints, a reference endlessly repeated and evoking endless comments. During the colonial era and the first decades of the republic, the poorest housing largely escaped notice since it often consisted of huts bordering the urbanized area. For the first time, a permanent poor section emerged within the heart of the city.

Following the example of a great many observers and onlookers, like Richard Henry Dana, author of *Two Years Before the Mast*, Charles Dickens, in 1842, carefully escorted by two policemen, "plunged" into the Five Points, where he discovered—with a fascination faithfully reproduced in his *American Notes*—Peter William's dance bar, Almack's. The district "is inhabited by a race of beings of all colours, ages, sexes and nations, though generally of but one condition, and that . . . almost of the vilest brute," noted a New York newspaper in the early 1830s.[22] Simple perceptions or prejudices influenced by the bourgeois values of these observers? The symbolic embodiment of the visible failure of republicanism, the Five Points nevertheless acquired an eminent place in American culture. Its slums and its rented rooms contrasted with the splendors of Broadway, always close at hand, and this opposition was the image of New York tensions.

The alternative to this critical view was a much more optimistic perspective. From the beginning of the century, New York symbolized the spectacular and apparently limitless growth of the young republic. "We are rapidly becoming the London of America," proclaimed the prominent New York merchant John Pintard in 1826. "I myself am astonished and this city is the wonder of every stranger."[23] To some extent, such remarks were nothing but pure convention, a rhetoric of urban promotion, the same type of discourse repeated by the tireless propagandists of thousand of real or imaginary cities in the American West, of which Chicago constituted the most successful example.

Nevertheless, in New York's case, there were not just declarations. Hundreds of brochures, books, lithographs, and soon, photographs celebrated its virtues. For example, the merchant Isaac C. Kendall published a pamphlet called *The Growth of New York City* that announced the city's advance to "metropolitan greatness."[24] The pro-urban bias merged with reports of New York's supremacy.

New York stimulated the national imagination by appearing henceforth as a city of infinite possibilities, a place where economic success and social advancement were within the grasp of those who aspired to them. Such an idea was basic to the egalitarian interpretation of American society, as embraced—at least since Benjamin Franklin's *Poor Richard's Almanac*—by all those impressed by its relative flexibility. Whatever the inequalities of the period, the idea of possible social advancement was commonly associated with New York. It constituted a framework for the edifying novels of Horatio Alger (1832–99), a former pastor with a Harvard diploma who took up writing in the late 1860s. In the 120 some novels that he published over three decades, Alger invented poor, young heroes who, through willpower, work, and virtue, went "from rags to riches" or, on the contrary, continued to languish miserably, through lack of ambition or moral qualities. The hero of his first novel, *Ragged Dick; or, Street Life in New York*, is thus heard to declare, "I hope, my lad, you will prosper and rise in the world. You know in this free country poverty in early life is no bar to a man's advancement."[25]

New York was also making its entry into literature. At the beginning of the century, the city was still only the pretext for literary jokes. Washington Irving's *History of New York* offers a lively description of a city springing directly from the author's satiric imagination, but basically bearing little resemblance to the real New York. All that changed after 1840, thanks to the "young America" movement, Melville's novels, and Whitman's poems. The son of a merchant, Melville was born in New York in 1819. He grew up there and, in 1830, witnessed his father's failure and madness, subsequently learned various occupations, sailed the South Seas, and returned home in 1845. In his work, New York is one of the ports where his characters, like the young hero of *Redburn*, can hope to embark on long voyages. Failing that, they still have the spectacle presented in the first lines of *Moby Dick*, "your insular city of the Manhattoes, belted round by wharves as Indian isles are by coral reefs," and its "silent sentinels" of "thousands upon thousands of mortal men" lost in "ocean reveries."[26] There the norms, conventions, and codes of life in society are made and unmade, as demonstrated by the hero of *Bartleby the Scrivener*, whose strange attitude disrupts the smoothly run operations of a Wall Street law office.

For Walt Whitman, the child of Brooklyn, New York held an even more central place. Even if the writer stated in the preface to his *Leaves of Grass* that "the United States themselves are essentially the greatest poem," New York is the setting, stimulus, and subject of his work and his life. "Ah, what can ever be more stately and admirable to me than mast-hemm'd Manhattan?" Whitman sang of the East River ferry, the scenes that Brooklyn and the streets of Manhattan offered to his muse, the trades and occupations of the New York working class.[27]

A NEW GRAMMAR

New York's entry into literature coincided with a growing awareness of the difficulty of perceiving the city. In the early 1830s, Gustave de Beaumont and Alexis de Tocqueville could still climb to the top of a New York church tower, "up small, dark and difficult staircases," and "after many tribulations," enjoy "an admirable view" encompassing the whole metropolis in one glance.[28] Then New York switched scale: its movement, its diversity, its sounds, its smells, its landscapes disoriented both New

Yorkers and visitors, torn between desire, admiration, and apprehension.

The city's lack of readability gave rise to the development of new tools for orientation and comprehension. This new grammar was first of all visual. Maps, drawings, and engravings, thanks to lithographic techniques, recorded transformations in the landscape. Thus in 1821, Theodore Fay published a volume of *Views of New York and its Surroundings* that contained some thirty-eight drawings and a map. In the early 1840s, the well-known company of Currier, later Currier & Ives, distributed lithographs of New York scenes throughout the country: City Hotel on Broadway, Central Park, and a view of Manhattan and the East River from Brooklyn Heights owed much to the talents of Frances Palmer, an artist of English origin.

Early photography, for which New York served as the capital, captured the city in various styles, scenes, and panoramas. With both lithography and photography, the bird's-eye view, aiming to capture the greatest possible amount of urban space, appeared side by side with representations of this or that building. In 1853, under the overall title of "New York in Daguerreotype," *Putnam's* magazine published a series of articles that combined a general view, taken from Union Square, with pictures of banks, theaters, and private residences. All its readers were thus given the opportunity to visualize the metropolis.

In publishers' catalogues, works on New York multiplied. Mary Booth and Martha Lamb each published, in 1859 and 1880, a *History of the City of New York*, and Henry Stiles published a *History of the City of Brooklyn* (1867–70). Even the very businesslike and austere *Manual of the Corporation of the City of New York*, published annually beginning in 1841 by the clerk of the Common Council, David T. Valentine, was brightened up with numerous maps and illustrations.

The first guides to New York—Goodrich's in 1818, Blunt's in 1828—were addressed specifically to merchants, businessmen, and manufacturers who were passing through town. Others were meant for one special category of visitors. Southerners, who rushed to New York in crowds each summer before going to take the waters in

FIGURE 30
View of New York from Union Square (1853)
© L'Illustration/Keystone

Saratoga, gleaned precious bits of information from Gideon Davison's guide, *The Fashionable Tour*, or William Bobo's travel account, *Glimpses of New York City, by a South Carolinian (Who Had Nothing Else to Do)*. Southern reviews—*Southern Literary Messenger, De Bow's Review, Southern Quarterly Review*—published columns on New York, thus demonstrating the metropolis's cultural hold. About 1840, sensing a significant market, major New York publishers issued generalist guides meant for Americans or foreign visitors who could read English, such as *Appleton's Guide* or *King's Guide to New York*.

The urban education so generously offered by all these guides did not claim to include all the city's secrets. Others guides had less respectable objectives. In 1839, a work was published under the deceptive title of *Prostitution Exposed; or, a Moral Reform Dictionary*. It described in detail the geography of mercenary sex and compared the advantages and disadvantages of the brothels in Five Points, the Lower East Side, and the shores of the Hudson. Because of its success, this kind of guide proliferated. A *Guide to the Harems* in New York, published in 1855, was followed two years later by a *Directory to the Seraglios in New York*. . . .

A fascination with the low life and shameful secrets of New York also explained the popularity of a new genre, influenced by *The Mysteries of Paris* by Eugène Sue, translated in London and New York in the early 1840s. *The Mysteries and Miseries of New York*, published by Edward Z. C. Judson under the pen name of Ned Buntline—subsequently well-known for his westerns—and other similar accounts of New York's shady side were intended to shock the bourgeoisie with complaisant descriptions of the city's low life, and to condemn the moral turpitude revealed there. Most importantly, they were meant to explain the urban mysteries behind the curtain and to put readers on their guard against swindlers of all kinds who thrived in New York. Their titles were explicit: *Sunshine and Shadow in New York* or *Lights and Shadows of New York Life*. They were so successful that they inspired German and French equivalents: *Asmodée à New York*, by Ferdinand Longchamp, recounting a visit to the city's underside with the devil as guide, was published simultaneously in Paris and New York in 1868. Plays and novels drew from the same inspiration. In 1848, *A Glance at New York* presented for the first time the two heroes from the Bowery, Mose and Lize. Countless gothic novels adopted New York as their setting, like *The Belle of the Bowery* (1846), in which Osgood Bradbury describes the fall of a young woman from the country, or Judson's *The B'hoys of New York* (1849).

These urban mysteries were not so far removed as it seemed from Horatio Alger's edifying novels, or from the numerous sentimental novels then published as serials by newspapers or in cheap editions by publishers. They all tried to include a moral dimension, even if the first genre emphasized the low life, the second social advancement, and the third affairs of the heart. *Ragged Dick* is also a visit to New York with a street urchin as a guide, who explains his city to other characters and to Alger's readers.

George Foster's writing merged the newspaper column and the urban mystery. Foster, a journalist who worked first in northwestern New York State and then in Alabama and Missouri before settling in New York in 1842, considered himself an expert on urban matters. It was after spending several years at the *Aurora*, and then at Horace Greeley's *Tribune*, and after a stay in Philadelphia, that Foster wrote *New York in Slices: By an Experienced Carver*, in the form of a serial that appeared in the *Tribune* in 1848, and then as a book in 1849. In 1850, *New York by Gas-Light and Other Urban Sketches* was published.

These two collections gathered together vignettes of New York night life that offered an expert reading of the city. They met with great and immediate success; more than 200,000 copies of them were sold. And they were quickly imitated: in 1854, Solon Robinson walked his reader through the seediest parts of the metropolis, showed them the consequences of excessive drinking on the families of ragmen, and made them listen to the common cries of New York that gave his book its name, *Hot Corn*—"Hot corn, here's your real hot corn, hot and steaming, right out of the pot!" But Foster was an "experienced carver" without equal. He was not content with just exposing the city's underside and its deceptive appearances by day and by night. He also proposed a social geography of New York at the time, centered around Broadway for the elite, the Bowery for the native working class, and Five Points for the immigrants. According to him, New York was a fragmented metropolis, a gigantic puzzle that had to be deciphered piece by piece without too much hope of being able to put it all back together.

THE VICTORIAN CITY

In 1893, the essayist and editor William Crary Brownell came to a similar conclusion. Thus the comparative essay that he devoted "to the traits of the French character" concluded with the idea that New York "is less like any European city than any European city is like any other," because "there is no palpable New York in the sense in which there is a Paris, a Vienna, a Milan. You can touch it at no point. It is not even ocular. There is instead a Fifth Avenue, a Broadway, a Central Park, a Chatham square." Moreover, the city demonstrated its capacity to accommodate foreigners but not absorb them. "It contrasts absolutely in this respect with Paris, whose assimilating power is prodigious; every foreigner in Paris eagerly seeks Parisianization," while in New York, the "noisy diversity" works against "any effect of *ensemble*."[29] The metropolis of the 1880s was divided by such great economic, social, and cultural gulfs that the parts could only prevail over the whole.

III
METROPOLITAN
MODERNITIES
1890–1940

FIGURE 31

Man waving from the Empire State Building construction site
© Hulton-Deutsch Collection/CORBIS

MAP 5

The New York area in the early twentieth century

6

GREATER NEW YORK

"The outline of the city became frantic in its efforts to explain something that defied meaning," observed the writer Henry Adams upon his return to the shores of the Hudson in 1903 after a long stay in Europe. "Power seemed to have outgrown its servitude and to have asserted its freedom. The cylinder had exploded, and thrown great masses of stone and steam against the sky. The city had the air and movement of hysteria, and the citizens were crying, in every accent of anger and alarm, that the new forces must at any cost be brought under control."[1] In this dawn of the twentieth century, New York was divided, fragmented, torn between multiple centrifugal forces and constant efforts toward unification and order.

NEW YORK THE MAJESTIC

Controlling New York "at any cost" was not a given. One of the strategies conceived by its admirers and promoters consisted precisely of inventing a new vision of the metropolis. The term itself, until then used without a second thought, now gave rise to existential questions. What defined a metropolis? Herbert Croly asked this question a few years before he became well known for publishing *The Promise of American Life* (1909), and then for founding and editing the weekly *New Republic* (1914). "In order to be actually metropolitan, it must not only reflect large national tendencies, but it must sum them up and transform them. It must not only mirror typical American ways of thought and action, but it must anticipate, define and realize national ideals. A genuine metropolis must be, that is, both a concentrated and selected expression of the national life."[2]

At the turn of the century, the staunch nationalism that led the United States to take over Cuba and the Philippines encouraged New Yorkers in their aspirations for greatness. They acquired a new self-awareness and a new sense of their own importance. Nothing better symbolized the heightened feelings of the time than the enthusiastic welcome some two million New Yorkers gave Admiral George Dewey on September 29 and 30, 1899. After a naval parade of unprecedented size, the "hero of Manila" and of the Spanish-American War made his way up Broadway, in an open carriage, to resounding cheers. He was then received at City Hall and for four hours reviewed the 35,000 soldiers and prominent figures who marched from President Grant's tomb, located at One Hundred and Twentieth Street, to Washington Square, passing under the triumphal arch—called the "Dewey Arch"—erected for the occasion on Madison Square and remotely inspired by the Arch of Titus. As the twentieth century dawned, New York imagined itself, not without grandiloquence, as the Rome of the new American empire.

It is true that the city had some experience in these matters. The year of 1898 opened, after all, with the annexation that, in fact, marked the creation of a Greater New York. Theoretically, this was only a merger between New York and Brooklyn, the first and third largest American cities at the time, respectively. But no one doubted that Brooklyn thus lost a share of that individuality of which it was so proud.

The mood was very different on the evening of December 31, 1897, on the two sides of the East River, where each city had decided to await the fatal hour of the union separately. In Brooklyn, there was no celebration. The Common Council had organized a sober ceremony in its chamber. The occasional poem on "the disappearance of

Brooklyn," the speeches given by the mayor, the editor of the *Brooklyn Eagle*, and the pastor of the First Reformed Church were all marked with a funereal melancholy. When the bells of City Hall rang at midnight, not only did they announce the birth of Greater New York and the borough of Brooklyn, they also sounded the knell of Brooklyn's former autonomy.

As for Manhattan, it rejoiced. Despite bad weather, thousands of New Yorkers gathered that evening in front of City Hall and on adjacent streets. Soon the marching bands arrived in good order, the battalions of retired firemen, the Irish, German, Italian, Hungarian, and French societies, followed by allegorical floats, like the one of Liberty lighting the world, or symbolic ones, like the one of Tammany Hall, displaying an enormous tiger with the portrait of the organization heads. "With the sky invisible and a fine, cold, stinging rain pelting from it," recounted the *New York Times* in a style worthy of the event, "with ceaseless showers of fire and stars of all colors of the rainbow, and huge fountains of shining silver and gold, sparkling, glowing, and flashing vividly amid the blackness around and above, with the crash of cannon and the roar of exploding bombs punctuating with quick periods the minor din of steam whistles, braying horns, and shouting men, the clash and throb of a huge brass band dominant over it all, and the mellow, distant chimes of Trinity Church heard now and then at intervals; with a cloud of smoke hanging low, tinted now red, now green, as the colors of the fire below changed with many flash lights throwing their long shafts of white everywhere, intersecting each other, making eccentric evolutions in the darkness, and finally concentrating in one great glare, the flag of Greater New York was officially unfurled over the New York City Hall at midnight by a touch of a button by the Mayor of San Francisco, 3,700 miles away, and the second city of the world came into existence."[3]

Henceforth, all the conditions were fulfilled for the "awakening of municipal vanity," noted by a caustic Herbert Croly.[4] Within a few years, New York was equipped with a monumental infrastructure meant to celebrate its grandeur. The new architecture drew its academic and neoclassical inspiration from the "White City," built in Chicago for the World's Columbian Exposition of 1893, which translated into marble an ideal of order and harmony, dignity and civic virtue. The Exposition buildings were intended as an attempt at architectural education on the national level, not just for Chicago. Under the leadership of the project director Daniel Burnham, they had been designed in part by New Yorkers—Richard Morris Hunt, George Post, Charles Follen McKim, William Rutherford Mead, and Stanford White. It was only natural for these architects to bring back to the shores of the Hudson those ideas that they had implemented on the shores of Lake Michigan.

Their achievements were numerous, and they transformed New York. In effect, at their instigation, a "city beautiful" movement developed, nurtured by town planning. They led it with the support of several organizations, such as the Municipal Art Society founded by Richard Morris Hunt, the Municipal Art Commission established in the 1898 charter, and its heir, the New York City Improvement Commission, created in 1904.

Of course the Commission could not achieve unanimity and never managed to impose its aesthetic views. "The vision of a local pseudo-classic Beaux Artists New Jerusalem" offers a "very insipid ideal," lamented Herbert Croly.[5] But despite the criticism, the city was provided with new symbols that came to be added to the Statue of Liberty and the Brooklyn Bridge. Thus, Grand Central and Pennsylvania Stations were conceived as monuments to its glory, and not only as utilitarian infrastructures.

The Grand Central building, at the intersection of Park Avenue and Forty-second Street, was renovated in 1898–1900, and then entirely rebuilt between 1903 and 1913, when it became necessary to provide electricity to all of Manhattan's railroad lines. The final results brought together impressive technical successes—a network of underground tracks conceived by the Central Hudson Company's chief engineer, William Wilgus—and a grandeur that corresponded to the concern of the architects,

FIGURE 32
Grand Central Station about 1910
© Roger Viollet

Reed & Stem and Warren & Wetmore, to make Grand Central New York's monumental entryway.

Pennsylvania Station, built between 1904 and 1910 by McKim, Mead & White, was also imposing, with its glazed concourse, its maze of corridors, and its neoclassical waiting room. But it was less well situated, between Seventh and Eighth Avenues from Thirty-first to Thirty-fourth Streets, and the commercial development that its construction was hoped to activate was slow to come about.

The first years of the twentieth century also witnessed the long-called-for construction of city administration offices. City Hall, built in 1811, was surrounded by a monumental group of buildings that made up a civic center finally worthy of the metropolis. The enterprise began with the Hall of Records (1899–1911), intended for the archives. With its seven stories, Corinthian columns, sculptures, mansarded roof, and great stairway, it was "perhaps the most Parisian thing in New York," judged the contemporary critic Montgomery Schuyler.[6] Next the Municipal Building was constructed between 1907 and 1914. Its symbolic dimension was affirmed by a colonnade on Chambers Street, and especially by a dome, topped with a statue of Civic Fame, that inscribed it into the New York skyline.

The other boroughs were not to be outdone. Besides a new courthouse in Manhattan, completed in 1926, imposing courthouses were built in Brooklyn, the Bronx and on Staten Island, where architects Carrère and Hastings also erected a Borough Hall that symbolized the integration of the island, still so provincial, into the greater city. Everywhere, various municipal services were moved into buildings considered worthy of the civic ideal they were supposed to embody: fire stations, police stations, school buildings constituted so many variations on the theme of municipal grandeur.

While Brooklyn was having a monumental museum built between 1895 and 1915, in Manhattan, Richard Morris Hunt adorned the Metropolitan Museum with a new facade that opened onto Fifth Avenue. Some forty blocks south, at the former site of the Croton reservoir, on the corner of Fifth Avenue and from Fortieth to Forty-second Streets, Carrère and Hastings raised the high walls of the New York Public Library in those same years. Initiated in 1895, it grew out of the collections of the Astor Library, open free of charge to the public since 1853, and the special collections of the Lenox Library, thanks to a gift of five million dollars from Samuel Tilden, "to establish and maintain a free library in the City of New York and to promote scientific and educational objects."[7]

The federal government helped to foster this vision of a monumental city by constructing a new customs building near Bowling Green, at the tip of Manhattan, the majestic Custom House designed by Cass Gilbert. On Ellis Island, where, since 1892, millions of immigrants who had previously arrived at Castle Garden had disembarked and been screened, architects Boring & Tilton constructed a new group of five buildings—replacing the original

Municipal Building, New York.

FIGURE 33
The Municipal Building and its statue of Civic Fame
© Hachette Livre

wooden structures that had been destroyed by fire in 1897. The central structure was crowned with highly decorative towers. For all those arriving from the Old World, this spot was, literally and symbolically, the doorway to the United States.

FIGURE 34
Ellis Island © Roger Viollet

PRIVATE GRANDEUR

Celebrating New York's glory and efforts to give it a certain formal unity were not the exclusive right of the
municipal or federal authorities. Large corporations, as
well, enthusiastically took up the charge of erecting monuments acclaiming the city's prestige, to the extent that
this prestige served their own image.

These corporations grew out of the turmoil the American economy experienced in the decades following the
Civil War. Growth in demand and accelerated technical
progress first revolutionized transport and communication, and then industrial production and distribution.
Large firms formed in all these sectors, either through
growth or merger, and the "visible hand" of the management replaced the "invisible hand" of the market so dear
to Adam Smith.

New York remained the heart of the new economy thanks to the incomparable advantages it offered with regard to the circulation and distribution of information, administrative and financial infrastructures, and technical and theoretical expertise. Large firms scrambled to open offices, and then to establish their headquarters there. The tobacco tycoon James Buchanan Duke began with a modest establishment in the mid-1880s before moving the headquarters of his American Tobacco Company from Durham, North Carolina to Broadway, and then into a spacious building on Fifth Avenue. By 1895, New York housed the headquarters of 298 firms with capital of more than one million dollars—that is, three times more firms than Chicago and four times more than Boston or Philadelphia. Managing the country's industrial economy was a New York affair.

Corporate America's expansion meant spectacular changes in the Manhattan landscape. Large businesses were greedy for offices. The short supply of available space in the Wall Street neighborhood, where most companies wanted to establish themselves, led to vertical growth. In the 1880s, Manhattan's skyline was still dominated by Trinity Church's neo-Gothic steeple, rising 220 feet over Broadway at the end of Wall Street. But over the course of the next three decades, a landscape of peaks and valleys emerged. Architects and large companies tried to outdo each other in audacity in the race to the sky. Their creations reached twenty-six stories in 1890, forty-seven in 1908, and as high as sixty stories in 1913, with the Woolworth Building.

This forest of skyscrapers left no one indifferent. Some observers were scathing in their criticism. The Frenchman Lazare Weiller claimed to know of "few things as downright ugly as these monstrous buildings that sometimes resemble ill-proportioned square towers and sometimes heavy, misshapen quadrilaterals, recalling those high blocks of solid soap that Marseilles provides to our housewives, the glory of grocery window displays."[8] Others with more equanimity admitted to the economic logic that ruled over the proliferation of these skyscrapers. The architect Cass Gilbert saw them accurately as "a machine that makes the land pay."[9] Still others were content to admire them.

The new giants also served to project into urban space the names of the large businesses thus directly associated with efforts to beautify New York. "Here the skyscraper is not an element in city planning," noted Le Corbusier later, "but a banner in the sky, a fireworks rocket, an aigrette in the coiffure of a name henceforth listed in the financial Almanach de Gotha."[10] In 1896, the sewing machine manufacturer Singer had the architect Ernest Flagg build a ten-story building, and then a few years later, a fourteen-story building next to the first; in 1906, the two buildings were joined and crowned with a forty-seven-story tower in the Beaux-Arts style, thus becoming one of Manhattan's landmarks.

The Metropolitan Life Insurance Company proceeded in the same way. Established on Madison Square since the early 1890s, the company multiplied its acquisitions of land and building properties over the course of the fifteen years of strong growth that followed. In 1906, Metropolitan Life hired the architect Napoléon Le Brun to build a fifty-story tower in the Italian Renaissance style; it was completed three years later. In an advertising brochure, the insurance company compared this new type of bell tower to "a great sentinel keeping watch over the millions of policy holders" insured by Metropolitan Life.[11]

As for Cass Gilbert, he chose the Gothic style for his commission from Frank W. Woolworth, the creator of a chain of stores in which all merchandise was sold at the fixed price of five and ten cents. Woolworth had dreamed of a copy of London's Parliament, but Gilbert built a "cathedral of commerce" which, with its inauguration in April 1913, became one of the peaks on the New York horizon.

During the 1920s and 1930s, this tendency did not flag, and many banks, shipping companies, and industrial firms—Cunard, Irving Trust Company, Chrysler, Manhattan Company, First National Bank, Bank of New York, etc.—inscribed their names on urban peaks. The skyscraper was the preferred mode of expression for triumphant American capitalism. It allowed an ever-growing

demand for office space to be answered. In 1913, Manhattan counted fifty-one buildings with anywhere from twenty-one to sixty stories, and nearly 1,000 buildings with eleven to twenty stories. In 1929, there were 188 buildings with more than twenty stories, and 2,291 with eleven to twenty stories. The city housed twenty-two million square feet of offices in 1920, and nearly twice that in 1935.

Skyscrapers sheltered the employees of the firms that gave them their names, but they also housed hundreds of other companies, large and small, that rented offices and prestigious addresses from them: Singer occupied only one of its tower's forty-seven floors, Woolworth only two of its fifty stories. In 1924, more than 400 companies were housed in the Woolworth Building.

Skyscrapers offered the space necessary for the expansion of corporate New York, for the thousands of white-collar workers employed by large firms or companies whose indispensable function it was to provide services and consultation. Insurance agents, lawyers, bankers, consulting engineers, industrial experts of every kind, architects, and advertisers—all wanted to be close to their best clients.

A second business district, near Grand Central Station, developed in the 1920s, under the combined effect of a strong demand for offices and growing real-estate speculation. Until then, the Metropolitan Life Insurance tower and its rival New York Life's skyscraper, on Madison Square, had seemed very isolated north of Wall Street. But within a few years, the line of skyscrapers multiplied along the streets and avenues located around Grand Central: in the heart of the "roaring forties," Forty-second Street alone accommodated the Chrysler Building—an elegant tower seventy-seven stories high, the tallest skyscraper in the world for two years—the Chanin, the Lincoln, and many other tall buildings.

Two more monumental projects soon put the midtown business district on the map—the Empire State Building and Rockefeller Center. The Empire State Building, erected on Fifth Avenue at Thirty-fourth Street, constituted a kind of aberration. The project, conceived by the businessman John Jacob Raskob—an ingenious financier, to whom the Du Pont Company owed its successful reorganization a few years earlier, and a skillful speculator—was launched in the fall of 1929, a few weeks before the financial crisis that provoked the Wall Street collapse on October 24 and 29—"Black Thursday" and "Black Tuesday." Despite the gloom that enveloped New York economic circles, the Empire State Building was inaugurated less than two years later, in May 1931, following the extraordinarily rapid construction of what became the tallest building in the world. Relatively far from Forty-second Street, it represented pure real-estate

FIGURE 36
Acrobat of the New York sky, at work on the Empire State Building,
as captured by the photographer Lewis Hine
© Avery Library, Columbia University

speculation, with no ties to any large business. Thus it was hardly surprising that this new symbol of New York remained three-quarters empty and lost money for its owners until 1950.

The dozen buildings of Rockefeller Center, between Fifth and Sixth Avenues, and from Forty-eighth to Fifty-first Streets, followed a different logic. According to the original plan, an opera house was to be built on the site, but because of the 1929 crash, that idea was abandoned. John D. Rockefeller, Jr., the backer, then decided to build a monumental ensemble that recalled, in a modern architectural language, the civic ambitions of the 1900s. The completion of the project in 1939 testified to the new significance of the Midtown business district: although in 1900, three quarters of the city's office space was located near Wall Street, by 1935, Midtown and Wall Street each accommodated about 40 percent of New York offices.

The demand for square feet of office space was not all that determined the evolution of the skyline. There were heavy constraints upon building in Manhattan. It was difficult to combine lots into areas large enough to build on, as was possible in Chicago, where the massive destruction of the 1871 fire had facilitated this process. In the Wall Street district, for example, architects built tall towers on minuscule plots. To consider an extreme case, the façade of the Gillender Building (1897) was twenty-six feet wide and eighty feet deep, for a building eighteen stories high.

It was also necessary to contend with regulations. Until 1916, backers and architects could give free rein to their imaginations, because those in favor of limiting the height of buildings had not managed to rally enough political support. But in the early 1910s, as skyscraper builders raced frantically to the sky, many lower Manhattan streets were transformed into dark, perpendicular gorges. Henceforth, the offices located in the shadows of the skyscrapers were difficult to rent because of their lack of light. Furthermore, the demand for office space had leveled off completely, and the owners of existing buildings obviously favored restricting new construction.

One skyscraper in particular came to symbolize this threat to real-estate values and the dangers of uncontrolled architecture. The forty stories of the Equitable Insurance Company building, constructed between 1913 and 1915, plunged the neighboring streets and skyscrapers into darkness. This was too much, and in 1916, the mayor signed an ordinance that regulated the use of land, and set height and area limitations on buildings. New York was divided into residential, industrial, and business districts, for which there were varying restrictions to prevent buildings from using up their entire sites. For each district, the maximum height of buildings was determined by the width of the street. Thus, in Manhattan's business districts, the authorized height before the first setback was two times the width of the street, and subsequent setbacks had to be proportional to the building's height.

This division of the city into zones was not a new thing in the United States. Los Angeles had adopted similar regulations in 1908, and the Supreme Court had declared them constitutional in 1915. But in New York, the idea was not so much to preserve residential neighborhoods as to resolve the conflicts between industry and the white-collar sector. Within a few years, the 1916 zoning ordinance had a profound affect on the style of skyscrapers. The buildings of the 1920s and 1930s were storied pyramids, soon known as "wedding cakes" or, more nobly and in reference to Babylonian architecture, "ziggurats."

THE "TENEMENT HOUSE PROBLEM"

While the new Babylon bloomed with civic monuments and towering "cathedrals of commerce," other New Yorkers tried to put their city in order by improving the living conditions of the very poor. It was the general opinion that the 1879 Tenement Act had not resolved the housing question. Sometimes it even aggravated the overcrowding in buildings on the Lower East Side and in the city's other working-class neighborhoods. In the 1890s, denunciations multiplied due to the efforts of reformers, often members of the middle class, who called for radical changes.

Some of them gathered their information firsthand, since they came to live among the working class, in one of the dozen settlement houses thriving in New York around 1910. Having appeared about twenty years earlier, these settlements were founded on the idea that middle-class values could be disseminated in working-class neighborhoods if the reformers lived in close contact with the immigrants. Some of the settlements were well-known at the time, like College Settlement, University Settlement, or the Henry Street Settlement, run by the radical reformer Lillian Wald. All of them increased the number of social-action and education programs in their neighborhoods.

In 1890, the publication of an important documentary work, *How the Other Half Lives: Studies in the New York Tenements*, marked a turning point in social awareness regarding this urban issue. Its author was the forty-year-old journalist, Jacob Riis. Born in Denmark, he came to the United

States in 1870, and got his training wandering the New York streets on behalf of the *New York Sun* and the *Evening Sun*, where he was the police reporter. In the chapters of *How the Other Half Lives*, graphically illustrated with photographs, and then in *The Battle of the Slums* and *The Children of the Tenements*, he described and sharply denounced the living conditions in the working-class buildings of lower Manhattan—the tenements—and called for housing reform.

Initiatives in this direction multiplied. In 1894, the New York state legislature established a new Tenement House Committee. A few months later, it published a report on the sorry condition of working-class neighborhoods in New York, beginning with a survey involving some 8,400 buildings where more than 250,000 New Yorkers lived. The following year, it was the federal government's turn to make public a report on *The Housing of the Working People*, conducted under the auspices of the Labor Department, and from the perspective of a comparison with European countries.

In 1896 and in 1900, two architectural competitions aimed at improving the tenements were organized by charitable reform societies, the Association for Improving the Condition of the Poor and the Charity Organization Society. The winner of the 1896 competition was Ernest Flagg, a young graduate of the Beaux-Arts School. Flagg tried hard to adapt the ideas of Parisian architects to the requirements of New York working-class housing. In the years that followed, his influence was considerable.

The 1900 competition featured a show on the tenements that presented photographs, maps, plans, diagrams, and models, and was a huge success. Its organizer, Lawrence Veiller, campaigned for housing reform for many years. Shortly thereafter, he was appointed secretary of a new commission on tenements, established by the New York state legislature under pressure from the Charity Organization Society, and presided over by the wealthy lawyer and reformer Robert W. DeForest. This commission's conclusions were published in a report of unprecedented depth, *The Tenement House Problem*, a huge two-volume work compiled by DeForest and Veiller.

Concurrently, in 1901, two reformers persuaded the state legislature to adopt a new law on tenement housing. With much stricter health and ventilation standards than the 1879 act, it created a new administrative authority, the Tenement House Department. DeForest was named as its head, with Veiller as assistant. But a few months later, reporters for the federal Industrial Commission on Immigration noted that the new law did nothing to resolve the problem of overcrowding and that it contained no measures for improving the approximately 60,000 dwellings, known as the "old law" tenements, built under the 1879 measure, despite their acknowledged shortcomings.

At the very least, the 1901 law opened the way for a radical redefinition of the "tenement house problem." Thus, more than 40,000 "old law" tenements were simply razed in the 1920s, and many thousands of others experienced the same fate over the course of the 1930s. All this demolition considerably transformed several working-class neighborhoods, especially on the Lower East Side.

Along with these measures came the development of working-class housing in Manhattan and other city boroughs as well. In the 1900s, some 10,000 three- or four-story, relatively comfortable apartment buildings were constructed in Manhattan and the Bronx. Some were the product of scientific philanthropic enterprises, like Forest Hills Gardens, built in Queens in 1908, under the auspices of the Russell Sage Foundation. Others were only the result of calculations by real-estate promoters, like the Queensboro Corporation, established in 1909 and originally located in Jackson Heights. But it was especially after World War I, in the 1920s, that these buildings experienced their boom: 600,000 housing units, two thirds of which were apartments, were created at that time, the combined result of increasing demand, new housing expectations on the part of individuals, strong fiscal incentives, and national economic prosperity. Styles varied from one borough to another: eighty percent of the construction in the Bronx consisted of four- to six-story apartment buildings, while in Brooklyn and Queens, forty and seventy percent of the new buildings, respectively, were for private houses.

The economic crisis of the 1930s temporarily halted these efforts to resolve the question of working-class housing—efforts that were generally very profitable for their promoters. But several budgetary and fiscal measures were adopted in the attempt to stimulate construction. A new administrative authority, the New York City Housing Authority, was created in 1934, and its role was strengthened three years later when the Wagner-Steagall Housing Act was adopted. Real-estate programs for low-income New Yorkers were launched. In their own way, the apartment buildings and, later, the housing projects that went up in Harlem, Williamsburg, Red Hook, and Queens provided a solution to the "tenement housing problem," but only by creating another one, the problem of the housing development. . . .

"THE SMALL MANUFACTURER'S PARADISE"

Growth or control? The tensions that characterized the development of the New York housing situation also existed in the industrial sector. Despite the expansion of the corporate sector, New York remained a major American manufacturing center: the city's workshops and factories put 420,000 New Yorkers to work in 1900, and more than a million in 1930.

One sign of the capacity for innovation was the growth of research and development laboratories linked to the big businesses established in New York. Thus, Bell Laboratories, a subsidiary of Western Electric and American Telephone and Telegraph (AT&T) opened on West Street in 1907. Adding innovative approaches in the area of the telephone and, more generally, electricity and electronics, Bell and the many cutting-edge companies that began in New York placed the metropolis at the forefront of American industrial research.

At the same time, industrial specialization was growing. This tendency, already apparent in the nineteenth century, was reinforced by the expansion of the national market. According to variations in production and delivery costs linked to the emergence of other industrial centers across the country, sector-based redeployment became necessary. Although consolidations and mergers increased on the national level, New York was "the small manufacturer's paradise." Its main asset remained the flexibility and competitiveness of its clothing and printing workshops, and its luxury- and specialized-product sectors. That was where growth occurred, and the other branches disappeared more or less rapidly.

In the 1930s, Manhattan was "still the favorite site for New York's industrial activities,"[12] noted a New York guidebook, but its place had diminished as Brooklyn's and Queens' had grown. In 1899, Manhattan had been the site of nearly three quarters of all industry jobs; by 1937, that number fell to less than three fifths, while Brooklyn's and Queens' share grew from a quarter to more than a third.

The companies leaving Manhattan often set up shop in Newark, Elizabeth, and Jersey City, New Jersey or, in New York State, in Brooklyn and Queens. Thus, an industrial belt grew up across the water from Manhattan, around New York bay. Beyond the natural inertia of invested capital, the proximity to the harbor and its services remained a decisive argument for attracting businesses.

In Manhattan, most of the workshops were located in the industrial heart of the island, south of Fifty-ninth Street—what city planners in the 1920s called South Manhattan—where they competed directly with the white-collar sector for use of land. The major branch was the garment industry: in 1922, this sector represented 40 percent of employment (and a fifth of the total employment in the metropolitan area). Until the 1880s, it was nearly exclusively a matter of men's clothing. But men's clothing manufacturing, easier to standardize, tended to leave New York for Chicago or Rochester, beginning in the 1920s. On the other hand, women's clothing experienced extraordinary growth. Coats, blouses, suits, aprons, dresses, and later, pants were produced in huge quantities in the workshops of Manhattan, which was destined to become the fashion capital of America.

Companies and workers remained concentrated in the neighborhoods of lower Manhattan until the 1910s. The Lower East Side abounded in cramped and overcrowded workshops, but also in larger sites that were evidence of the tendency toward concentration. The Triangle Shirt-waist Factory, for example, employed hundreds of workers in the same building. During the 1910s and 1920s, the center of the garment industry moved north, between Sixth and Ninth Avenues, and between Twenty-fifth and Forty-first Streets. In this district, soon known as the "garment district," manufacturers and subcontractors, wholesalers and retailers, all set up shop. All day long, people crossed paths with garment workers pushing loaded clothes racks.

Despite appearances, the garment district was very well organized. It housed those businesses that were particularly dependent on the dictates of fashion, concerned with flexibility and not standardized—in short, the extremely sensitive sector of women's clothing. What remained of the men's clothing industry in New York, and that part of the women's clothing industry less sensitive to fashion, like apron-making, tended to leave Manhattan for Brooklyn or Queens, if it did not abandon the New York region entirely.

Besides the clothing industry, many New Yorkers worked for companies that specialized in printing or publication, or in the food industries. These sectors experienced identical development. Publishing remained solidly established in Manhattan, where it profited from a privileged situation with regard to sources of information essential to it. But printers set up shop increasingly in Brooklyn or Queens, where the price of property and rents were much lower.

This relative decentralization on the metropolitan level resulted in the formation of two types of industrial landscapes, still visible in New York today. In Manhattan, lofts proliferated. These buildings were often more than ten stories high, but could reach fifteen, thirty, and even fifty stories on rare occasions. Each was occupied by workshops, often renovated over the course of the 1920s, when service elevators and adequate loading docks were added.

During this same decade, Midtown lofts experienced spectacular development in the new garment district: within a few years, dozens of buildings were constructed near Seventh Avenue between Thirtieth and Forty-fifth Streets. Their symbolic and architectural heart was a group of buildings erected in 1921, the well-named Garment Center Capitol, the work of the architect Walter Mason. These two industrial buildings, seventeen and twenty-four stories high, housed nearly seventy companies where more than 20,000 workers labored. A few years later, the architect Ely Jacques Kahn made his reputation as a modernist by erecting numerous lofts in the garment district at the request of property developers, who were often former garment manufacturers who had made their fortunes.

Outside of Manhattan, factory buildings generally accommodated industrial activity. These buildings were not tall but very extensive, thus allowing for continuous production. The neighborhood of Long Island City, in Queens, was a veritable "labyrinth of industrial plants," to quote a New York guidebook of that time. Some 1,400 New York factories—most of them industrial bakeries, paint and varnish manufacturers, pasta companies—were clustered on a few square miles.[13] Further north, the Astoria district housed the Edison Company's gigantic gas-manufacturing plant. As for Brooklyn, it prided itself on its U.S. Navy Yard, with its dry docks, tidal basins, wharves, and foundries, where 10,000 people were employed at the end of the 1930s.

THE WORLD'S PREMIER PORT

The big factories in Brooklyn and New Jersey were located there because, in 1900, New York was the world's premier port—still centered in Manhattan. The banks of the Hudson had definitively supplanted those of the East River, even if the latter still accommodated barges and the fishing boats that supplied the fish market on Fulton Street. From the tip of Manhattan to Sixtieth Street, the Hudson was lined with docks and warehouses through which passed most of the merchandise that entered or left New York. Washington Market, "the belly of New York," could be found there, with all its wholesalers and retailers stocking up. West Street, the main thoroughfare for the port district, rang all day long with the noise of trucks loading and unloading in endless cycles. The "banana docks" of the United Fruit Company bordered the piers used by coastal traffic.

North of Fourteenth Street, the Chelsea piers were the domain of the transatlantic maritime companies: spacious at the time they were built, between 1902 and 1907, they had become too cramped a quarter-century later, and the largest liners in the 1930s, like the *Normandie*, preferred the wharves built to their scale between Forty-fourth and Fifty-seventh Streets.

The port already extended much further. "Your average New Yorker thinks of the shores of Manhattan and Brooklyn, and lets it go at that," noted *New York Panorama* in 1938. "But not so the scientific student of port affairs. Considered as an economic unit, the Port of New York port embraces the entire area within a 25-mile radius of Statue of Liberty. It extends westward beyond the Passaic River and southward beyond Perth Amboy in New Jersey, farther than Jamaica Bay on the east, northward to Tarrytown on the Hudson River, and as far as Port Chester on Long Island Sound."[14]

In fact, the New York port was the point of convergence for many shipping and railroad line systems: Brooklyn possessed dozens of wharves, warehouses, and silos, like the Bush Terminal, begun in 1890, and through which about a fifth of all commercial port traffic passed in the late 1930s. As for the New Jersey shores, they chiefly accommodated the large railroad-company terminals.

The port's role in international commerce tended to diminish. New York lost ground with regard to exportation beginning in 1890, even while it retained a dominant role in importation for a much longer time. Yet, despite the growth of the ports in the Houston, San Francisco, and Philadelphia areas, New York remained the leading port for domestic and international commerce throughout the first half of the twentieth century.

Still, it was necessary for the port to operate smoothly. But in fact, continual conflicts over New York freight tariffs set the states of New York and New Jersey at odds. In 1916, New Jersey filed a complaint with the Interstate Commerce Commission, in the hopes of attracting the bulk of the metropolis's maritime and railroad freight.

This conflict prompted a plan for creating a bistate port authority, launched by the counsel for the New York

State Chamber of Commerce, the lawyer Julius Henry Cohen. Concerned about the metropolis's economic and administrative efficiency, and influenced by the model of the Port of London Authority, created in 1908, Cohen was responsible for establishing an ad hoc commission and inspiring the proposals that this commission submitted in December 1918.

Thus, in 1921, after two years of difficult negotiations, the Port of New York Authority was born. This bistate authority was given responsibility for improving operations of the infrastructures within the metropolitan port area, which then included seventeen counties and more than a hundred municipalities on both sides of the Hudson. Even though it was authorized to issue guaranteed loans on these infrastructures, the Port Authority never managed to organize the railroad system, due to opposition from the companies involved. But it did succeed in completing a huge bridge project begun in 1925 and intended for road traffic over the Hudson. Constructed by the engineer Othmar Ammann, the George Washington Bridge, connecting Manhattan at One Hundred and Seventh-ninth Street to Fort Lee in New Jersey, was inaugurated in 1931 by the governors of New York—at the time, Franklin Delano Roosevelt—and New Jersey.

PLANNING THE FUTURE

New York went from 2.5 million inhabitants in 1890 to 7.5 million in 1940. During this half century, Manhattan experienced only weak growth, from 1.4 million to 1.9 million, after a peak of 2.3 million in 1910, whereas the populations of the other boroughs exploded: Brooklyn went from 840,000 to 2.7 million inhabitants, the Bronx and Queens from 89,00 and 87,000 respectively to 1.4 million inhabitants each. The only relatively slow growth occurred in the borough of Richmond—that is, Staten Island, whose population only tripled (from 51,000 to 174,000 inhabitants). If Greater New York had existed in 1890, six out of ten New Yorkers would have lived in Manhattan; in 1940, three out of four New Yorkers lived in some other borough.

This transformation, visible everywhere along the coast—the region that the geographer Jean Gottmann later dubbed the "megalopolis"—contributed to a general awareness as the century began that urban development called for better planning. The municipality of New York had long made attempts in this direction—the 1811 grid map or the 1842 Croton reservoir testified to such efforts in the past. In the early twentieth century, this disposition toward rational order and urban renewal resurfaced and took concrete form in New York, as in other American cities, Chicago in particular. The plan for Chicago, created in 1909 by the architect and city planner Daniel Burnham at the request of local business circles, conveyed an ideal of metropolitan harmony and an overall vision of regional development that was readily accepted as a model.

Chicago's example deeply influenced some of New York's municipal administrators in the early 1910s. In 1914, the reform mayor John Purroy Mitchel created an advisory committee on urban planning, which succeeded another committee whose recommendations had resulted in the 1916 ordinance on the height of skyscrapers. At the head of this new committee, Mitchel placed Charles Dyer Norton, a Chicago businessman who had supported the Burnham project before locating in New York and becoming vice president and then president of First National City Bank.

The advisory committee's significance increased after port traffic was paralyzed in the spring of 1917, drawing attention to the urgent need for action. Thus the Port Authority was created in 1921. But translating a general recognition of the problem into real solutions was not easy. A solution comparable to Chicago's, where Burnham was able to work with great freedom, seemed ill-suited to New York, where the professionalization of urban planning coincided with a growing sense that it was important to draw on the expertise offered by the social sciences.

Thus Norton turned to private foundations capable of providing financing for a large-scale planning enterprise. In 1921, the Russell Sage Foundation, already well-known for its support of a major sociology study conducted in Pittsburgh from 1907 to 1909 on the lives of steel workers, agreed to finance the project and granted it one million dollars.

Norton now had the means to convene a research group, which he presided over until his death in 1923. His successor, Franklin Delano, was an engineer, but also a businessman and former Federal Reserve Board commissioner. A Columbia University economics professor, Robert Murray Haig, and a city planning specialist from Harvard, Thomas Adams, were responsible for the group being both lively and efficient. After several years' work, the Committee on the Regional Plan of New York published the results of its research—twelve volumes of analysis, maps, and statistics that analyzed in detail the development of the New York region since the end of the nineteenth century, and ventured predictions and suggestions for the years 1925–65.

The project's aim was to maintain Manhattan's central position and its role as economic nexus by favoring the white-collar sector over manufacturing and industry, who were thus called upon to leave the island. At the same time, the plan insisted upon maintaining manufacturing in the region. Those enterprises were to locate in specific outlying districts of the metropolis. The overall outline of regional coordination provided for three distinct zones: the heart of Manhattan, to the south of Fifty-Ninth Street, devoted to the white-collar sector; an industrial belt about eighteen miles in diameter around the island; and finally, an outlying region reserved for agriculture, outdoor recreation, and large estates.

No suburban development was envisioned. To the contrary, the authors of this regional plan counted on the city's tendency toward centralization. In their eyes, the key to their project's success lay with the railroads—both passenger and freight transport by rail. They resumed the projects conceived a few years earlier by the engineer William J. Wilgus, who had proposed constructing two concentric railroad belts, as well as establishing a regional transportation authority with sufficient power to manage the flow of people and merchandise.

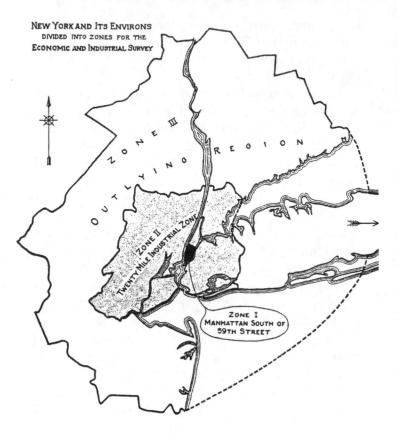

MAP 6

The development plan for the New York area and its three zones

---

The Committee's project for the regional plan prompted loud criticism. The harshest objections came from a young architectural historian, Lewis Mumford, and from a group of architects and city planners who considered the committee too attentive to the demands of big business. Mumford and his friends, who founded the Regional Planning Association of America in 1923, defended the idea of a decentralized metropolis, with a periphery of urban centers capable of counterbalancing it.

In fact, neither Mumford's vision nor the Committee's ever became reality, because of the considerable economic stakes involved in regional development. The railroad companies refused to organize their lines in any rational way or to relinquish any control to public or semi-public administrative authority. Likewise, property developers, who speculated on suburban development, contested the idea of a centralized metropolis where suburban properties were not meant to be subdivided. This dual opposition within the economic circles that initially supported the planning project led the planners to renounce their grand railway projects and focus on automobile and truck routes instead.

Planning efforts thus resulted in a doubly paradoxical outcome: the creation of a highway infrastructure, even though the plan had banked on the railway, and the expansion of the suburbs—a phenomenon neglected by the experts, who underestimated the taste of many New Yorkers for individual houses and misjudged the power of economic interests, always ready to satisfy the demand for real estate. More importantly, in the 1930s, the gradual deterioration of New York's industrial belt led to the appearance of industrial wastelands, whereas the plan predicted a dynamic recentralization and increased economic development. This was good evidence that the plan's projects had become obsolete, or at the very least, diverted from their objective.

AN URBAN ARCHIPELAGO

Despite the misadventures of planning, New York changed scale. The 1898 merger created a new metropolitan area, and it was necessary to provide infrastructures equal to it.

From the 1890s to the 1920s, this was largely a matter of building on efforts begun in the preceding decades involving public transport, in Manhattan as well as in Brooklyn. Electric trolleys replaced the horse-drawn streetcars of the 1850s, and then the cable cars of the 1880s. Trolleys remained the principal means of transportation for millions of New Yorkers until almost 1920, despite competition from the subway, which was opened in 1904. Measured by the miles of rail or by the millions of passengers they carried, their peak came in 1919, before the widespread use of automobiles led to their decline.

Like the streetcar lines, the elevated railway—the famous "el"—was converted to electricity at the turn of the century to respond to ever increasing demand. It continued to play an essential role in the lives of New Yorkers until the early 1920s: the 384 million passengers who used it in 1921 marked its height, before a decline, comparable to that of the trolleys, resulted in the closing of the lines.

The great innovation in the years 1890 to 1920 was undoubtedly the metropolitan underground railroad—the "subway"—which constituted the chief means of integrating the New York archipelago. The underground solution was an effective response to the congestion that threatened the city, because the hundreds of miles of above-ground, or elevated, rail networks were not sufficient.

The first subway line was inaugurated in 1904, but plans for it had begun as early as the late 1880s—following a spectacular snowstorm that paralyzed New York for two weeks, in March 1888, when the mayor of the city, Abram S. Hewitt, first suggested building an underground railroad. A businessman and industrialist, coming from modest means, Hewitt had married well and made his fortune in metallurgy before entering politics and becoming New York's mayor in 1886. He considered the subway New York's only hope in the long run for maintaining its supremacy. It had to facilitate the movements of New Yorkers and keep the middle class from settling in the suburbs, which threatened to diminish the city's fiscal base and promote its economic decline and property-market collapse. Hewitt considered the project so essential that he proposed abandoning the usual formula of franchised concession, and dividing the ownership of the property and the lines themselves, which would remain with the municipality, from the construction and financing of the lines, granted to private enterprises.

As conceived, Hewitt's project drew hostile reactions from some business circles and property developers, who were opposed to all forms of public intervention that they deemed contrary to the principles of free enterprise, as well as New York political circles. Only the New York State Chamber of Commerce was interested, and this was the city's most powerful business association. At its instigation, a law passed in 1894 authorized public investments to implement the project, and entrusted control of the operation to the Chamber of Commerce.

Many years passed before the Chamber clinched a deal in 1900 with the financier and entrepreneur August Belmont, who agreed to build and operate the first subway network. The Interborough Rapid Transit Company (IRT), inaugurated in 1904, experienced immediate success, but Belmont refused to open new lines, hoping to make the most of his monopoly. In 1907, progressives, worried about contending with monopolies, set up a commission granted regulatory powers over transportation: under its leadership a second line was built, beginning in 1913; the Brooklyn Rapid Transit Company soon became the Brooklyn-Manhattan Transit Company (BMT). The subway, which thus went from having 275 to 600 miles of lines, extended into new areas of the Bronx, Brooklyn, and Queens.

In the 1930s, a third group, the Independent Subway System (IND), was financed by public capital. Unlike the BMT, the IND did not try to reach new districts, but rather reinforced the existing lines. No doubt this was not the best choice, since the enterprise immediately faced financial difficulties.

Beginning in 1934, New York's new mayor, Fiorello La Guardia, launched a reorganization operation for the subway infrastructure in order to unite the three existing enterprises (IRT, BMT, IND) under one political authority—the municipality's. After years of debate and negotiations, La Guardia achieved his ends in June 1940.

The construction of these different networks had profound consequences for the development of the metropolis. The IRT ran along the east side of Manhattan from City Hall to Grand Central Station, and then passed under Forty-second Street, heading west to Times Square, before following Broadway as far as Ninety-Sixth Street, and then dividing into two branches that entered the

Bronx. The opening of the line unleashed a spectacular real-estate boom on the Upper West Side of Manhattan in the early 1900s: a huge number of apartment buildings meant for the wealthiest New Yorkers and the middle class sprang up between Fifty-ninth Street and One Hundred and Tenth Streets, from the Hudson to Central Park.

In the Bronx, the proximity of the IRT lines also dictated the construction of apartment buildings for skilled and semi-skilled workers. In the 1910s, the IRT-BMT opened to real-estate speculation parts of Brooklyn and Queens that were still uninhabited, such as Corona or Canarsie. Henceforth, the whole urban area of New York was accessible by subway.

After 1920, the focus was on developing infrastructures for facilitating the movements of individuals throughout the region. New York progressively became a city of automobiles. The city counted 2,400 automobiles in 1900, 31,000 in 1910, and 213,000 in 1920. It was necessary to pave and asphalt the roads and build bridges and tunnels. The Brooklyn Bridge was soon flanked by the Williamsburg, Manhattan, and Queensborough bridges, all completed in the 1900s. Roadway connections to New Jersey were made possible by building the Holland Tunnel (1927), the George Washington Bridge (1931), and the Lincoln Tunnel (1937), which facilitated road traffic between New England, the New York area, and Pennsylvania. Projects for landscaped expressways, or "parkways," were carried out in the Bronx and on Long Island, such as the Bronx River Parkway, which followed the river's twists and turns as far as Westchester County. Other followed, under the instigation of Robert Moses, head of the New York State Council of Parks and the Long Island State Park Commission. It was during this time that the Northern and Southern Long Island Parkways were built.

Over the course of the 1930s, the city itself became a grid of infrastructures, at Mayor Fiorello La Guardia's initiative and also Moses's, who was named New York's Park Commissioner in 1934. Beginning in 1934–35, thanks to an influx of federal grants meant to create jobs, Moses

FIGURE 37
The New York archipelago: from top to bottom, the ferry pier, the
Manhattan Bridge, the Brooklyn Bridge © Roger Viollet

and La Guardia multiplied the number of expressways, freeways, and bridges. One of the most grandiose projects was the so-called Triborough Bridge—in fact, a group of three bridges that connected Manhattan, Queens, and the Bronx. Construction began the same day as the Wall Street stock market crashed—October 25, 1929—and then stopped, due to lack of funds.

In 1933, Moses had New York State create the Triborough Bridge Authority, which was granted the power to borrow money from federal institutions created by Roosevelt: the Reconstruction Finance Corporation and the Public Works Administration. Work could resume, and the bridge was inaugurated in 1936. Its success was evident in its first year of existence, over the course of which tolls brought in nearly three million dollars. Moses used this opportunity to restructure the Triborough Bridge Authority and launch other projects, such as the Bronx-Whitestone Bridge, opened in 1939.

All these transformations encouraged the growth of the suburbs, henceforth accessible by rail or road. In New Jersey, the opening of the Holland Tunnel and the George Washington Bridge facilitated the development of Bergen and Morris counties. In New York State, the counties of Rockland and Westchester witnessed the arrival of more and more New Yorkers. Some of these suburbs had been there a long time, but others were newly created, like Radburn, New Jersey, which proudly proclaimed itself "the city of the automobile age." Most of them were also places conceived for the white, Catholic, and Protestant middle class: neither African-Americans nor Jews were widely tolerated in these bastions that aspired to homogeneity. Though still limited in the 1920s and 1930s, the growth of the suburbs only heightened the fragmentation of the metropolis.

THE 1939–1940 EXPOSITION

In April 1939, an international exposition opened in New York. Its central theme, "building the world of tomorrow with the tools of today," was an indirect way of showcasing the metropolis, its present and its future. "No other city has advanced nearly so far along the road that leads to the world of tomorrow," proudly proclaimed the impressive "City of Light" diorama, presented, appropriately enough, by the Edison Company. For its part, Democracity, the model imaginary city of 2039, offered a vision of a decentralized metropolis well supplied with networks of highways. And Futurama, an exhibition of an American city in 1960 financed by General Motors, constituted unadulterated praise for the automobile's influence on urban civilization. With 25 million visitors, this was the most popular attraction at the Exposition.[15]

The idea of organizing an international exposition in New York originated in 1935. The ambitious project was supported by business circles, who saw it as a way of fighting the economic slump, by city planners, who hoped to use it as a forum for spreading their ideas, and by Robert Moses, who wanted to use the opportunity to transform the marshy site he generously proposed, Flushing Meadows, into a modern park. In *The Great Gatsby*, Francis Scott Fitzgerald described this well-known Corona dump as "a valley of ashes." Debates immediately raged between advocates of a neoclassical style, who wanted to create a scene recalling the Chicago Exposition, and modernists, who mocked the idea of constructing "a Parthenon on a Flushing swamp."[16] The final result was a compromise—a general plan featuring time-tested classicism and graced with modernist buildings.

Thus the Exposition paid homage simultaneously to the two approaches—the classical eloquence of the 1890s and 1900s, and the triumphant modernity of the 1920s and 1930s—that had tried to shape the metropolis during the last half century. It gave the place of honor to science and technology, and made no distinction between them and the uses that commerce and industry put them to. Thus it demonstrated to its millions of visitors that social engineering had to come to terms with the objectives of big business. Even while summarizing the changes that had taken place in the metropolis over the course of the last fifty years, the Exposition emphasized the continual tensions between the many efforts to impose a kind of rational order on New York and the reality of a city that never ceased diversifying.

7

THE PROMISED CITY?

Rational order or diversification: the tension between these two tendencies also provided the key to the social and political changes in a metropolis whose population grew from 3.5 to 7.5 million between 1900 and 1940. "New York City is inhabited by 4,000,000 mysterious strangers," ironically observed the columnist William Sydney Porter, alias O. Henry, in 1910. "They came here in various ways and for many reasons—Hendrik Hudson, the art schools, green goods, the stork, the annual dressmakers' convention, the Pennsylvania Railroad, the love of money, the stage, excursion rates, brains, personal column ads, heavy walking shoes, ambition, freight trains—all these have had a hand in making up the population," engaged in an endless "duel" with the city "to decide whether you shall become a New Yorker or turn the rankest outlander and Philistine."[1]

THE NEW NEW YORKERS

"A map of the city, colored to designate nationalities, would show more stripes than on the skin of a zebra, and more colors than any rainbow," noted Jacob Riis in 1890. "The city on such a map would fall into two great halves, green for the Irish prevailing in the West Side tenement districts, and blue, for the Germans on the East Side," but there would also be red for the Italians, gray for the eastern European Jews, not to mention yellow for the Chinese, or black for the African-Americans.[2] In the years that followed, the city became even more diverse: a map of nationalities drawn in 1920 or 1930 would have been dominated by red and gray, with touches of green, blue, and black. Never had New York experienced more dynamic migratory activity.

The city's magnetic attraction, felt by millions of Americans and Europeans over the decades, continued to grow. In villages in Sicily and Campania, in southern Italy, in Poland and Bessarabia, in the towns and the rural areas of continental Europe, the metropolis's name was often pronounced with fervor or curiosity. People gathered to dream about America, and they never tired of reading letters or listening to stories from those who had gone there and returned, or had written to tell about their new lives. New York was first of all a rumor that spread across Europe.

And for the multitudes who chose to confront the reality of the dream, New York was a brutal and staggering discovery. Louis Adamic arrived from Slovenia in the New York harbor in 1913. Twenty years later, he recounted the reactions of his traveling companions: "They crowded against the guardrails, turning and stretching their necks to catch a glimpse of this new country, this city; hoisting up their children, even the babies, so they could see the Statue of Liberty; the women wept with joy, the men fell to their knees to give thanks and the children shrieked, cried, danced."[3] For these immigrants, as for millions of others, New York represented the city of all hopes and promises.

Henceforth, many of them came from central, southern, or eastern Europe, and no longer from the northern or western regions, as in the past. This evolution resulted from political circumstances and Europe's growing integration into the north Atlantic economy. It was soon conveyed by New York population statistics. In the 1880s and 1890s, Germans and Irish still made up 70 to 80 percent of the immigrant population. Then the Italians flooded in: from 40,000 in 1890, their number grew to 250,000 in 1900; in 1920, there were 800,000 first- and

FIGURE 38
The American dream: immigrants arriving at Ellis Island and
the Statue of Liberty © Roger Viollet

second-generation Italians. The second largest immigrant
population in the metropolis, the Italians were only out-
numbered by the Jews who came from the Russian and
Austro-Hungarian Empires, and who, according to census
officials, formed the largest ethnic group in the New York
urban area in 1910.

Moreover, New York continued to attract Germans and
Irish, as well as Armenians, Lithuanians, French, Syrians,
Scottish, Finnish, Rumanians, Welsh, Russians, Swiss,
Swedish, Spanish, Greeks, Danish, Serbians, Hungarians,
and many more. Over the course of the 1920s and especially
the 1930s, the waves of immigrants tended to slacken under
the effect of the 1921 and 1924 laws that imposed quotas
according to nationalities. But the millions of foreigners
who had arrived in the previous decades were enough to
ensure the apparently infinite diversification of New York's
population.

European immigrants were not the only ones to feel the attraction of the New York magnet. New York's Chinese population was limited, due to the 1882 law prohibiting them from entering the country: 6,000 in 1900, less than 20,000 in 1940. More significant was the wave of immigrants coming from the island of Puerto Rico, ceded by Spain at the end of the 1898 war. Becoming American citizens in 1917, and therefore not subject to the quotas of the 1920s, these Puerto Ricans numbered 7,000 in 1920, and more than 60,000 twenty years later.

The most impressive growth was that of the blacks. In 1890, there were 36,000 blacks in Manhattan and Brooklyn, less than two percent of the total population. The "great migration" of African-Americans from the South to northern cities began in the 1890s, and then accelerated between 1915 and 1930. Leaving the rural areas of Virginia, the Carolinas, Georgia, and Florida, hundreds of thousands of men and women converged on New York, with the hope of improving their living conditions and escaping the discrimination they were subject to in the South—or to satisfy their curiosity with regard to the big city. Others came from Jamaica, Barbados, or the Virgin Islands. In total, New York counted 61,000 blacks in 1900, 152,000 in 1920, and 460,000 in 1940—that is, six percent of its population. For all these new arrivals, too, New York was the promised land.

NEW YORK IN WHITE . . .

Because of their scale, these migratory movements profoundly reshaped the New York ethnic landscape. The same neighborhoods witnessed different groups of Europeans succeeding each other.

In lower Manhattan, Little Germany was abandoned by a large portion of its occupants, who moved out and took over Harlem and Yorkville—the upper Manhattan neighborhood located along the East River, near Eightieth Street—or the Williamsburg and Bushwick districts in Brooklyn. The majority of these German immigrants, or their children, had not become rich, but they were certainly not as poor as they had been when they or their parents had arrived. Relocating was evidence of their upward social mobility and their desire to continue to live close to one another, but in different neighborhoods according to their degree of social success.

In lower Manhattan—Greenwich Village, Chelsea, and Hell's Kitchen—the Irish, for whom economic mobility was often more limited, left their neighborhoods more slowly and in fewer numbers than the Germans. But they did move to Yorkville, Washington Heights in upper Manhattan, new districts in the Bronx (Mott Haven, Fordham, Morrisania), and Brooklyn.

At the same time, Italian and Jewish immigrants flooded into the old Irish and German neighborhoods. Beginning in 1880, the former Little Germany became the Jewish quarter of the Lower East Side, that lower-Manhattan protuberance that, for many new arrivals, was synonymous with New York. Reformist observers or nativists at the turn of the century were convinced that new arrivals were incapable of assimilating the values they themselves associated with American democracy. Their harsh view of the Lower East Side did not take into account the district's diversity. Just as Little Germany assembled Bavarians, Prussians, Württembergians, and Hessians, the Lower East Side was inhabited by immigrants with a wide variety of origins.

"All around the Brooklyn Bridge, crowded into narrow, airless streets stinking with the stench of food and miserable dwellings, live pell-mell and as well as can be expected the most cosmopolitan and mixed populations imaginable," noted the Frenchman Charles Huard in 1906, in his *New York as I Saw It*, a bit given to the expected picturesque and not exempt from ethnic and racial prejudices. "Mixing their idioms and their native characters, all the races of the world rub elbows; Italians and Irish, Spanish and Swedish, thin Egyptians beside stout Germans, Russian peasant children rolling in the mud with little Negroes, women from the lands of the sun, wrapped in rags of brilliant colors, blues, reds, yellows, greens, chatting in the doorways of shops run by dark Dutch Jews."[4]

A description more strictly limited to sociological observation and less concerned with stylistic effects would still

FIGURE 39
Hester Street, in the heart of the Lower East Side (1914)
© Roger Viollet

have noted the extraordinary diversity of the Jewish quarter. Hungarian Jews lived primarily in the northern part of
the Lower East Side, in the Eleventh Ward, within a quadrilateral formed by the East River, Houston Street, Avenue B,
and Tenth Street. Jews from the eastern borders of the
Austro-Hungarian Empire, Galicia in particular, lived in
the Thirteenth Ward, in an area defined by Houston, Grand,
and Clinton Streets, and by Hamilton Fish Park. Their
neighbors in the Tenth Ward, Jews from Rumania and the
Levant, settled between Allen Street and the Bowery. The
large majority of arrivals from the Russian Empire lived
south of Grand Street, in an area bounded by Monroe
Street and the Bowery.

Similarly, the former Irish district of the Fourteenth
Ward became the "New Italy" in the early 1880s, but
there again, "the Italians gather in provincial groups," as
Kate Holladay Claghorn noted in 1901, in a report on
"The Immigrant in New York City," which she wrote for

the very official Industrial Commission on Immigration. "For instance, in the Mulberry Bend district are to be found Neapolitans and Calabrians mostly; in Baxter street, near the Five Points, is a colony of Genoese; in Elizabeth street, between Houston and Spring, a colony of Sicilians. The quarter west of Broadway, in the Eighth and Fifteenth wards is made up mainly of North Italians who have been longer in New York and are rather more prosperous than the others, although some Neapolitans have come into Sullivan and Thompson streets to work in the flower and feather trades. In "Little Italy," One hundred and tenth to One hundred and fifteenth streets, South Italians predominate. In Sixty-Ninth street, near the Hudson River, is to be found a small group of Tyrolese and Austrian Italians."[5]

Beginning in the 1900s, it was the Italians' and the Jews' turn to leave the enclaves of lower Manhattan for new neighborhoods. The Lower East Side, which housed three quarters of New York's Jews in 1892, gradually lost its demographic significance as the "Jewish Quarter": only half of all Jewish New Yorkers still lived there in 1905, and only a quarter in 1915. The others settled in upper Manhattan, the Bronx, Brooklyn, and New Jersey.

Brownsville, in east Brooklyn, was built, beginning in the 1890s, by Jewish developers who had managed to attract garment workshops and their Jewish labor force there. Brownsville counted nearly 50,000 Jews in 1905, that is, 80 percent of its population. The proportion remained the same twenty years later; the district then counted 200,000 Jews, many of Russian origin, employed in the district's garment workshops, building firms, printing shops, and graphics industries.

Also in Brooklyn, Boro Park was a very different neighborhood, originally a residential suburb that developed along a trolley line, and then a district that experienced full expansion in the 1920s. In 1925, 60,000 Jews lived there, or half its total population. It was a residential district where fairly wealthy inhabitants diligently observed their religious practice, evident by the number of synagogues, and owned or rented private homes. The Bronx offered similar contrasts: many workers, unionists, or politically active

Jews settled near Van Cortlandt Park or Bronx Park; the wealthiest Jews came to live on the Bronx's "art deco"–style Grand Concourse, unless they opted for the luxury apartments in Manhattan's Upper West Side, between Seventy-ninth and One Hundred and Tenth Streets.

. . . AND IN BLACK

Until the end of the nineteenth century, there were not many blacks and no black district in New York. In 1900, the city's 60,000 blacks were relatively evenly distributed between Manhattan and Brooklyn, with a stronger presence on Manhattan's West Side. In contrast, there were 460,000 blacks by 1940: more than half lived in Harlem, between a quarter and a third lived in the Bedford-Stuyvesant district of Brooklyn, and the others were more widely scattered. These clusters resulted for various reasons: demographic expansion, beginning in 1890; exclusion from the skilled industrial jobs and white-collar employment that helped European immigrants in their upward social mobility; the city's racist atmosphere; and, very simply, personal choice.

In fact, the construction of what Chicago School sociologists called the "ghetto" was a complex phenomenon extending over three decades. Racism was not the only factor. The formation of the ghetto was also tied to the influx of Southern black migrants and European immigrants as well as the condition of the real-estate market.

Harlem's ghetto was built in many stages. The Nieuw Haarlem of the Dutch colonists long remained a village where rich New Yorkers liked to build their country houses. After the New York & Harlem Railroad opened in 1837, it gradually became a suburb. In the early 1880s, the elevated railway connected Harlem—two lines, to the East Side, at Second and Third Avenues, the other to the West Side at Ninth Avenue. In a few years, East Harlem, south of One Hundred and Twenty-fifth Street, was transformed as tenement housing went up. Irish, Germans, and Italians moved in, these last creating a new "Little Italy" between One Hundred and Fifth and One Hundred and Twentieth Streets. Farther west, developers built very middle-class city

FIGURE 40
Silent protest march against racism, Harlem, July 1917
Schomburg Center, New York Public Library

houses that attracted wealthy German-American immigrants moving north from lower Manhattan.

Beginning in the mid-1890s, some Lower East Side
Jews, in their turn, relocated to Harlem, where real-estate
development followed the progress of the trolley lines
and, a few years later, the subway line. The wealthiest settled to the west of Lexington Avenue, the poorest to the
east. Harlem, with 17,000 Jews in 1900 and 100,000 ten
years later, became the second largest Jewish district in
New York, behind the Lower East Side.

That was also when the first African-Americans arrived.
There were only a few families at the beginning of the century, but by 1910, there were 22,000, more than 15,000 of
whom lived in a quadrilateral bordered by One Hundred
and Thirty-third and One Hundred and Fortieth Streets,

Park Avenue, and Lenox Avenue—that is, the northern part of Central Harlem and East Harlem. Until World War I, this constituted the black quarter, which hardly intersected with the Jewish quarter of lower Harlem at all.

The first arrivals were explained by a local real-estate market crisis, linked to an overabundance of construction projects. In a tight spot, some developers agreed to open the market to blacks in 1904–1905, notably through the intervention of a black real-estate agent, Philip A. Payton. In 1904, he founded the Afro-American Realty Company and launched the movement, even though he went bankrupt in 1908. Within a few years, more than 20,000 blacks had settled in Harlem.

About 1910, Harlem was a very diverse district, with strong, locally dominant clusters—Italians in the southeast, Jews in the south, blacks in the north. A small number of Jews still lived in the part of Harlem where blacks were the most numerous. After 1915, the balance was lost, and over the next fifteen years, Harlem was transformed into a black district, simultaneously dynamic and in decline—dynamic because the black population grew more than 120 percent between 1920 and 1930, due to the "Great Migration" of African-Americans from the South. World War I had interrupted European immigration. Afterwards, the American government's hostile immigration policy and changes that had taken place in Europe combined to prevent the return of the great migratory waves of Jewish and Italian immigrants. The massive arrival of blacks brought about major demographic changes in Harlem.

As for Harlem's decline, that had another explanation. The establishment of a war economy in 1917 redirected all resources. Real-estate development programs were suspended, and this came at a time of heavy demand, since the war industries needed manpower. Manhattan experienced unexpected growth, even if New York in general and Harlem in particular were hit by a real-estate crisis since supply was inadequate. Property owners could keep increasing rents and stop maintaining their buildings, which began to deteriorate.

Beginning in 1921, the adoption of fiscal incentive

measures led to renewed construction in Manhattan, Brooklyn, and the Bronx. As white New Yorkers saw their standard of living improve and Harlem properties deteriorate, they gradually left the district. In a few years, Jewish Harlem lost its inhabitants and welcomed increasing numbers of black residents, whose arrival no doubt accelerated the departure of the remaining Jews. As for the blacks, Harlem was the only neighborhood open to them because of the deep-rooted prejudices they faced everywhere else. Thus property owners could demand high rents, which led to overcrowding, and then further decline in living conditions: a vicious spiral that completely disrupted Harlem.

FROM THE "SOCIAL QUESTION" . . .

The various migratory movements, changes in the New York landscape, and developments in the American economy all helped to reshape the social groups. The impact of growth was felt in particular among the working class. In 1910, four out of ten employed New Yorkers aged sixteen or over were blue-collar workers, and in 1930, the year when the symbolic bar of one million men and women workers was crossed, three of ten still were. How could the working class, already so diverse in 1890, not become even more heterogeneous over the half century that followed?

In job sectors such as printing, brewing, light metallurgy, or the cigar industry, many German or Irish workers had high professional skills and solid union experience. Their organizations—like the Allied Printing Trades Council, established in the mid-1890s—validated the occupation and the skills. Their impact became even greater in the last years of the nineteenth century, when they obtained work agreements that made union membership obligatory, and the unions responsible for hiring. In these sectors, the workers managed to maintain a significant degree of autonomy in the workshops, and to partially control the production process. This system, known as the "closed shop," involved tens of thousands of workers early in the century, but it was not the norm.

In the clothing industry, the heart of New York activity, the situation was, in fact, very different. The various subcontracting systems and the growth of demand beginning in the 1880s made the organization of the work very complex, all the more so because the price of land at this time prohibited production from becoming recentralized. Moreover, the expansion in women's ready-to-wear clothing coincided with the mass arrival of tens of thousands of Jewish workers from the Russian and Austro-Hungarian Empires, and, to a lesser extent, Italian immigrants. Within a few years, these two groups occupied almost all the jobs in the sector. For many decades, because of the importance of the garment industry in the metropolitan economy, Jews and Italians were the major constituent of the New York working class.

The middle classes were also disrupted by the transformations in American capitalism that led to a proliferation of white-collar jobs. To be able to operate at the national scale, railroad and insurance companies, banks and industrial firms, distributors and large stores, and countless businesses, large and small, had to call on thousands of men and—in ever growing proportions—women, to give New York capitalism its human face. As of 1910, for example, many thousands of employees worked at the main offices of the Metropolitan Life Insurance Company, where they were distributed among the various services located in the tall skyscraper on Madison Avenue: every day, shorthand typists and telephone operators, actuaries and cashiers, accountants, and various other employees crowded into the forty-eight elevators and the hundreds of offices on the forty-five floors of the vast Metropolitan beehive. Together, they gave birth to a new culture, the culture of office work.

Few immigrants attained these white-collar positions, which required a good mastery of English. But their children, and their daughters in particular, attained them in growing numbers after 1910, thus putting their experience in the New York schools to good use. In 1930, more than 500,000 white-collar workers were employed in New York. Henceforth, they constituted a much more significant social circle than the immigrant small businessmen—the Germans, Irish, and even eastern European Jews—who had succeeded in the garment industry, and they made up another facet of the metropolis's middle class.

The expansion of large corporations also changed the composition of the economic elite. At the turn of the century, next to the merchants and industrial leaders of the preceding decades, rose the bankers, financiers, executive managers, stockbrokers, business lawyers, and other experts and members of the professions. Some of them, no doubt a majority, came from the merchant elite of the past, such as the associates of Cravath, Shearman & Sterling; of Strong, Bidwell & Strong; or of Cadwalader, Wickersham & Taft, among other prestigious law firms. Others, Jewish or Christian, were originally German. Except for their economic activity, everything was against them: the German Jews were isolated by the anti-Semitism to which they were subject, while German Christians, Catholic or Protestant, could not move in the same circles as Anglo-American Protestants, who were themselves divided and regrouped according to birth, fortune, or culture.

Such deep contrasts between social groups created bitter tensions. These affected the clothing industry in particular, one of the branches of industry where, at the turn of the century, working conditions were the most difficult. Whether employed in the central workshops or at home, workers at that time worked sixty to seventy hours per week, risks of accident or fire were high, and the necessary flexibility of this sector made it structurally unstable. Because there were laws regulating working conditions for women and children and for working at home, the tendency was toward centralization in the industrial workshops. But these workshops hardly offered greater safety, as the fire at the Triangle Shirtwaist Company made tragically clear on March 25, 1911. Trapped in the business's workshops on the eighth, ninth, tenth, and top floors of a building at the corner of Greene Street and Washington Place, 146 young women died in the blaze.

Nevertheless, workers' efforts to obtain better working conditions only met with success slowly. Until 1909, the attempts of organized labor failed or faltered in the garment industry. The International Ladies' Garment Workers' Union (ILGWU), founded in 1900, experienced difficult early years. The rapid turnover of its members, the profession's relative mobility, personal conflicts within the leadership, and its complex relations with the socialist movement all hindered its growth.

The situation improved under pressure from young Jewish and Italian women workers in the shirt-making business, one of the newest branches in the women's clothing industry, which was organized in central workshops and not in homes. In autumn 1909, these workers launched a protest movement aimed less at low salaries and long hours than at democratizing the business, and winning worker representation and respect for the labor force. During a meeting at Cooper Union on November 22, one of them, Clara Lemlich, called on her companions to join the fight. "I am a working girl, one of those who are on strike against intolerable working conditions," she cried in Yiddish. "I'm tired of listening to speakers who talk in general terms. What we are here for today is to decide whether we shall or shall not strike. I offer a resolution that a general strike be declared—now."[6] By the next day, the workshops involved had initiated a strike that lasted three months.

During the conflict, the ILGWU managed to mobilize women reformers from the middle classes, such as Jane Addams, Mary Dreier, and Lillian Wald, who tried to create a sympathetic climate around what New York soon called "the Uprising of the Twenty Thousand." When the women workers became victims of police violence, the city reacted strongly. Public opinion and the press sided with the strikers, forcing the employers to negotiate. Formed into an association, these employers had no intention of giving in on the question of union recognition, because that finally amounted to granting the union control of hiring and production procedures, but they agreed to improved working conditions. The Uprising of the Twenty Thousand ended with a compromise in February 1910—an important success for the workers.

A few months later, in the summer of 1910, another sector of the women's clothing industry rose in revolt.

On July 7, the coat makers stopped working, in order to obtain the right to unionize. After several weeks of dead-lock, the two parties began to negotiate. At the end of August, while public opinion still favored the strikers, employers and worker representatives came to an agree-ment on a "protocol of peace" conceived by the conflict's two mediators, Louis D. Brandeis and Lincoln Filene. It provided for higher salaries, improved working conditions with the institution of a fifty-hour week, union recogni-tion, and the establishment of arbitration and mediation authorities. Other sectors of the garment industry imme-diately signed protocols of peace.

Over the course of the three decades that followed the events of 1909–1910, the garment-industry sector experi-enced other conflicts and a troubled history. The men's clothing workers organized, beginning in 1914, as part of the Amalgamated Clothing Workers of America (ACWA). The president of this union was Sidney Hillman, who popularized the idea of "industrial democracy" and pas-sionately defended the principle of collective negotia-tions. But in the 1920s, the repercussions of the Russian revolution, the hostility of owners and federal authori-ties, and many attempts by communist activists to take control weakened the ACWA, and the ILGWU as well. The Depression further weakened the unions, and it was not until the New Deal, which Hillman and the ILGWU's new president David Dubinsky enthusiastically sup-ported, that they played an important role once again. The establishment of well-structured unions in the clothing-industry sector in the 1910s nevertheless helped to defuse social tensions in the metropolis.

. . . TO MORAL REFORM

In the same period, men and women from very different backgrounds led very different attempts to avoid social upheaval. Sparked by a shared desire for reforms, their main concern was spreading their ideas and values, but they were also very pragmatic. Some considered the "social question" or the "urban question" to be a matter of organization, regulation, and efficiency. Some advocated a moralization of society, a purification rendered necessary in their eyes by urban growth. Others considered the main problem to be political, and thought the most important thing was to create conditions for a "good government" in the city, even if they could not agree on an exact definition of it. They were all convinced that New York risked a serious social crisis if nothing was done to reduce the tensions.

Among these reformers, many came from evangelical Protestantism, and put forward plans for moral reform. In their eyes, the principal dangers threatening society were prostitution and alcoholism. Initiatives to limit the many temptations the city offered proliferated in the 1890s. In March 1892, Charles Parkhurst, the pastor at the Madison Square Presbyterian Church, launched from his pulpit a virulent campaign against prostitution. Two years later, the New York State Chamber of Commerce financed a huge inquiry, named after its president, Senator Clarence Lexow. The inquiry resulted in five thick volumes of testimony underlining the collusion between the world of prostitution, the police, and New York politicians. In 1896, John Raines, a New York State senator, tried to reduce prostitution by increasing regulations for saloons. Thereafter, their owners had to apply for a permit from state authorities, as the Raines law only authorized hotels with more than ten beds to sell alcohol.

The results of the Raines law were antithetical to the reformers' expectations. The saloons turned into hotels and, more often than not, accommodated prostitutes and their clients. But the reformers did not give up. In 1899, New York State created a new commission, placed under the authority of Senator Robert Mazet. The following year, the Committee of Fifteen was set up; then beginning in 1905, the Committee of Fourteen, which met some success in tackling the hotels that had appeared under the Raines law. Although it did not disappear, prostitution became less visible, before falling into the hands of powerful organized-crime networks in the 1920s. Thus, the efforts of Victorian reformers only resulted in more structured organization for the commerce of sex.

With regard to the struggle against alcoholism, the results

FIGURE 41
New York hotel bar, before Prohibition (1918)
© Roger Viollet

were no more satisfactory to those who defended temperance. New York, in fact, did not show much enthusiasm for the passionate crusade of those active in the Woman's Christian Temperance Union, who succeeded in getting the Eighteenth Amendment adopted in 1919, scheduled to go into effect in 1920. Prohibition did not keep New Yorkers from drinking alcohol—the metropolis counted as many as 32,000 clandestine bars, or "speak-easies," at the end of the 1920s—it simply made their habits more complicated.

Above all, it led to a reorganization of the underworld. Until then, its hold was local: gangs controlled the shady business of gambling and racketeering at one racecourse or in a single neighborhood. Lower Manhattan had its Italian gangs, like Paul Kelly's (born Paolo Vaccarelli), and its Jewish gangs, led by Arnold Rothstein, Herman Rosenthal, or Monk Eastman, "the purveyor of iniquities" noted by Jorge Luis Borges in his *Story of Infamy*.

With Prohibition, the scale changed. Small racketeers began to organize alcohol traffic on a national level, and their gangs quickly became structured. Meyer Lansky and

"Bugsy" Siegel, Louis "Lepke" Buchalter and Albert Anastasia, Frank Costello and "Lucky" Luciano were the talk of the town. They had direct ties to the various Mafia families in the city, and provided them with the necessary manpower to conduct the short but violent gang wars that erupted periodically. Luciano and his henchmen won lots of money in these wars, as well as their nickname, "Murder Incorporated."

The end of Prohibition in 1933 did not bring an end to organized crime, but it forced those involved into partial conversions. Luciano was convicted in 1936, and sentenced to several decades at Sing Sing, following a spectacular investigation led by Thomas E. Dewey, a young assistant prosecutor (and future United States presidential candidate). This effectively shut down his flourishing racketeering enterprises, after which Frank Costello and Meyer Lansky were somewhat successful in reorganizing and returning to classic pre-1920 gangster activities.

. . . AND TO MUNICIPAL PROGRESSIVISM

Unlike the attempts at moral reform, those aimed at organizing the metropolis more rationally sometimes succeeded. Over the course of the 1890s, efforts in this area multiplied. Under the leadership of skilled engineers, who often held their posts for several decades, hundreds of miles of new sewers and water mains were installed. The city's capacity for conveying water grew in a spectacular manner, thanks to the construction of new reservoirs and aqueducts that carried water from the Catskills and completed the Croton system built in the 1840s. At the end of the century, despite technical constraints, inhabitants of New York had much more water at their disposal than Londoners, Parisians, or Berliners, and the capacity of the reservoirs continued to grow. By the mid-1930s, the system distributed several hundred millions gallons of water each day.

Asphalt was often used to replace the bad pavement of earlier decades, to the great satisfaction of pressure groups like the Good Roads Association, formed by Brooklyn cyclists, and including among its members several aldermen. New York was also equipped with thousands of electric lamps and hundreds of miles of underground cable for providing electrical power.

These efforts at creating order were not limited to the construction of various technical networks. It was also necessary to see that the streets were cleaned, a task poorly performed in the nineteenth-century city, when the job of city street sweeper was for a long time a modest sinecure tied to the favor of Tammany Hall. In 1895, the reform mayor William Strong put George Waring, a specialist in public health and hygiene, in charge of street cleaning. Waring reorganized his department in a quasi-military manner, stressing the professionalism of the operation and instituting a white uniform that earned city street sweepers the very poetic nickname of "white wings."

At the same time, the municipal health department experienced an increase in its resources. Hundreds of municipal inspectors visited the city's markets, dairies, slaughterhouses, and sanitary installations every day. In 1892, the cholera epidemic that took thousands of lives in Hamburg only killed nine New Yorkers, thanks to a very effective organization. That same year, the municipality created a bacteriological laboratory within the department of health, directed by Dr. Hermann Biggs, who declared war on diphtheria, tuberculosis, rabies, and typhoid. At the turn of the century, he had dozens of employees, twenty-five of whom were doctors. He soon earned an international reputation. Robert Koch, the German bacteriologist who discovered the tubercle bacillus and the cholera bacillus, cited the New York laboratory as exemplary to the authorities in his own country.

Efforts like these to fight diseases and improve hygienic conditions were part of a huge network of measures meant to combat poverty and provide New Yorkers with a relatively secure education and lifestyle. In 1902, aware of the necessity and the importance of making playgrounds, public gardens, and parks accessible to working-class children, the municipality took over facilities created by private initiatives and added new ones. About 1930, New York counted more than a hundred such playgrounds, and this number increased again during the Depression, thanks to a combination of federal funds and initiatives by Robert Moses. Moses also expanded the sports and recreation fields in Central Park, which had been poorly equipped until then.

Other initiatives aimed at improving minds. The New York Public Library, founded in 1895, opened neighborhood libraries a few years later, thanks to the munificence of Andrew Carnegie, who financed their construction. In the early 1920s, the New York Public Library counted about forty branches throughout Manhattan, the Bronx, and Staten Island. In the same period, the boroughs of Brooklyn and Queens enlarged their own public library systems, forming a very extensive system of neighborhood branches.

More important still was the question of education, the key to a democratic society in the eyes of progressives like the philosopher John Dewey. The educational challenge in New York was impressive, if only because of the numbers: beginning with the creation of Greater New York in 1898, more than half a million children attended municipal schools, not including the large number that preferred parochial schools, especially Catholic ones. In the early 1890s, the faults of the system, based on a very decentralized organization, prompted reflection, controversy, and decisions. Grade schools were integrated into the municipal system in 1893, and, three years later, the ward boards of education were abolished under pressure from advocates of centralization, regrouped into a Committee of One Hundred.

In 1898, academic education in Greater New York was placed under the direction of a superintendent of schools, assisted by a board of forty-six members—too many to be effective. The real power was in the hands of the superintendent, William Maxwell, who held the position from 1898 to 1917. By 1917, the school board had been reduced to seven members, but education professionals had had almost twenty years to take control of the municipal education structures and to develop them according to their preferences, which were supposed to be scientific and objective. Under their impetus, dozens of primary schools and then secondary schools were constructed, a whole range of special programs, especially for the benefit of immigrants, was put into place, and teacher training was professionalized, resulting in the creation of a union in 1916, the New York City Teachers' Union.

All these endeavors affected New Yorkers in very unequal ways. The middle classes benefited from them more than the poorer classes, and whites more than blacks. In Harlem, there were too few public schools in the 1920s and 1930s to respond to the district's demographic growth, but no new construction was initiated.

As for the struggle against poverty, for a long time it seemed limited. As in the past, it was a matter of private initiatives, some of which benefited from partial funding by the municipality. For a long time, public intervention was limited to the poorhouses, which sheltered many thousands of individuals early in the century. The city did not build its first public baths until the 1900s, following the example set in the Lower East Side by the Association for Improving the Condition of the Poor. In fact, the principal initiatives remained those of associations like the Charity Organization Society (COS), a federation of charitable societies founded and directed in New York by Josephine Shaw Lowell—or the Salvation Army, which opened several shelters for the homeless in working-class neighborhoods.

It was the age of scientific charity. The COS in particular tried to gain a better understanding and exact measurement of poverty. Under the instigation of Josephine Shaw Lowell and Robert DeForest, the association was largely responsible for the professionalization of social work. The summer school it organized became the New York School of Social Work in 1898, and was later affiliated with Columbia University. This type of initiative and the support given to the new profession a few years later by the Russell Sage Foundation, established in 1907, allowed for the creation of social services—however modest—on a citywide scale during the 1910s and 1920s.

The Great Depression completely altered this situation. The stock-market crash in October 1929, which brought to an end many years of rising speculation, ruined thousands of New Yorkers—both modest and wealthy investors whose assets disappeared abruptly with the collapse of the stock market. While the United States settled into the crisis, hundreds of thousands of other inhabitants of the metropolis were soon out of work. In March 1936, nearly one out of five New Yorkers (that is, 1.5 million people) received some form of public assistance, and more than a million still did in 1938. The number of homeless people exploded, and soup kitchens multiplied. In 1931–32, shantytowns—nicknamed "Hoovervilles" in New York as elsewhere, in a bitter reference to President Hoover— sprang up even in the heart of Central Park. The crisis affected New Yorkers to varying degrees, blacks being most hurt by it and receiving the least assistance in proportion to their need. The overall need was immense, and overwhelmed private associations' capacities to assist, whether it was a matter of charitable organizations or mutual-aid societies.

An impressive public assistance system was thus put into place, first with funds granted by New York State and by its governor, Franklin D. Roosevelt, in 1931, and then with major federal financing obtained before and after Roosevelt was elected president of the United States. New York became the great laboratory for the New Deal's social policies. In the past, private assistance had represented three quarters or four fifths of total aid; henceforth, public funds accounted for eight or nine tenths of the total. Private organizations set about revising their objectives and their practices, resulting in the 1939 merger of the COS and the Association for Improving the Condition of the Poor into the Community Service Society.

No one more accurately embodied the era's social policy than Harry Hopkins, a New Yorker by adoption, who became one of the leading figures in Washington. A former resident of a settlement house in the 1910s, he was made head of the New York State Temporary Emergency Relief Association by Governor Roosevelt in 1931. After Roosevelt became President, Hopkins directed several federal programs of great importance to New York: the Federal Emergency Relief Administration, the Civil Works Administration, and then in 1935, the Works Progress Administration, the famous WPA. At the instigation of

FIGURE 42
"Hooverville" in Central Park by Robert Wiseman
© Museum of the City of New York/CORBIS

Hopkins and New York's mayor, La Guardia, the WPA poured millions of dollars into New York each month: as many as 250,000 people were employed, most of them in the construction and improvement of urban infrastructures, others in developing social and cultural programs like the Federal Arts Project or the Federal Writers' Project.

A NEW DEAL

In the area of public affairs as well, the metropolis of the 1930s had come a long way from what it was in 1890.

At the turn of the century, political life was characterized by the fragmentation of the urban elite, the growing power of the unions, the tendency of parties to become professional, and of course the mosaic of the ethnic landscape. By the late 1880s, many influential representatives of the New York socioeconomic elite—the Swallowtails—had abandoned the two major parties that they had indirectly controlled until then. The Swallowtail Republicans were opposed to the efforts of Boss Thomas C. Platt to make their party a more effective organization, because they preferred attempts to establish nonpartisan, reformist pressure groups, relying on organizations like the Good Government City Club, the German-American Reform Union, or the Charity Organization Society. As for the Swallowtail Democrats, they had abandoned their party after the relative failure of their leader Abram Hewitt's mayoralty in 1886–88, and moved closer to the former Republicans.

Throughout the 1890s, political players of this new cast increased their attempts to assemble an electoral majority. Sometimes they met with temporary success, as with the election of Mayor William Strong in 1894, and especially of Seth Low, the former president of Columbia University, in 1901. Over the long term, however, their efforts proved futile, largely because their constituents' objectives were too diverse. Beginning in 1903, the former Swallowtails abandoned their separatist attempts and returned to the two major parties, even though it meant resorting to pressure groups for specific issues.

The parties they rediscovered were very different from the ones they had left fifteen years earlier. For the Democrats, the departure of Hewitt and his friends had allowed Tammany Hall leaders to extend their political grasp. Richard Croker (1884–1901) and especially Charles Francis Murphy (1902–1923) had much greater freedom than their predecessor John Kelly. Nevertheless, Tammany did not rule undivided. Its victories gave it control of many posts, and allowed it to operate its patronage system successfully, but the organization only stayed in power by becoming the representative for New Yorkers of modest means and foreign backgrounds, and by accepting the election of mayors who were only nominally subordinate to it.

Murphy argued for improved working conditions, and actively supported the commission formed to investigate the Triangle factory fire in 1911. Thus he was a proponent of an important law on industrial labor, supported at once by middle-class feminist groups, the unions, and the men of Tammany Hall—Robert F. Wagner, a member of the New York State Senate at the time, and Alfred E. Smith, his colleague in the House of Representatives. Despite his effectiveness in Albany, Murphy had to accept independent-minded and strong-willed New York mayors, like George McClellan (1904–1909) and the former State Supreme Court judge William Gaynor (1910–13).

Only in the 1920s did Tammany's control over the New York mayor's office become less sporadic. Mayor John Hylan (1918–25) was Murphy's creation. His successor, James J. Walker, known as Jimmy Walker or "Beau James," was the puppet of George Olvany, who replaced Murphy when he died in 1923, Edward Flynn, patron of the Bronx Democrats, and Al Smith, New York State governor, future unsuccessful U.S. presidential candidate (1928) and true head of the New York Democrats. Better known for writing the hit song, *Will You Love Me in December as You Do in May?*—and for his escapades with the dancer Betty Compton—than for his administrative skills, Jimmy Walker embodied the carefree attitude of New York's Roaring Twenties, during which he ran the city from the Central Park casino.

But after his easy reelection in the autumn of 1929, even though Wall Street had just collapsed, Walker became the focus of a detailed investigation for corruption in the following year, conducted by the judge Samuel Seabury. In 1932, while the charges mounted, he chose to resign and leave for Europe. Tammany was discredited.

Fiorello La Guardia's election as mayor of New York in the autumn of 1933 thus marked a political turning point—with false modesty, La Guardia spoke of it as the "small New Deal." The son of a Jewish mother and Italian father, this Republican lawyer, elected to the House of Representatives in 1916, was a progressive. A Washington outsider during the 1920s and a member of a political party generally hostile to immigrants and in favor of a laissez-faire economic policy, La Guardia failed to win the New York mayorship in 1929—and even lost his House seat in the 1932 elections, which saw the Democrats triumph. Running as an independent in the 1933 mayoral race, he owed his victory to the popular rejection of Tammany Hall, and was easily reelected in 1937 and 1941, against Democratic candidates and with the help of a coalition made up of Republicans, progressives, anti-Tammany

Democrats, unionists, independents, and the American Labor Party.

Clever and jovial, easy to talk to, the mayor whom New Yorkers nicknamed "Little Flower" owed his popularity to his activism and his interventionism in economic and social matters during the years of the Depression. He knew how to successfully combine a desire for organization and efficiency, very much in the tradition of progressive ideas, and a belief that he himself embodied the social and cultural diversity of New York. Did he not, after all, enjoy the support of a majority of Jewish, Italian, working-class, Republican, and reformist voters?

Above all, La Guardia embodied the alliance formed with the federal administration in Washington during the 1930s, so essential to the economic survival of the metropolis. The massive injection of federal funds was not enough to bring New York out of the Depression, but La Guardia was very effective in helping to partially preserve the social fabric, under great strain at the time. As the *Panorama of New York*, published in 1938 as part of the Federal Writers' Project, soberly noted, La Guardia's successive terms coincided with "a great realignment" that "synthesized" many political visions. Henceforth, "there was acceptance of the municipal government as a functioning agent for social welfare and unemployment relief. There was evident approval of the large-scale public works program, especially an increase of recreational facilities, undertaken by the municipality. There was recognition of the city's responsibility in labor disputes, through appointment by the Mayor of special fact-finding committees and his active intervention in some disputes."[7] In many respects, the La Guardia era witnessed the height of New York progressivism.

METROPOLITAN COMPROMISES

The nature of the social fabric in the late 1930s undoubtedly suggested that the promises of modernity were only partly kept, through excessive audacity or, alternatively, through default. Observers did not hesitate to note this. In 1925, Mayakovsky considered New York futurism to be cautious and unfulfilled: "No, New York is not modern, New York is unorganized," sneered the poet. "Simple machines, subways, skyscrapers and so on are not enough to make a true industrial civilization. This is only the external aspect. America has gone through a fantastic material development that has changed the face of the world. But people have not grasped what this world was. . . . Intellectually, New Yorkers are still provincial. Their minds have still not accepted all the implications of the industrial age. That is why I say that New York is disorganized—it is a gigantic accident trampled by children, and not the mature product of men who would have understood what they wanted and what they imagined as artists."[8] Others, following the example of Georges Duhamel in *Scènes de la vie future*, focused on the view that New York offered to horrified eyes. Fritz Lang, who visited the city in 1924, delivered a phantasmagorical vision of it in his film, *Metropolis*, three years later.

Nevertheless, New York's modernity may have resided less in the vision of its urban landscapes—magical or Dantesque, depending on one's point of view—than in the way the city managed to negotiate the continual tension between its physical growth and its social and political evolution. More than promises, it was a matter here of compromises—significant or minor, temporary or permanent, sporadic or daily—often produced by the pluralist and progressive efforts of all New Yorkers who were conscious of the risks of unrestrained growth. It is true that the authentic "metropolitanites" were those who understood the stakes: the possibility of "taking all their busy lives to appropriate a little of this intoxicating boundlessness to themselves," of giving in to the attraction of the lights of the city.[9]

8

THE LIGHTS OF THE CITY

—————————

"Since we have failed up to the present to develop genuine regional cultures," noted Lewis Mumford in 1922, "those who do not wish to remain barbarians must become metropolitans. That means that they must come to New York, or ape the ways that are fashionable in New York."[1]

In the last years of the nineteenth century, New York confirmed its cultural domination. Its vitality stemmed from its economic dynamism, its social heterogeneity, and its capacity for innovation. It was also explained by the desire to explore and understand what contemporaries anxiously perceived as modernity. Modernity involved a rejection of the social conventions of the Victorian era and a reaction against American cultural dependence on Great Britain and Europe, as well as a new attitude with regard to consumption. Thus the New York cauldron kept all sorts of cultures in tumultuous coexistence.

A NEW POPULAR CULTURE

On a visit at the end of the 1920s, Paul Morand was fascinated with the lights of Broadway: "Not only white lights, but yellow, red, green, mauve, blue; not only fixed, but moving, hanging, revolving, flowing, zigzagging, rolling, vertical, horizontal, dancing, epileptic." New York, that "perpetual thunderstorm" was overloaded with electricity.[2]

No doubt Morand found Broadway vulgar and vaguely threatening, but even against his will, he knew how to appreciate the energy and novelty of it.

What the spectacle of Broadway offered was truly a new form of popular culture. Inseparable from New York's commercial development, present in the heart of the city and outlying regions alike, it resulted from the expansion of mass production, distribution, and consumption, beginning in the 1890s.

The function of the amusement parks and beaches on nearby Coney Island, in the south of Brooklyn, was to entertain the masses. The place had long lost its mid–nineteenth century reputation for respectability, when wealthy New Yorkers went there on vacation. Sometimes called the "Sodom on the Sea," Coney Island was subsequently transformed into a mecca for prostitution, gambling, and crime, before sensible developers tried to attract a less dubious clientele. In the mid-1880s, big hotels bordered the beaches of Brighton Beach and Manhattan Beach, the latter more family-oriented, the former more chic. Many train lines connected them to the city. Visitors who were not drawn to the pleasures of bathing could always visit the famous racetracks. A short distance away, West Brighton Beach was more popular, with its restaurants, bars, saloons, and various distractions, like Lucy, a colossal wooden elephant almost 100 feet high.

One of the first amusement parks, Steeplechase Park, created by George Tyliou, opened its doors in 1897. Luna Park, created by Fred Thompson and Elmer Dundy, followed in 1903, and Dreamland in 1904, owned by a consortium of New York investors. These parks offered all sorts of attractions: Steeplechase Park's carousel, Luna Park's "Electric Eden," Dreamland's artificial lagoons and the minaret on its gigantic tower—a copy of the Giralda of Seville. In their own way, Luna Park and Dreamland attempted to be educational, with their Eskimo or Irish villages, but their primary purpose was to amuse. In that way, Coney Island was very different from Central Park, conceived a generation earlier by the very pedagogically-minded Frederick Law Olmsted.

FIGURE 43
Luna Park's electric tower on Coney Island
© Roger Viollet

Developers promoted the idea of a "new Coney," entertaining and nevertheless respectable, where one could
come with family or friends. But the Victorian era was
over: men and women met there to have fun, together or
separately. It was a good place to leave everything behind
or at least to challenge the usual proprieties. Dance halls
and outdoor cafés sprang up around the parks. Visitors

FIGURE 44
Times Square, about 1920: the Paramount Building (right),
the Times Building (rear) © Roger Viollet

abandoned themselves to the turkey trot, the grizzly bear,
or the next newest dance. The Coney Island Bowery, thus
dubbed in honor of Manhattan's pleasure spot, attracted
young Jewish, and sometimes Italian, working-class
women. "They know the bad reputation of some of them,
but the dancing floor is good, there are always plenty of
men and there are laughter and liberty galore," observed

the militant reformist Belle Israels in 1909.[3] This liberty
was within the reach of every New Yorker after the arrival
of the subway in 1920. Coney Island, with its huge board-
walk, opened in 1923, its restaurants, hotels, and parks—
Luna Park and especially Steeplechase Park, outlasting
Dreamland, which was destroyed by a fire in 1911—
attracted tens of thousands of visitors each day for a modest fee, until World War II.

The Coney Island attractions formed the more modest
part of the commercial culture that overran New York. But
the bulk of it was elsewhere, at Times Square. This district,
which developed early in the century at the intersection
of Broadway and Forty-second Street, became the center
of New York nightlife. Times Square was originally called
Longacre Square and was, in fact, quite disreputable until
the *New York Times* moved there and renamed it in 1905.
The *Times* thought the spot should become New York's
civic center. Its transformation into the mecca of the new
commercial culture was an expression of the growth of a
cultural industry conceived and managed as just that.
Now Times Square was easily accessible, thanks to the
proximity of Grand Central Station and the arrival of the
subway in 1904, and was located north of the garment
district and its industrial lofts. Developers and speculators, who had not mapped out its growth, quickly took
note of the commercial area's evening and nighttime
profitability. The combination of convenience and profit
could only stimulate the district's development.

In a few years, Times Square became the heart of an
industry involved in the production and consumption of
cultural goods. Thanks to the magic of electricity, Broadway, "the Great White Way," arrayed itself, as night fell, in
its garments of light. The quarter served as the home base
for the hundreds of traveling theatrical or vaudeville
groups that organized tours, hired actors, and held
rehearsals in New York. Theaters proliferated. In 1899–
1900, Manhattan counted twenty-two theatrical halls,
only one of which was near what was still called Longacre
Square. Ten years later, Manhattan's thirty-four theaters
were nearly all found around Times Square, and the trend

continued and increased after that—there were fifty theaters in 1919–20, seventy-one in 1929–30.

These were often monumental buildings, on the model
of the Hippodrome, the "department store in theatricals"
opened in 1905 by Fred Thompson, of Coney Island's
Luna Park. Each year, Broadway produced dozens of plays
and musicals—as many as 200 yearly in the 1920s. According to proven formulas, the shows tried to avoid any artistic innovations that might threaten profits. Producers also
made a specialty of a genre that was formerly discredited:
the variety show. The most spectacular of these, the
Ziegfeld Follies or Earl Carroll's *Vanities*, won over the public. In the 1920s, revues and musical comedies sometimes
merged, as with certain Marx Brothers shows like *I'll Say
She Is!*, *Coconuts*, or *Animal Crackers*, which were made into
successful films. These shows were aimed at middle-class
audiences, not a wealthy or intellectual elite. But beyond
the big productions that made it famous, Broadway began
to offer less conventional shows, such as plays by Eugene
O'Neill, or musicals by George Gershwin.

As the hot spot for theater, Times Square was also the
epicenter of the city's nightlife. Beginning in the 1890s,
the range of distractions offered to night owls had broad-
ened to the extent that high society, turning its back on
Victorian proprieties, abandoned balls and private soirees.
Other kinds of nightlife entrepreneurs worked frantically
to respond to the elite's desire to amuse itself in public
places. Suddenly there were restaurants and cabarets, outdoor cafés on the roofs of apartment buildings, like the
Casino, the Madison Square, or the Paradise. New Yorkers'
only problem was choosing. One could dine at the very
refined but quite conservative Delmonico's, in its new
restaurant on Fifth Avenue, or choose from the new spots
on Broadway or elsewhere, like Murray's Gardens, opened
in 1907, or the Basque restaurant, Bustanoby's, not to
mention the countless luxury hotels built around Times
Square, Grand Central and Pennsylvania Stations, and
along Fifth Avenue. These hotels all welcomed visitors day
and night—wealthy resident clients, or simply curious
New Yorkers who wanted to be seen there: the Waldorf-

Astoria, with its famous maitre d', Oscar, and its "peacock alley" where rich and beautiful New Yorkers paraded; the Savoy, the New Netherland, the Plaza, the Saint-Regis, the Ritz-Carlton, the Imperial, the Astor, the Knickerbocker, the Belmont, the Vanderbilt, the Pennsylvania, and the McAlpin; or the grandest of them all, the Biltmore, opened in 1913.

With Prohibition, of course, the nature of nightlife changed. Literally as well as figuratively, it went underground. For New Yorkers, who were hardly inclined toward temperance and who had little respect for a law they largely opposed, the clandestine consumption of alcoholic beverages was an additional attraction that the metropolitan night offered. Thus, in the cellars of Harlem or Times Square, many "speakeasies" appeared—clandestine bars sometimes hidden in the back rooms of those lively restaurants where women and men belonging to or on the fringes of high society launched into wild Charlestons or Bostons on the dance floor.

The revolt against Victorian cultural codes and Prohibition extended to sexuality. Many visitors came to Times Square to "live it up." Loose morals and homosexuality were flaunted for all to see. "Another woman was dancing indecently with a man," reported a police investigator sent to a Harlem bar in 1928 . . . "Several of the men were dancing among themselves. Two of the women were dancing with one another going through the motions of copulation. One of the men [invited me to dance]. I declined to dance. I also observed two men who were dancing with one another kiss each other, and one sucked the other's tongue." Homosexuals did not hide away and no longer confined themselves to the saloons and dance halls in the Bowery, the targets of moral reformers at the turn of the century who denounced the shamelessness of "fairies" and other "degenerates." They now took their place at the heart of nighttime culture in Harlem and around Times Square.[4]

The Depression sounded the death knell for these wild years, and the end of Prohibition (1933) restored the legitimacy of the Broadway cabarets. Nightlife in the metropolis regained an appearance of normality. New York authorities waged war against homosexuality, stepping up harassment, inspections, and arrests. Once the mystique of the forbidden vanished, New York's high society abandoned Times Square and withdrew to the private clubs that opened on the East Side. Restaurants and cabarets attracted wider audiences, often from out of town and just passing through, who appreciated the pleasures of the Back Stage Club or the Casino de Paree, masterminded and managed by the soon-to-be-famous Billy Rose, who embarked on productions of big Broadway shows at the same time.

Times Square was also the home of the musical industry, nicknamed "Tin Pan Alley." The success of a song by Charles K. Harris, *After the Ball* (1892), which sold five million scores in a few years, prompted musicians and their publishers to invent increasingly more sophisticated commercial methods: newspaper advertising, promotional tours in theaters, nightclubs, or music stores, participation in musical productions, plays, or vaudeville shows.

In the 1920s, Tin Pan Alley turned simultaneously to radio, cinema, and recording, and gave many young and talented immigrants their start. Having arrived from Russia in 1893 at the age of five, Irving Berlin became a successful composer and songwriter. His songs, such as *Alexander's Ragtime Band* (1911), *God Bless America* (1918), *Manhattan Madness* (1932) and *Harlem on My Mind* (1933) accompanied Tin Pan Alley's evolution toward recording and musicals. George Gershwin, born in Brooklyn in 1898, also passed through Tin Pan Alley's school of hard knocks working as a "song plugger" and a rehearsal pianist before his songs (*Oh, Lady, Be Good*, 1924) and orchestral works (*Rhapsody in Blue*, 1924, *An American in Paris*, 1928) won him success. Following the example of Berlin and others like the Gershwin brothers, Cole Porter, Oscar Hammerstein, and Duke Ellington, New York composers and songwriters excelled in adapting to the new technologies.

THE MECCA OF JOURNALISM AND LEISURE

For a long time, New York had been the mecca of American journalism, thanks to its information agencies, the Associated Press, United Press, and International News Service, as well as its hundreds of newspapers, many of which were published for various immigrant groups in their own languages.[5] The readership for the major daily newspapers, the *World*, the *Herald*, and the *Times*, increased again after 1880. Joseph Pulitzer bought out the *World* in 1883 and upped the number of daily editions. He was the great figure in New York journalism until William Randolph Hearst entered the scene. Having taken over the *Morning Journal* in 1895, Hearst further heightened the sensationalism for which the New York press had long been hankering. Soon the *Journal* began a jingoistic campaign in support of the Cuban struggle for independence from Spain. Hearst did not hesitate to mix facts with fiction to push for war, feeding into the martial patriotism of the times. After the United States formally declared war on Spain on April 25, 1898, Hearst continued to publish saber-rattling reports that earned his newspaper a record circulation.

Pulitzer was not to be outdone. The *World* and the *Journal* quickly entered into bitter competition, and their continued success testified to their readers' taste for the popular dailies. Beginning in the mid-1920s, they were dethroned by newspapers with a new format—the tabloids, such as the *Daily News* or the *Mirror*. As for the *New York Times*, it was in a very sorry state when Adolph S. Ochs took it over in 1896. Opting for a different strategy of responsible reporting, its new owner made it the nation's standard daily paper.

New York also continued to dominate the world of magazines and reviews of all kinds. *Vogue*, founded in the early 1890s and aimed at fashionable New Yorkers, saw its influence expand, beginning in the 1910s, under the direction of Condé Nast and Edna Woolman Chase. In 1936, it absorbed its great rival, *Vanity Fair*. In the 1920s and 1930s, several news magazines in their turn captured the consumerist mood of modern American society. The inspired innovator Henry Luce founded the news weekly, *Time*, in 1923, followed a few years later by the monthly *Fortune* and, in 1936, by the weekly *Life*, which brought photojournalism into its own. It was also in New York that the *Reader's Digest* was born in 1922. The cultural emblem of the new middle class, this magazine moved its offices a few months later to Westchester County.

New York also became the American capital of radio. It was "a central node" in the "world's intricate spider web of radio communication," noted the authors of *New York Panorama* in 1938.[6] Appearing at the end of the 1920s, the large networks of NBC and CBS (National Broadcasting Company and Columbia Broadcasting System) soon extended their hold over the entire country, to the detriment of local radio stations. In the early 1930s, CBS and NBC established themselves at Rockefeller Center, soon nicknamed Radio City. From this new complex, programs were broadcast "direct from New York" or prerecorded. They often bore the mark of their metropolitan origin and conferred upon their stars, like Eddie Cantor, rapid national renown. After 1935, CBS and NBC began to relocate some of their programs in California, but their offices remained in New York. When, in the autumn of 1938, Orson Welles announced that New Jersey was being invaded by Martians, the panic that he unleashed in the area testified to the size of New York radio audiences.

It was a different situation with the cinema. Despite the development of Hollywood, which gave California incontestable dominance with regard to production, New York retained a certain financial and promotional control over the southern-California film colony until World War II. It housed many studios, such as those the Edison Company owned in Manhattan and then in the Bronx until the 1960s, or the Studio Astoria, opened in 1920 by the Famous Players–Laski Corporation (which became Paramount in 1927), where several of the Marx Brothers movies were shot. Most importantly, there were hundreds of movie theaters in New York. Some were tiny, like the nickelodeons of the first years of the century; others were huge palaces. Built by entrepreneurs convinced that cinema would be a success— such as Mitchell Mark or Samuel "Roxy" Rothafel—the Loew's King Theater in Flatbush, or the Rialto, Paramount, Astor, Roxy, and Capital in Manhattan could accommodate spectators by the hundreds, or even by the thousands.

The city itself—its landscapes, its actors, and accents— was henceforth a movie theme: the Empire State Building owes part of its renown to the famous *King Kong*. Movie actors and actresses often came from Broadway theater— from Douglas Fairbanks to Clark Gable and Cary Grant, from Mae West to Claudette Colbert, Mary Pickford, or Ginger Rogers, to name a few. As the authors of *New York Panorama* commented in 1938, movie gangsters came to be identified with two native New Yorkers, James Cagney, "the embodiment of the Great American Male during the Babylonian years of the Coolidge era," and Humphrey Bogart, who, in the 1942 movie *Casablanca*, played one of his most memorable roles as Rick Blaine, a New Yorker in exile. As for Groucho Marx, "with his be-moustached aplomb, his cocked eye and his ominous walk," he summarized all by himself, and with genius, "metropolitan ambition and pretense."[7] The heroines were not to be outdone, however—imaginary ones like Betty Boop or very real ones like Louise Brooks, a former dancer for the *Ziegfeld Follies*, who embodied the allure of the New York woman in the 1920s, or a bit later, Katherine Hepburn.

Other New Yorkers, or sometimes the same ones, preferred the stadiums to the cinemas. Sports became a mass spectacle. and offered a few athletes the hope of rapid social advancement. As in the past, boxing continued to fascinate many spectators, but the favorite sport of New Yorkers, and a majority of Americans, was baseball, which won over the new middle classes and a portion of the working-class world. Both the National League and the American League, the two major associations of professional clubs, had New York teams. The famous Giants dominated the two first decades of the century, the Yankees proved the best team in the 1920s and 1930s, and the Brooklyn Dodgers were legendary for their erratic performance. Racial discrimination led to the creation of several clubs for black players in the 1920s and 1930s— the Lincoln Giants, the Cuban Stars, and the Black Yankees were members of leagues that organized their own championships. All these teams drew large and faithful crowds to the stadiums (Ebbets Field, where the Dodgers started playing in 1914, the Giants' Polo Grounds, or Yankee Stadium), and fans were quick to go wild over their heroes. It was during these same years that player worship became a major phenomenon, thanks in particular to exceptional figures on the Yankees' team, like Babe Ruth, Lou Gehrig, or later, Joe DiMaggio.

THE METROPOLITAN MOSAIC

Alongside all these new forms of popular culture, older practices, tied to the various immigrant groups, made New York into a gigantic mosaic of ethnocultural traditions that adapted to and profited from certain innovations, like the radio.

These cultures were solidly based in the new arrivals' districts. It did not take Jews, Italians, and African-Americans long to establish associations, newspapers, and social centers. On Manhattan's Lower East Side and, to a lesser extent, in the neighborhoods of Brownsville or Williamsburg in Brooklyn, thousands of associations, or *landsmanshaftn*, assembled Jewish immigrants who had come from the same city or even the same village. Beyond the guarantee of financial security in case of accident, disease, or death, they provided them with the warmth of a friendly presence and eased their integration into the metropolis. There were also fraternal organizations, like B'nai B'rith, or institutions that provided assistance or advice, such as the Educational Alliance or the United Hebrew Charities, founded with contradictory feelings of solidarity and scornful reticence by German Jews present in New York for many generations. In 1908, the various Jewish societies united to form one central organization, the Kehillah.

In New York's Little Italies in lower Manhattan or Harlem, Williamsburg or Sunset Park, the Italians wove a network of mutual-aid and social organizations, often local or regional, that were combined into one federation, the Sons of Italy, in 1905. For its part, Harlem counted numerous black associations, beginning in the 1910s and 1920s, with many different objectives: mutual aid, social and leisure activities, health and social work. Many of them had previously been located in lower Manhattan, and moved when the black population became concentrated in Harlem.

Each quarter had its own places of worship meant for the new arrivals. In the Lower East Side and Brooklyn, hundreds of Jewish congregations provided for the immigrants' spiritual needs. Some continued to practice orthodox Judaism; others, who wanted their faith to accord with the world that surrounded them but were not drawn to the reformed Judaism that developed in New York during the 1850s, followed a more conservative middle path.

As for the Italians, they constituted a major portion of the two million Catholics the metropolis counted in 1920, with its 200 parishes and parochial schools. Italian immigrants sometimes came up against the hostility of a clergy dominated by the Irish, even if a succession of New York archbishops—Mgr. Michael Corrigan (1885–1902), John Cardinal Farley (1902–1919), and Patrick Cardinal Hayes (1919–38)—tried to respond to the demands of separate, so-called ethnic parishes, drawn up by their new flocks. These tensions reinforced the religious fervor and virulent anticlericalism among many immigrants. This mix, already present before immigration, was particularly visible each year on the big holidays honoring a patron saint of a city or a village. To celebrate Saint Paulinus, immigrants from Nola, near Naples, marched down the streets of Williamsburg carrying on their shoulders a high tower crowned with a statue of the saint, the *giglio*, while in Harlem, Italians turned out en masse for the festival of Our Lady of Mount Carmel.

In the same period, black Harlem witnessed the proliferation of Protestant churches, traditionally the principal structures of the African-American community. Some churches, long established in New York, opened missions in Harlem and then moved there in the 1910s, like the African Methodist Episcopal Zion Church. They often located in imposing buildings, acquired or built with the profits they earned by selling their properties in lower Manhattan. Other, less well established or less wealthy, contented themselves with a suite, a room, or even the back of a store. The Baptist and Methodist churches were the most influential, such as the Abyssinian Baptist Church established on One Hundred and Thirty-eighth Street in 1920, led by the pastor Adam Clayton Powell, Sr. But in

FIGURE 45
Harlem's elegant women, 1927
Schomburg Center, New York Public Library

fact, Harlem housed churches of every conceivable Protestant denomination, as well as Catholic parishes.

Each group had its newspapers. In Harlem, the *New York Age*, a Republican weekly published by Thomas Fortune and then Fred Moore, or the Democratic *Amsterdam News* of John Henry Anderson and Sadie Warren Davis, defended black interests and the principle of equal rights. New York published many Italian newspapers, most importantly the *Progresso Italo-Americano*, and many Yiddish newspapers, such as the conservative *Tageblat*, the more liberal *Tog*, or *Forverts*, closely tied to the socialists. They had a considerable readership: in the early 1910s, the *Progresso's* circulation was about 80,000, and Abraham Cahan's *Forverts* 140,000.

Besides these organizations, places of worship, and newspapers, Brownsville, the Lower East Side, and other Jewish districts in the city supported a very vital secular culture. In the cafés, former members of the Bund—a Jewish political party in Tsarist Russia that defended Yiddish and fought for Jewish autonomy—endlessly debated the best way of instituting socialism in the capitalist metropolis; garment-industry workers crowded into the many dance halls. In the 1910s, about twenty Yiddish theaters existed in Manhattan; they were extraordinarily popular and had rich repertoires of light comedies and more ambitious dramatic pieces. Streets and shops rang with the tones of Yiddish, eventually mixing with American terms eagerly adopted by those immigrants who no longer wanted to pass for new arrivals, or "greenhorns."

Italian sociability was just as visible in the Mulberry Street district or the streets of East Harlem. In the grocery shops, the bakeries, the butcher shops, and the cafés, immigrants often from the same city or region—*paesani*—ran into each other and reconnected. The neighborhood was the natural extension of the home, a world that felt familiar and mastered.

Long established, the Germans maintained their cultural vitality until World War I. A majority of them left Manhattan then for Brooklyn and Queens, but their various athletic and cultural societies remained active. In 1914, many of them supported Germany and wanted the American government to maintain a strict neutrality. But when the United States entered the war in April 1917, loyalty to their adopted country generally won out, even though New York witnessed a surge of anti-German fever. Coney Island hamburgers were renamed "liberty sandwiches," German-American institutions and associations Americanized their names, German-language newspaper sales diminished, as did the use of the language in schools and churches.

Following the conflict, immigration from Germany never regained its former significance, and the German cultural presence in New York weakened. This decline accelerated still further in the 1930s when a fraction of the New York German-American community took a pro-Nazi position, joining Fritz Kuhn's German-American Bund. This movement organized parades in support of the Hitler regime, and instigated anti-Semitic incidents. Many New York Germans refused to be identified with these extremists and thus distanced themselves from German-American institutions. As for the many thousands of Jews who fled Nazi Germany and settled in the Washington Heights district in the 1930s, like Paula and Louis Kissinger and their son Henry, they had little desire to be linked with New York Germans, and preferred to live through a difficult adjustment period by themselves.

Unlike the Germans, the Irish continued to immigrate to the United States over the course of the 1920s, particularly to New York. Less geographically concentrated than the last wave of immigrants, they were also better established. Their significance among New York Catholics was substantial, as was their political clout, since they represented about one out of five voters at that time. They formed vital community networks, such as the Friendly Sons of St. Patrick or the United Irish Counties Association, which, beginning in 1904, brought together the various local associations that were at the center of New York Irish social life. Most importantly, the events in Ireland in 1916 kindled nationalist sentiments throughout the 1920s and 1930s, and led to the demands for Irish recognition of many first-, second-, and third-generation immigrants, among them Eamon De Valera, the head of Sinn Fein, who was himself born in New York. The Irish presence was no less visible in urban life, thanks to newspapers, radio stations, and the countless bars in the metropolis.

THE BIRTH OF THE NEW YORK INTELLECTUALS

New York gradually made a name for itself as an intellectual capital, even if this new image emerged slowly and was rife with contradictions.

At the turn of the century, ideas and ideologies abounded and competed on the streets, in the cafés and the meeting halls of Manhattan and Brooklyn. There was no great debate that did not have its New York incarnation. The stormiest ones involved the vote for women and what was then called "the relation between labor and capital," or again, "the social question."

The suffragettes organized in the 1900s, increasing the numbers of meetings and associations. Passing through New York, the Englishwoman Emmeline Pankhurst electrified her listeners. The suffragettes marched down Fifth Avenue on many occasions, prompted by the Progressive Woman Suffrage Union. Merged in 1909 into the Women Suffrage Party of Greater New York, presided over by Carrie Chapman Catt, they narrowly lost a 1915 referendum on voting rights in New York State after a campaign lasting many months on the city's streets. Two years later, they prevailed, thus opening the way for the adoption of the Nineteenth Amendment in 1920.

Socialist ideas also flourished in New York, where the Socialist Labor Party had been founded in 1877, bringing together especially the German-Americans. In the 1890s, under the leadership of Daniel De Leon, it adopted a political line that was overtly revolutionary and hostile to reformist trade unions, and it exerted only a weak influence upon Jewish immigrants newly arrived from Eastern Europe. Among these latter, many were favorably disposed to socialist ideas. The news from Russia fascinated them: the 1905 revolution filled them with enthusiasm, its failure with despair. To protest against the bloody repression carried out by the tsarist regime, 100,000 Jews from the Lower East Side demonstrated on Fifth Avenue on December 4, 1905. Many Jewish voters supported the new Socialist Party of America. Created in 1901, it was reform-oriented and closely aligned with the unions. One of its members, the lawyer Meyer London, was elected to the House of Representatives in 1914, and in the 1917 municipal elections, its candidate, Morris Hillquit, won more than 20 percent of the votes.

In the 1920s and 1930s, New York was home to a very active communist movement. The Communist Party established its headquarters near Union Square in the late 1920s, and numbered tens of thousands of sympathizers throughout the metropolis. The Party was an important political influence due to its following among first- and second-generation Jewish immigrants who worked in the garment industry and among blacks in Harlem—also its clout in the Congress of Industrial Organizations, the attraction felt by many New York intellectuals and writers for the communist ideal, and the alternative it offered to fascism's increasing threat. This political influence translated into communist support—through the intermediary of the American Labor Party—for the outgoing mayor, Fiorello La Guardia, in the 1937 municipal elections; into the presence of communists elected to the city council, like Benjamin Davis of Harlem; and into the election of Vito Marcantonio, an East Harlem politician and Party fellow traveler, to the House of Representatives in Washington.

Beginning at the turn of the century, New York witnessed the formation of an intellectual circle whose liberal and secular ideas contrasted with the literary culture of the Victorian era, still exemplified by the writer Edith Wharton until she settled in France in 1913. This new circle distinguished itself by the diversity of its members, Jewish and Christian, and by the cosmopolitan ideal that informed it. "Cosmopolitanism": the word was coined by the brilliant young critic Randolph Bourne, a shooting star in the New York sky, dead in December 1918 at the age of thirty-two, never having witnessed the cultural revolution that he called for. The cosmopolitan ideal that he defended was neither assimilationist, like the nativist credo that wanted to destroy all cultural distinctions, nor pluralist, like the one proposed in the same period by Horace Kallen, envisioning a society of groups practicing mutual tolerance. For Bourne and his friends, it was more a matter of transcending the distinctions without making them disappear.

In New York from 1910 to 1940, following Bourne, Van Wyck Brooks, and Ezra Pound, this demanding ideal attracted writers, literary critics, and intellectuals. The famous lost generation described by Gertrude Stein was first distinguished by its hostility to all provincialism. Some of its members found European exile to be the only solution, like Pound, who always considered London the artistic and literary capital of the United States. Others, such as Van Wyck Brooks or Lewis Mumford, remained in New York, where they evolved their vision of a dynamic and national American culture, respectful of differences without being submissive to them, capable of integrating newcomers without being constrained.

This cosmopolitan ideal captivated Jewish intellectuals like Walter Lippman, descendant of German immigrants, Harvard graduate, and author of an important essay, *Drift and Mastery*, written in 1914 when he was twenty-five. It found a wider response among certain Jews recently arrived from Russia who, even before emigrating, had discovered a culture distinct from their own in the *shtetl* or the ghettos of Russian cities. Their model was the philosopher Morris Cohen: born in Minsk in 1880, arriving in New York in 1892, a graduate of City College with a doctorate in philosophy from Harvard, Cohen taught philosophy at City College from 1912 to 1938. There, he exercised considerable influence over generations of students, often Jewish, to whom he passed on his rationalist convictions and his progressive ideas.

Founded on faith in progress and rejection of their respective provincialisms and distinctions, this cosmopolitan ideal was at the heart of the dialogue between intellectuals born in the United States and those newly arrived there between the two world wars. They all found or created in New York the places for these exchanges—newspapers, journals, and universities. The last of these—Columbia University, New York University, and City College of New York—had witnessed great changes during the final decades of the nineteenth century. Between 1870 and 1910, they acquired considerable intellectual and civic influence. In that interval, they moved to new campuses. Over the course of the 1890s, New York University became established in the Bronx, at the University Heights site that it occupied until the 1970s; in 1897, Columbia left its Madison Avenue and Fifty-seventh Street premises to set up its present-day campus in northwest Manhattan's Morningside Heights at One Hundred and Sixteenth Street; and City College moved to St. Nicholas Heights at One Hundred and Thirty-eighth Street in Harlem.

FIGURE 46
The acropolis of knowledge (1908): Columbia University campus on
Morningside Heights; President Grant's tomb, front right
© Roger Viollet

These relocations symbolized the intellectual and institutional transformations that the three establishments were then experiencing. Under Seth Low's presidency (1890–1901) and especially under Nicholas Murray Butler's (1902–1945), Columbia emphasized professional and scientific expertise, even while establishing quotas for Jewish students in the 1910s. For its part, City College, presided over by the former journalist John H. Finley, accepted primarily young immigrants or the children of immigrants, among them Bernard Baruch, Morris Cohen, Robert Wagner, Felix Frankfurter, and Ira Gershwin.

New York became a center for cutting-edge research in most disciplines, thanks to the matrix of higher education that was put into place. Columbia was transformed into a true university and acquired a reputation for excellence in medicine, law, chemistry, and physics. The Rockefeller Institute for Medical Research, the future Nobel Prize breeding ground founded in 1901 by John D. Rockefeller and directed for more than thirty years by Simon Flexner, added to the number of state-of-the-art laboratories in biology and medicine.

Another innovation was the 1923 creation of the Social Science Research Council (or SSRC), whose ambition it was to bridge the gap between this type of research and public policy. When the New York publisher Macmillan published an impressive *Encyclopedia of Social Sciences* in the early 1930s, it was a sign of how far the field had come. Appearing in New York in the 1840s, anthropology was first developed within the American Museum of Natural History before finding its chosen place at Columbia, under the leadership of Franz Boas, who taught there beginning in 1896. By separating anthropology from racist and biologistic theories, Boas founded a school with an international reputation. At Columbia, he trained most of the following decades' great anthropologists, including Ruth Benedict, Melville Herskovits, Margaret Mead, and Edward Sapir. Columbia's influence was no less significant in psychology, because of John Cattell; in philosophy, thanks to John Dewey; or in history, with James Harvey Robinson already promoting a "new history," and Charles Beard specializing in political history.

The universities played an essential role in training future intellectuals, but they rarely welcomed them back during the course of their careers. They were also the battlegrounds where certain academics defended their leading role in the sciences (like Columbia's president Butler) and others, like Dewey or Beard, fought for civic and progressive ideals. This opposition between experts and intellectuals was not without casualties: during World War I, one conflict led to Beard's and Dewey's departure from Columbia, to found a new institution in 1921, the New School for Social Research.

Publishing houses offered New York intellectuals other places to express themselves and hold forth, thanks to editors like Bennett Cerf who founded Random House in 1927, or Maxwell Perkins of Scribner's. Reviews had a long tradition of political and social critique, on the model of magazines like *McClure's* or *Cosmopolitan*, which made a specialty of investigative reporting at the turn of the century, denouncing scandals and corruption under the sharp pen of muckraking journalists like Lincoln Steffens and Ida Tarbell. Others specialized in political thought and cultural critique, like *The Nation*, a liberal weekly founded in 1865, or *The New Republic*, launched by Herbert Croly and Walter Lippmann in 1914 to spread the ideas of the New York intelligentsia. The creation of *The New Yorker* in 1925—sophisticated, literary, profoundly metropolitan (the column entitled "Talk of the Town" was one of its most popular)—further enriched an extraordinarily diverse range of publications.

Originally, a great number of intellectuals were progressives, like Beard or Dewey, or even radicals embracing socialist ideas. But the Russian Revolution, Stalinism, fascism, and Nazism reshuffled the deck. Henceforth, socialists and communists split and opposed each other through their respective parties, both of which retained significant electoral and union support. In the early 1930s, communism exerted a strong pull on intellectuals and artists who were captivated by the soviet experience and mobilized against fascism. Most of them soon broke away, following the example of the *Partisan Review*. Inspired by communism when it was founded in 1935, the review stopped publishing due to lack of funds in 1936. When it reappeared the following year, the *Partisan Review* severely criticized Stalinism. Following suit, a large portion of New York intellectuals evolved under the effects of anti-Stalinism and anti-fascism, and then under the new nationalism in the war years and the horror that followed the discovery of the Final Solution. That was how postwar liberalism, with its profoundly anticommunist strain, took shape.

THE AVANT-GARDE

In half a century, New York had also become a cultural and artistic mecca, following the private negotiations that writers and artists conducted with modernity.

Here again, it began with an anti-Victorian reaction that

led to a reorientation of American culture in the 1890s. It took the form of a rejection of social and cultural conventions, but also of neocolonial dependence on Europe (and particularly Great Britain) as experienced by American literature, music, and painting. Even as late as 1910, American literature was not taught in the universities. Melville was unknown and Twain scorned. New York modernity was first of all a revolt, an attempt at liberation as manifested by the rejection of the Victorian cultural corset. It involved the quest for autonomy and the discovery of a cultural Americanism, bringing with it a certain degree of nationalism.

Of course, this revolt owed more to the Victorian culture than it wanted to admit. It was indebted to it for establishing many renowned cultural and artistic institutions in New York, against which modernity could rebel. At the turn of the century, the metropolis could pride itself on concert halls like Carnegie Hall, founded in 1891 thanks to the munificence of the steel magnate who gave it its name, or its Metropolitan Opera, which owed much to the generosity of Otto Kahn. Subsequently, the city could boast of numerous first-rate orchestras. The founding of the Institute of Musical Art in 1905, better known by its later name, the Juilliard School, contributed to New York's reputation among musical candidates. The musical scene attracted the best artists in the world, such as the tenor Enrico Caruso, who starred regularly at the Metropolitan Opera from 1903 until his death in 1921. With regard to the visual arts, the Metropolitan Museum, bordering Central Park, was soon on a par with the best museums in the world, thanks to the generosity of donors who made its collections the most renowned in the country.

In reaction against these various institutions, many attempts at emancipation began in the heart of Manhattan, more precisely in the artistic and literary Bohemia of Greenwich Village. The Village, nicknamed the "American district" in the mid-nineteenth century because of the low percentage of immigrants who settled there, was transformed in the 1880s when Irish and Italians came there to live, and when the rows of town houses were replaced by industrial lofts and tenements.

Early in the century, painters, writers, and rebels of all kinds set their sights on the district, where countles cafés, tearooms, galleries, theaters, and bookstores opened. The "Latin Quarter of Manhattan," as John Reed called it, was as much a state of mind as a place, characterized by a great tolerance for rejecting conventions, whether they were social, sexual, or cultural. During those pre-war years, less famous than the 1920s when Greenwich Village was home to Ernest Hemingway, John Dos Passos, and Willa Cather, the first claims for literary and artistic modernity were conceived. Djuna Barnes, who later became a well-known journalist and lived in Paris from 1918 to 1940, noted in 1916 that "the greater part of New York is as soulless as a department store, but Greenwich Village has recollections like ears filled with mute music and hopes like sightless eyes straining to catch a glimpse of the Beatific Vision."[8]

Thus the Village was the heart of a veritable cultural insurrection. Socialists and feminists, homosexuals and lesbians, celibates and champions of free love, the anti-establishment and the avant-garde, painters and writers met and mixed there, all united in their rejection of commercialization and their desire for independence. "We are free who live at Washington Square,/We dare to think as Uptown wouldn't dare," wrote John Reed, the revolutionary journalist and future author (and witness) of *Ten Days that Shook the World* (1919), who lived in the Village in the 1910s.[9] The district accommodated many artists' studios, as well as several places that soon symbolized its restlessness. First on Nassau Street and then on Greenwich Avenue, the radical review, *The Masses*, founded in 1911, had its offices. Writers, artists, and cartoonists held endless discussions there. Beginning in 1912, Mabel Dodge Luhan's literary salon at 23 Fifth Avenue welcomed Emma Goldman, Alfred Stieglitz, Margaret Sanger, John Reed. At 291 Fifth Avenue, Alfred Stieglitz's studio exhibited work by American and European painters and photographers.

Reacting against the landscape, neoclassical, and impressionist traditions that dominated painting in New York in 1900, the Village witnessed the birth of two modernist movements. The first, realism, emerged in the first years of the century, after a group of Philadelphia painters established themselves in New York, gathered around the group's theoretician, Robert Henri. Opposed to the ambient academicism, Henri and his friends, soon nicknamed the Ashcan School, sought to take into account in their painting the noises and smells of New York, the reality of the city and its inhabitants. Their message was social and political. In 1908, the National Academy of Design refused to show Henri and seven other painters (George Luks, William James Glackens, John Sloan, Everett Shinn, Arthur B. Davies, Ernest Lawson, and Maurice Prendergast); they thus adopted the name of the Group of Eight and went on to exhibit their canvases at the Macbeth Gallery. A second tendency, semi-abstract and cubo-futurist, emerged around artists like John Marin, Abraham Walkowitz, Joseph Stella, and Max Weber, who owed their discovery of Henri Matisse to Alfred Stieglitz and his Gallery 291, and adopted in their works and as their motto Francis Picabia's characterization of New York as a cubist city.

The militancy of all these defenders of pictorial modernism was conveyed by their decision to organize an international exhibition of modern art in New York. The Armory Show, which opened in February 1913 at the Sixty-ninth Regiment Armory on Lexington Avenue, included European artists like Matisse, Braque, Picabia, Picasso, Redon, and Marcel Duchamp, and Americans like John Sloan and John Marin. Perhaps because of the icy reception that the New York press reserved for this initiative, the exhibit's success took the form of scandal (Duchamp shocked viewers with his *Nude Descending the Stairs*) and testified to the gradual emancipation of American painting.

Over the course of the twenty-five years following the Armory Show, modern art slowly acquired a prominent place for itself in New York. An extraordinary individual, Gertrude Vanderbilt Whitney (1875–1942), played a decisive role in this development. Born into high society, Whitney decided in 1900 to become a sculptor; she set up a studio in Greenwich Village in 1907. During the years that followed, she became a recognized artist but also a patron and collector who invested her family fortune in modern art. She first created the Whitney Studio in 1914, then the Whitney Studio Club in 1918, and then the Whitney Studio Galleries in 1928, where she received artists whom she assisted through purchases, shows she organized for them, and grants she gave them. In 1930, after the Metropolitan Museum refused to house her collection, she founded the Whitney Museum of American Art.

Other patrons, who were not themselves artists, displayed a growing interest in modern art. In 1929, the Museum of Modern Art (the famous MOMA) opened, the initiative of Lillie Bliss, Abby Rockefeller (daughter of an eminent Rhode Island senator, Nelson Aldrich, and wife of John D. Rockefeller, Jr.), and Mary Quinn Sullivan. Unlike the Whitney Museum, the MOMA was interested in all the visual arts and not just painting and sculpture. Ten years later, in 1939, Solomon R. Guggenheim, a businessman who had made his fortune thanks to judicious industrial and mining investments, opened his collections to the public, gathered together in a museum for nonobjective painting that exhibited in particular works by Kandinsky, Klee, and Modigliani.

New York also emerged as a subject for art as much as a setting. Its association with the idea of modernity, essential to the cultural emancipation of the city, evolved. The impressionist paintings of Childe Hassam or the art photography of Alfred Stieglitz captured the new urban verticality and registered its strangeness. The realist paintings of the Ashcan School, John Sloan's *Fifth Avenue*, for example, or George Bellows's *New York*, tried to recreate the city's intensity and speed. And finally, the cubo-futurists set about defining an artistic modernity in keeping with the urban modernity around them. To do that, they resorted to a use of abstraction that led them to imagine veritable New York hieroglyphs—skyscrapers, the Brooklyn Bridge, the energy and the masses. In the same way, the skyscrapers painted by Georgia O'Keefe, John Storrs, or Charles Sheeler in the 1920s, were pyramids in which all nature was absent. New York was modernity, and modernity was American.

Corresponding to this emancipation in painting was a demand for literary emancipation embodied, for example, by the Provincetown Players, who performed one-act plays by Eugene O'Neill in theaters in the Village between 1916 and 1920. The situation with the novel was more complex, because many American authors, temporary or permanent expatriates, preferred to write about New York from Paris. The 1910s witnessed the blossoming of a very creative literary scene in Greenwich Village. Bustling, always in motion, noisy and revitalized, New York became a setting and a subject for the novel as well. It inspired a whole generation of writers, from F. Scott Fitzgerald to Edmund Wilson, from John Dos Passos to e. e. cummings, not to mention Hart Crane and Sherwood Anderson. From the Dos Passos of *Manhattan Transfer* to the Fitzgerald of *The Great Gatsby*, all were confronted with the challenge of metropolitan modernity.

All these writers could rely upon a vast network of reviews. Even though their life spans varied, reviews like *Others*, *Seven Arts* (1917), *The Little Review*, or *The New Yorker* helped to make New York a literary center. During the 1920s, the Algonquin Hotel regularly welcomed around its famous roundtable successful authors and critics like Dorothy Parker, Alexander Woolcott, and Robert Sherwood, who set the tone for the literary and theatrical trends of the day.

THE HARLEM RENAISSANCE

At the same time as artists fought these battles in the name of a modernist ideal opposed to all provincialism, other New Yorkers sought to redefine the respective places of white and black cultures and their mutual influence. This discovery, or rediscovery, of the significance of the African-American tradition was accompanied by a militant affirmation by blacks of that tradition, from a perspective that was rarely separatist. Instead, the point was to build bridges, and open pathways, to express demands for recognition, and then to satisfy them.

For the first time, the black cultural heritage was recognized as a distinct tradition, worthy of respect, that exerted its influence on white culture. This awareness came about within a society and a city often racist and in conflict, but where some latitude for maneuvering and negotiating existed.

"Whether Americans admit it or refute me," noted Jean Cocteau, "Harlem is the machine's boiler and its Black youth stamping their feet, the coal that feeds it and determines its movement."[10] From the silent protest march against racism that brought thousands of people together on Fifth Avenue on July 28, 1917, to the race riots that shook the district in 1935 and 1943, Harlem acquired a new meaning. The growth of "Black Manhattan" so dear to James Weldon Johnson brought with it cultural ferment. Particularly significant in literature and in music, this movement was tied to the political context of the 1920s, noticeably marked by the psychocultural impact of World War I, Wilsonian principles of self-determination for nations, and the "Great Migration" of Southern blacks to Northern cities.

Many of Harlem's important places came to embody this ferment. The New York Public Library Extension on One Hundred and Thirty-fifth Street acquired the collections of Arthur Schomburg beginning in the 1920s; these were exceptional for their history of black culture. The location, later renamed the Schomburg Library, was a place for research, but especially for intellectual and literary discussions, as was the Harlem branch of the Young Men's Christian Association Harlem was also home to numerous clubs, cabarets, and dance halls. Some, like Connie's Inn and the Cotton Club, where Cab Calloway and his orchestra earned their reputation, were limited to white audiences, but others, like the Apollo, welcomed whites and blacks.

Jazz became integral to American culture. It was born in New Orleans, St. Louis, and Chicago, but Harlem's boom and the growing cultural domination of New York made the metropolis the center of what soon became a cultural phenomenon.

Ragtime was one of the first examples of interactions between white and black music, symbolically consecrated by the Chicago Exposition in 1893. Ragtime's success came by way of the recognition of its African-American origins and its nationalism, but its Americanization was less an appropriation by whites than the result of cross-breeding between white and black music, exemplified by the works of George Gershwin and Irving Berlin. When, reacting against the slightly mawkish sentimentalism of the day's popular tunes, Berlin adopted the syncopated—or "ragged"—rhythm of ragtime, he mixed English, Irish, and Jewish influences with the musical traditions of white and black America. This hybrid genre, which triumphed in 1911 with *Alexander's Ragtime Band*, earned him the nickname of "king of ragtime." Ragtime's influence was also evident in Al Jolson, "the jazz singer," a Russian Jew like Berlin, and Fred Astaire. Son of an Austrian immigrant who settled in Omaha, Astaire learned to dance from Irene and Vernon Castle, dancing instructors for the New York socialites in the 1910s and conveyors of culture, who taught African-American dances to their black students. He was then influenced by two black artists, John Bubbles and the famous actor and tap dancer Bill "Bojangles" Robinson, nicknamed "the mayor of Harlem."

Ragtime influenced European composers like Darius Milhaud and set off a wave of enthusiasm in Europe in the aftermath of World War I. Its success was also a result of its commercial development. It was New York that ensured its national influence, first in the form of musical scores (Scott Joplin, a New Yorker from 1910 until his death in 1917, sold more than a million copies of his *Maple Leaf Rag*, composed in 1899), then in the form of player-piano rolls, and finally as phonograph records, making Eubie Blake, James P. Johnson, and Fats Waller famous.

The history of the blues, originally more rural than ragtime, was quite similar but only began in the 1920s. Coming directly from oral African-American culture, the blues first gained commercial success within the black community. In 1920, Mamie Smith's recording of *Crazy Blues*, which sold more than a million copies in a few months, started a trend. More than 5,000 blues records were produced over the course of the next two decades. In its turn, the blues influenced white musicians, resulting in

Gershwin's *Yankee Doodle Blues* (1922) and Berlin's *Shakin' the Blues Away* a few years later. During the 1930s, the economic crisis closed a large number of clubs and cabarets in Harlem that had served as cultural intermediaries between whites and blacks, but the role of ragtime and the blues in redefining what American music could be did not disappear.

In the 1920s and 1930s, Harlem was home to an extraordinary number of poets, novelists, and playwrights, who figured prominently in what was soon known as the "Harlem Renaissance." Their works testified to their situation and the condition of blacks in the United States, from *The New Negro* anthology, published by Alan Locke in 1925, to the novels of Walter White or Jean Toomer, from works by Nella Larsen and Zora Neale Huston to poems by Langston Hughes, Claude McKay, and Countee Cullen. Black and white authors connected with and influenced each other, thanks to a mutual desire and imaginative conveyors of culture like Carl Van Vechten, a very popular critic at the time and author of a successful novel situated in Harlem, *Nigger Heaven* (1926).

Some saw these literary and artistic interactions as a potential turning point, an indication of the way to get beyond the racism that permeated New York and America. "Nothing," wrote James Weldon Johnson, "can go farther to destroy racial prejudices than the recognition of the Negro as a creator and contributor to American civilization."[11] Others were less optimistic. Developments in the 1930s justified their skepticism. The fragile bridges collapsed one after the other, affected by the economic crisis and cultural and political impasses. Interest in race or the hybridization that characterized the "jazz age" gave way to an emphasis on social realism, leading a portion of the New York literary world to uncompromised criticism of a capitalist system that everyday life proclaimed a failure. Harlem was no longer in vogue. Throughout the 1930s, the place and the role of its writers changed. Some soon became participants in the Federal Writers' Project; others left New York or gave up writing. All the same, the Harlem Renaissance had transformed the role of blacks in American culture.

NEW YORK, 1940

"New York is not a completed city . . . It is a city in the process of becoming. Today it belongs to the world," noted Le Corbusier in 1937. "Without anyone expecting it, it has become the jewel in the crown of universal cities . . . Crown of noble cities, soft pearls or glittering topazes, or radiant lapis, or melancholy amethysts! New York is a great diamond, hard and dry, sparkling, triumphant." The cultural domination that it exercised was achieved "rather by in- than by exclusiveness," observed the English writer Ford Madox Ford.[12]

Four years later, in 1940, France's defeat and the fall of Paris confirmed in the eyes of many the transfer of sovereignty between the two metropolises. It was partly a matter of circumstances, the direct consequence of the tragedies that racked Europe and brought a long wave of exiles to New York, from Bartok to Chagall, and including Isaac Bashevis Singer and Hannah Arendt. But it was also the result of five decades of invention, dispute, and redefinition that made the semiprovincial city of 1890 into the irresistible magnet of 1940, whose universal attraction fascinated Otto Preminger and Claude Lévi-Strauss alike. A few months before Pearl Harbor, when Henry Luce, publisher of *Time*, *Life*, and *Fortune*, proclaimed the advent of the "American century," it was clear to the eyes of the world that New York was at the heart of it.

IV
CAPITAL OF THE
AMERICAN CENTURY
1940–2000

FIGURE 47
New York by night
© Hachette Livre

9

THE PHOENIX

On August 21, 1948, New York inaugurated an exposition in its own honor at the Grand Central Palace, at Lexington Avenue and 43rd Street, to celebrate the fiftieth anniversary of the 1898 merger that gave birth to the contemporary city. Never had it appeared so powerful. After an old-fashioned torchlight procession down Lexington Avenue—its electricity was cut for the occasion—William O'Dwyer, the mayor of New York, Trygve Lie, the secretary general of the United Nations, David Lilienthal, president of the Atomic Energy Commission, and General Leslie Groves, one of the founders of the Manhattan Project, took their places, in the company of thousands of invited guests and 50,000 onlookers, before a long ribbon that stretched to the middle of the avenue in front of the exhibition building.

"Atop the Empire State Building and in a Navy 'truculent turtle' bomber overhead telescopes were trained on the star Alioth, just fifty light years away," reported the *New York Times*. "At 8:30, light which left the star in the year that New York's five boroughs were united, was admitted to the telescopes. It activated photoelectric cells and sent radio impulses to the exposition, where it triggered an atomic pile, split a uranium atom and ignited, electrically, a mass of magnesium in the ribbon. With a flash and a loud crack, the ribbon flew apart and the invited guests, 6,000 strong, poured into the building to see the four floors of exhibits put on by city departments and atomic energy agencies."

The symbolism escaped no one: in his speech, General Groves emphasized the new context that mastering atomic energy created, while the secretary general of the UN hailed the present and future "capital of the world."[1] Three years after the end of a conflict in which its citizens and arsenals had played a major role, the metropolis seemed at its zenith. Berlin was in ruins, London, bled dry, had renounced its financial supremacy, and Paris its cultural dominance. New York seemed invulnerable. Three different events that took place during the summer of 1945 attested to that, each in its own way: the spectacular accident on the morning of July 28 involving a bomber that crashed into the seventy-eighth and seventy-ninth floors of the Empire State Building, taking fourteen victims, but never threatening the solidity of the tallest symbol of New York; the gathering of two million people at Times Square on August 14 at the announcement of Japan's surrender; and a few weeks later, the crowning in Atlantic City of a young woman from the Bronx, Bess Myerson, the first Jewish Miss America in the history of the competition.

CHRONICLE OF A DECLINE . . .

For more than twenty years, the apparent omnipotence of New York dazzled most observers and New Yorkers themselves. After all, wasn't the metropolis the economic capital of the greatest postwar power? Used to the morose grayness of a devastated Europe, Simone de Beauvoir marveled at the "treasures of the Thousand and One Nights" that she discovered there. "In New York at that time, in those years right after the war," Claude Roy reminisced later, "there was in the air an electricity of victory and the winds of the future."[2]

The headquarters for the Organization of the United Nations, which was built on the shores of the East River, symbolized New York's worldwide calling. Nevertheless, the UN had almost found a home elsewhere. Throughout 1946, it had been a question of various places in the United States, from Boston to Philadelphia to San Francisco,

several New York suburbs, or Flushing Meadows, where the
1939–40 World Exposition had been held. It was thanks to
the Rockefellers that New York was finally chosen: at the
price of some 8.5 million dollars, they quickly acquired
property owned by the developer William Zeckendorf
where the New York slaughterhouses formerly lined the
East River, between Forty-second and Forty-eighth Streets;
and they offered it to the United Nations. The Rockefellers'
offer was accepted on December 14, 1946, and a few weeks
later, a group of prestigious architects, including the Brazilian Oscar Niemeyer and the Swiss Le Corbusier, met to work
under the direction of Wallace Harrison, a New Yorker. At
the end of summer 1947, the project they submitted was
approved by the United Nations General Assembly, and
work could begin. When they were completed in 1952, the
tall glass Secretariat Building, the Conference Building, and
the General Assembly Building became the political heart of
the world.

In economic matters, continuity prevailed. Small
industry still dominated New York, employing nearly a
million workers in 1950 and 900,000 in 1960. The principal industries remained garment-making and printing,
but the war years had also witnessed the formidable
growth of heavy industry to serve the national effort: in
the Brooklyn Navy Yard, the biggest in the United States,
tens of thousands of men and women built and repaired
aircraft carriers and battleships. Other enterprises adapted
their production to the needs of the moment, which
ranged from munitions to medications, like the penicillin
made in the Pfizer laboratories in Williamsburg.

The relocation of certain firms undoubtedly continued
after the war, but this decline did not worry New York officials because it had begun in the mid-nineteenth century.
Of course, the women's clothing industry in its turn began
to leave Manhattan. But the pessimism about New York's
industrial future expressed by certain experts encountered
only indifference or criticism. In a large study on the future
of the region, which paralleled the one conducted by the
Committee on the Regional Plan during the 1920s, the
economist Raymond Vernon and his collaborators sought
to draw attention to industrial decentralization, but they

were not very convincing. *Anatomy of a Metropolis*, the work that Vernon and Edgar M. Hoover published in 1959, received some publicity, as did the French geographer Jean Gottmann's *Megalopolis*. But they themselves considered New York's industrial decline to be inevitable, and they did not think it called into question the national and international domination of the metropolitan area.

For most New Yorkers, the somber predictions of the experts had little bearing, given the feeling of abundance and prosperity that contrasted so sharply with not too distant memories of the Great Depression, Twenty-five years after the exposition in 1939-40, the International Exposition of 1964-65 opened. Celebrating in its own way New York's continuing economic domination, it was organized, in theory, around the theme of "Peace through mutual understanding." The large industrial firms, like Bell, Coca-Cola, General Electric, IBM, Kodak or General Motors, who found it an excellent opportunity for advertising, each had a pavilion there. But the exposition's mastermind, Robert Moses, whose last great project it was, prompted criticism from observers who denounced its commercial character and absence of ideals.

Nevertheless, the 1964-65 World's Fair turned a page more than it hinted at the future, because it was precisely in the mid-1960s that the structural transformation of New York's economy accelerated, in the face of general circumstances that were unfavorable to the city. Paradoxically, New York actually profited very little from the international economic order established after World War II. Worse, industrial activity in the metropolis experienced a worrisome decline. Henceforth, the advantages New York offered, in terms of quick access to information especially, were not always enough to compensate for the costs of production, so much higher than elsewhere. In addition, direct and indirect imports grew enormously in the 1960s to the detriment of New York-based firms. In a few years, numerous Manhattan clothing workshops closed their doors. Brooklyn's factories and breweries followed, and even, in 1966, the Navy Yard, the pride of an entire borough. Between 1968 and 1977, 600,000 industrial jobs disappeared.

At the same time, the role of the port diminished. Its activity was now confined to the western shore of the Hudson, in New Jersey, where Newark Bay offered more available space for managing the containerized-cargo revolution. On the Manhattan and Brooklyn wharves, tens of thousands of dockers, carriers, and warehouse employees lost their jobs in the 1970s, while the decline in industrial and port activity also led to a decline in employment in railway and highway transport, and in the warehouses. For their part, some large corporations abandoned their New York locations, tempted by other cities or by the suburbs. Out of the 500 top industrial corporations in America listed by *Fortune* magazine, 136 had their headquarters in New York in 1956, 125 in 1969, and 80 in 1977. Among those that left in the years 1968–70 were such giants as American Can, PepsiCo, Shell Oil, and US Tobacco, whereas others, like Uniroyal, announced their intention of following suit.

This weakness in the New York economy went hand in hand with an increasingly uncontrolled rise in New York expenditures. The number of municipal employees and the cost of social-assistance programs grew continuously—in fact, following a tendency that began during the Great Depression, and resulting from past financial agreements between La Guardia and the federal government. In ten years, between 1958–59 and 1968–69, the municipal operations budget grew by 200%, two times more than the gross national product. And this growth still continued into the early 1970s, at a time when the city could hardly count on federal aid any longer.

The New York–Washington axis, established at the beginning of the century by Theodore Roosevelt and strengthened during the New Deal thanks to privileged ties between Franklin Roosevelt's and Fiorello LaGuardia's teams, now fell on hard times. Under the presidencies of Richard Nixon and especially Gerald Ford and Ronald Reagan, the federal government abandoned the cities, formerly coddled by the Democrats, leaving the financing of social-assistance programs largely up to them. In New York, this withdrawal proved dramatic, all the more so because strained relations between municipal and New York State authorities did not make the search for solutions any easier. To meet its obligations, the city thus resorted regularly to short-term loans between 1965 and 1975, leading to a dangerous spiral of excessive debt.

After the economic reversal of 1969–70 and the 1973 recession, which prompted a market downturn on Wall Street and a real-estate crisis, the city was on the verge of bankruptcy. Certain intellectuals, like the writer Norman Mailer who ran for mayor in 1969, spoke of the city secession from the state and its transformation into an autonomous state within the United States. The New York banks, convinced that the city no longer had the means to pay the interest on its debt, stopped supplying municipal funds. In the spring of 1975, New York's governor, Hugh Carey, created the Municipal Assistance Corporation (nicknamed, unsurprisingly, "Big Mac"), directed by the financier Felix Rohatyn, a partner of the investment bank Lazard Frères & Co. and a future ambassador to France. Under Rohatyn's leadership, "Big Mac" placed New York under its effective supervision and tried to stabilize the situation.

Nevertheless, by autumn, the city had to ask Washington for help. At first, President Ford refused to intervene and suggested that bankruptcy procedures should be initiated. The *Daily News* immediately ran the headline on October 30, 1975: "Ford to City: Drop Dead." A month later, when bankruptcy seemed inevitable, New York, Albany, and Washington reached a last-minute compromise.

. . . AND A REVIVAL

Bankruptcy avoided, New York set about putting its finances back in order. Expenditures were strictly controlled and many municipal jobs were cut. In a few years, "Big Mac" and the city succeeded in drastically reducing the city's debt and, in 1981, balancing its budget. Thanks to fairly sustained favorable economic conditions, income soon exceeded expenditures, and New York could even begin to reduce taxes. Improved city management did not create growth, but it accompanied it.

Nevertheless, the causes for the crisis in the early 1970s did not disappear altogether. For example, the industrial

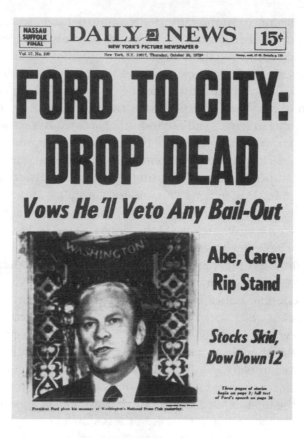

FIGURE 48
The *Daily News* headlines, October 30, 1975
© New York Daily News, L.P.; reprinted with permission

sector continued to decline during the 1980s. More precisely, hundreds of thousands of jobs were cut, but others
were created. The enterprises that survived, or new ones,
were those that knew how to take advantage of external
economics linked to New York's situation. For clothing,
furs, and jewelry, the only workshops not leaving the city
for the South or Asia were those that produced limited
lines and maintained direct ties with the fashion sector—
its designers, buyers, and distributors. Many of these benefited from renewed immigration, the traditional source
of cheap labor.

Beginning in the early 1990s, industrial activity stabilized. This equilibrium was dependent on very specialized production. As in the past, good access to information was enough to restore New York's advantage over American and foreign competition. But the city's economic renaissance over the course of the last twenty years was primarily due to service and not industrial activity. Its formidable growth at the end of the twentieth century confirmed tendencies apparent at the end of the nineteenth century, but suspended for a time during the Great Depression and the war. Thus, in the 1950s, millions of square footage of office space was renovated or created in Manhattan, where big businesses like Mobil, Seagram, and Union Carbide built new and prominent skyscrapers.

In lower Manhattan, the financier David Rockefeller, his Chase Manhattan Bank, and the developer William Zeckendorf united efforts to renovate the office districts, most of which dated back to the early part of the century. "New York," insisted Zeckendorf, "is and must be a gigantic 'national headquarters.'"[3] The Chase Manhattan Bank Tower, in 1960, was the symbol of their aspirations. Many other skyscrapers followed, for the most part constructed in the international modernist vein which had appeared in Europe during the 1920s but was slow to be explored in the United States due to the Depression. Within a few years, under the leadership of architects like Skidmore, Owings and Merrill, and Emery, Roth and Sons, lower Manhattan was covered with high steel and glass towers. The minimalist architecture of these new skyscrapers was very far removed in the end from the ideals of Gropius, Le Corbusier, or Mies van der Rohe, but, like the Lever House on Park Avenue (1950–52), they perfectly embodied the rise in power of the bureaucracies.

Beginning in 1957, David Rockefeller could rely upon the Downtown–Lower Manhattan Association, created to support his remodeling projects for lower Manhattan. If his plans failed for a large central market in the Bronx— the project's aim was to free up the space still occupied by the markets near the Hudson—and a new expressway through lower Manhattan, he successfully launched his project for a World Trade Center, two twin towers with

FIGURE 49
Model of the World Trade Center
© Keystone

more than one hundred floors, opened in 1970 and officially inaugurated three years later. The renovation of office buildings was also tied to the continual expansion of Wall Street, which led to growth for banks, stock exchange companies, and other financial intermediaries. Half the offices built after World War II went up in three years, between 1967 and 1970. No doubt supply exceeded demand since the stock market fell in the early 1970s, many finance companies merged, and some building projects launched in the good years were now open for occupancy. But recovery soon followed.

The expansion of the service sector in New York's economy never really slowed down. In the early 1980s and—after an interruption due to the 1987 stock-market crisis—throughout the 1990s, office construction continued, especially centering on large projects like the South Street Seaport, the West Side Conference Center, and the Marriott Hotel at Times Square. As the twenty-first century began, Manhattan's central business district employed more than two million people, and the metropolitan region employed some eight million, all working in the various service activities, including financial organizations, insurance companies, law offices, consulting firms, information and computer businesses, advertising agencies, and public accounting firms, indispensable to the operations of big business and administration.

Thanks to technological transformations, New York's financial service companies continued to extend their reach. In fact, New York rested upon the expansion of the global and the American economy: an international city, it profited from global competition, the technological revolution, the growing place of finance in relationship to production, the centralization of financial markets, and the growth of ever more sophisticated and innovative communications systems, like the fiber-optics networks that now served the metropolis. More than ever, multinational firms and American and foreign banks needed to open offices in New York, if only to take advantage of the liquid assets available on the New York stock markets, due especially to investments realized by pension funds. Since the 1980s, financial deregulation won for New York large sums that, in the past, had often been invested in tax havens. The city was "the major synapse in the nervous system of the world's major information flows," asserted one of those responsible for these impressive transformations.[4] Moreover, the communication industry, in the broader sense, brought together in New York the majority of the country's leading newspaper, television, and radio journalists, as well as editors and literary agents.

This vitality allowed New York financial services to diversify and grow, in significance as well as size. Conversely, insurance companies, for example, saw their relative place shrink due to the lack of innovations needed to maintain activities in New York and the prohibitive costs of administrative tasks easily performed outside the metropolis. All in all, the service sector did not escape the specialization phenomenon that affected industry. The technological revolution in communications encouraged the removal or the networking of formerly centralized tasks. Even when they did not leave New York, the central offices of large corporations employed fewer white-collar workers than in the past. It was not unusual for routine operations to be relocated, while innovative and specialized activities in legal, commercial, or financial areas gained in importance. In other words, the white-collar world gained in adaptability and flexibility what it lost in certainty.

At the same time, New York developed other services based on an unusual stock of know-how and knowledge, especially in the areas of health, education, social services, tourism, and nonprofit organizations. For the city, this was a matter of economic activity of vital importance. In the area of medicine, the range of expertise was particularly diverse. Thanks to an old tradition, financing from Medicare and Medicaid programs, public subsidies and the generosity of countless private donors, the metropolis counted tens of thousands of beds, dozens of hospitals, many highly regarded medical schools and state-of-the-art research centers—the Sloan-Kettering Institute of Memorial Hospital, for example, in cancer research, or the Mount Sinai Hospital, or the Cornell Medical Center. Likewise, in the area of higher education, the large number of New York universities attracted many hundreds of thousands of students and created tens of thousands of jobs. Columbia University, which alone employed more than 11,500 people, pumped many hundreds of millions of dollars into the New York economy each year.

The economic renewal of the 1980s and 1990s was accompanied by a resumption of all commercial and service activities, from the hotel and restaurant to the luxury-product sector, which had never been so active. Better yet, the growth of the U.S. commercial deficit during the Reagan years meant that New York saw the expansion of already spectacular port and air-freight activity. Three international airports served New York—Newark International in New Jersey, and, in Queens, La Guardia (formerly North Beach) and John F. Kennedy (called Idlewild until the early 1960s). The port saw its role expand, benefiting New Jersey, of course, where containerized cargo was unloaded, but also the city of New York, where the shipbrokers, financiers, and maritime law offices remained.

THE CITY AND THE SUBURB

The change from an industrial city to a service-sector city was accompanied by a vast transformation in the New York metropolitan region. The most spectacular sign was the growth of suburbs beginning in the 1950s. The often isolated planned communities of the nineteenth and first half of the twentieth century were replaced by countless housing developments and satellite towns. The city's limits began to disappear. These new suburbs, lacking any specific architectural originality, responded to the strong postwar demand for private homes. On Long Island, for example, in Suffolk and Nassau Counties, the population grew by more than a million people in less than a dozen years.

One of the first, and no doubt the most famous, of these mass suburbs was Levittown, a development located on Long Island twenty-five miles from New York; its developers, the brothers William and Alfred Levitt, modestly decided to name it after themselves. From the time their project was announced in 1947, their four-room houses won immense popular success, undeniably linked to their reasonable price, the relatively high quality of their construction, and the easy payment terms offered potential buyers, especially if they were war veterans. Thanks to production methods inspired by the automobile industry— William Levitt spoke of his enterprise as "the General Motors of the building industry"—Levittown soon grew to more than 17,000 houses and 82,000 inhabitants, all white, because of very effective segregation.

These suburban developments were both a cause and a consequence of the completion of a network of roads and expressways that linked New York to its suburbs, or one suburb to another. In the 1950s, highways also were opened through the Bronx and Long Island, while the new Throgs Neck Bridge stood at the confluence of the East River and Long Island Sound, between Queens and the Bronx. New York's last great bridge, the Verrazano-Narrows, joining Long Island and Staten Island, was built between 1958 and 1964. Its inauguration marked the end of the relative isolation of Staten Island, which was totally transformed within a few years by real-estate speculation.

Such undertakings, as well as postwar economic prosperity, multiplied the number of automobiles coming and going from Manhattan each day. At the instigation of the municipal traffic commissioner T. T. Wiley, New York adopted a series of measures—"alternate side of the street" parking to facilitate city street cleaning, along with more parking meters, and synchronized traffic lights. First and Second Avenues became one way streets in 1951, Fifth Avenue in 1966. All these efforts hardly made driving in Manhattan any less of a nightmare, where parking places were sorely lacking and the parking garages built in the 1950s only drew new, and uncontrollable, waves of vehicles. A sign of the system's failure: Wiley, who had been commissioner since 1949, had to resign following a huge traffic jam on December 27, 1961. New York traffic was "madness," observed the sociologist Daniel Bell.[5]

The postwar years were also a period of significant demolition and construction in New York's working-class neighborhoods. Backed by the first article in the 1949 federal housing law and the federal financing that accompanied it, Robert Moses, chairman of the New York City Slum Clearance Committee, launched ambitious "urban renewal" programs. His method consisted of privatizing public housing by entrusting to private developers the responsibilities of freeing up occupied sites, finding homes for the tenants, planning and building new housing, and choosing the new occupants.

It was no surprise that Manhattan's Lower East Side was the first target for Moses's projects: many unlivable apartment buildings were torn down to make room on the shores of the East River for several large complexes like Stuyvesant Town (a 50-acre, 18-block area of towers and buildings belonging to Metropolitan Life) between Fourteenth and Twentieth Streets, or the Lillian Wald (Sixth Street), Alfred Smith, Baruch, Corlear Hook, or Jacob Riis residential apartment buildings. In 1950, Lewis Mumford sharply attacked these new constructions in a *New Yorker* article, fearing they formed nothing but a "broken palisade of red brick."[6] But such attacks were rare, because the big complexes seemed a sign of progress in a period of very heavy demand for housing.

The Washington Square neighborhood experienced similar changes. North of the square, a real-estate owner as rich as it was discreet—Sailors' Snug Harbor, a private foundation that provided a hospital and retirement home for seamen, had several apartment buildings built on property it had owned since the nineteenth century. But Moses was to be credited (or held liable) for the most spectacular changes, which involved destroying several properties south of Washington Square and replacing them with superslabs built with the self-interested support of neighboring New York University.

In the end, Moses's policy unleashed a barrage of criticism. Despite the number of recent housing projects (nearly 100,000 dwellings between 1940 and 1960), Moses was accused of not having resolved the housing crisis and benefiting private developers at the expense of the common good. His policies were also blamed for destroying the life of various neighborhoods by requiring major population shifts, as in Bay Ridge, for example, where thousands of Brooklynites were displaced by the construction of the Verrazano Bridge. They were criticized as well for creating huge complexes in which living conditions rapidly deteriorated. The 1961 publication of Jane Jacobs's book, *The Death and Life of Great American Cities*, gave substance to these criticisms and marked a turning point.

Under pressure from neighborhood associations, Robert Moses was forced to abandon his plans for surgically transforming the West Side; he lost the battle for renovating the West Village, won after a tough fight in the autumn of 1961

by Jane Jacobs and other residents determined not to relinquish their neighborhood to cranes and excavators; and he
failed to convince the public of the need to open an east-
west expressway through lower Manhattan, connecting
the Holland Tunnel to the Manhattan and Williamsburg
Bridges on the East River. The idea for this Lower Manhattan Expressway originated in the 1929 *Regional Plan of New
York and Its Environs*. It was approved in 1940 by La Guardia
and remained alive for almost thirty years. But it came
under severe attack in the early 1960s—according to Jane
Jacobs, its construction "would Los Angelize New York"[7]—
and was abandoned for good in 1969.

Due partly to the decline of the railroad, Pennsylvania
Station—one of the crown jewels of imperial architecture
at the beginning of the century—was demolished in 1963.
But its loss and its replacement by a very banal Madison
Square Garden Center shocked many New Yorkers into
mobilizing to better protect the architectural heritage of
their city. Symbolically, Moses quit most of his positions in
May 1960, with the exception of the presidency of the
1964 World's Fair and the chairmanship of the Triborough
Authority, which he relinquished in 1968 when he retired,
though he remained active as a consultant.

The 1960s also saw a decline in low-rent public-housing
programs. The new apartment building projects, whether
entirely private or partially financed through public funds,
were carried out by private developers or by organizations
like the United Housing Foundation, a consortium of
unions. The end of the decade was marked by the initiatives to rehabilitate neighborhoods in difficulty, especially
those inhabited by blacks and Puerto Ricans. Thanks to
Senator Robert Kennedy, the Bedford-Stuyvesant neighborhood benefited from substantial private, federal, and
municipal financial support in 1967, and soon a shopping
center, a computer-equipment factory and several social
services were in operation there. Also, between 1966 and
1974, New York participated in the federal program for
"model cities," thus securing for itself a certain level of
funding.

From the early 1970s, the New York urban landscapes
continued to differentiate themselves. During the crisis that

struck the city, many construction programs were halted and the real-estate market collapsed in poor neighborhoods, henceforth mostly inhabited by Afro- and Latino-Americans. These included the South Bronx, the extreme north of Manhattan, the Lower East Side, and certain parts of Brooklyn. The South Bronx, the setting for Tom Wolfe's *Bonfire of the Vanities*, became the symbol for urban decay.

At the same time, New York urban infrastructures, rarely and poorly maintained since the end of Fiorello LaGuardia's mayoralty, deteriorated rapidly, the subway in particular, even though the price of a token went from a nickel to a dime to fifteen cents in only a few years, and a $500 million improvement plan had been adopted. A project for a new line running the length of Second Avenue, launched in 1970, had to be abandoned in 1974 at the height of the urban crisis. As for other infrastructures, they were in no better shape, even though the Brooklyn Bridge was renovated beginning in 1950. The water and sanitation systems dated back to 1900–1920 for the most part, and their maintenance left much to be desired. The holes in the roads—the famous "potholes"—were legion. An alarming and spectacular sign of New York's infrastructural decay was the collapse of a section of the West Side Highway in 1973.

At the same time, however, and for the first time in New York's history, many preservation and renewal programs were aimed at preventing the complete disappearance of buildings associated with the city's identity. They were financed privately, but they benefited from fiscal measures. A certain number of old residential buildings were renovated, and industrial spaces were transformed into housing. The results were contradictory, however: although they helped to halt the decline of certain neighborhoods in Manhattan and Brooklyn, they primarily benefited wealthier New Yorkers.

SoHo (SOuth of HOuston) is the best example of this. After barely escaping total destruction as part of the lower Manhattan expressway project, the neighborhood attracted artists' studios, galleries, restaurants, residences, and boutiques in the 1960s and 1970s—perhaps a more productive grouping than the industrial workshops of the past. In

1971, artists were officially authorized to live in SoHo, a district restricted to industrial activities by zoning regulations. Two years later, many cast-iron buildings were officially protected by the creation of the SoHo historic district. Henceforth fashionable, SoHo became one of the most chic neighborhoods in Manhattan.

Throughout New York, thousands of tenant, apartment-building, and neighborhood associations were formed. About fifty community councils, composed of members named by the presidents of the five New York boroughs, directed budget priorities and policies for using space. In the context of the economic revival that New York experienced beginning in the early 1980s, the most effective of these councils, soon nicknamed "little city halls," came from the middle-class neighborhoods. Indeed, for the last two decades, New York's neighborhoods have evolved differently according to the ups and downs of the local economy. The areas directly or indirectly connected to the impressive growth of the service sector benefited greatly from it—as suggested by the many conversions of industrial buildings into luxury apartments in SoHo or Chelsea, the renovations of Victorian brownstones in Brooklyn Heights, and the new buildings on the Upper West Side. Even in Harlem, the Sugar Hill neighborhood north of One Hundred and Forty-fifth Street was transformed, beginning in the early 1990s, thanks to restoration efforts launched by African-Americans, often professionals, who profited from the newfound growth and prosperity. Conversely, the areas of New York without ties to the "global village" continued to decline.

THE CITY'S PULSE

New York landscapes are inseparable from its population. But in this matter, the figures are deceiving. Certainly they indicate that, for the first time in its history, the city ceased to grow significantly, stagnating between seven and eight million people between 1940 and 2000. During these decades, Manhattan and Brooklyn lost 360,000 and 240,000 residents respectively, the Queens population leveled off in 1970, before gaining almost 300,000 new residents during the 1990s, and the Bronx remained in 2000 at its 1940 level; only modest little Staten Island saw its population grow between 1940 and 1990, from 174,000 to 443,000 residents. Thus while Manhattan's population was at its peak in 1910, Brooklyn's in 1950, and the Bronx's in 1970, Queens and Staten Island reached their peak in 2000.

The limited growth of New York City was not synonymous with languor. In fact, it masks the importance of departures and arrivals, powerful diastolic and systolic movements that balanced each other long before departures gained the upper hand in the 1970s—when New York lost ten percent of its population, a portion of which was regained in the 1980s before the city added another ten percent in the 1990s. Furthermore, it ignores the uninterrupted growth of the New York metropolitan area, and most importantly, it does not take into account the evolution of the New York population.

Most of those who left New York after mid-century were white. The new arrivals were essentially blacks or Puerto Ricans in the 1940s to 1970s, and immigrants from Asia, Latin America, and the Caribbean from 1970 on. Thus the majority were not European, even if, in the postwar years, hundreds of thousands of Europeans—survivors of the Holocaust, people displaced by the Cold War or more traditional economic immigrants—also settled in New York, where, for example, a major Hasidic Jewish community developed.

It was the conjunction of the attraction to New York, agricultural and demographic changes in Puerto Rico, and a direct air connection between San Juan and New York that prompted the Puerto Rican great migration and the spectacular increase in the presence of islanders in New York. The Puerto Rican population leaped from 60,000 to 254,000 between 1940 and 1950, and exceeded 600,000 in 1960. As in the past, they willingly took up residence in East Harlem's El Barrio, Washington Heights, or the south Bronx, as well as Brooklyn. Likewise in the 1950s, New York became the first American city to number a million blacks, the effect of natural population growth and immigration from the South. Blacks constituted 13 percent of the population in 1960 and 20 percent in 1970. For the most part, they lived in Harlem, Bedford-Stuyvesant, Crown Heights, Brownsville, and certain neighborhoods in Queens and the Bronx.

Beginning in the late 1960s, New York drew an increasingly more significant proportion of immigrants, who could enter the United States more easily because of a new immigration law adopted by Congress in 1965. The effects of this measure were unexpected and considerable: the metropolis once again became a city of immigrants and regained the heterogeneity it had lost somewhat since the 1930 implementation of laws adopted a few years earlier, limiting immigration through quotas. Unlike the early part of the twentieth century, migrants came from the West Indies, Latin America, and Asia, but also still Europe, with Jews arriving from Russia, as well as Italians, Polish, and Irish. The major groups in decreasing order were Dominicans, Jamaicans, Chinese, Haitians, and Italians, not to mention immigrants from Trinidad and Tobago, Colombia and Ecuador, and also the Soviet Union. Conversely, the migratory flow from Puerto Rico slackened and the relative proportion of Puerto Ricans diminished, both in terms of the total population and the number of New York immigrants from the West Indies.

All these immigrants embodied in their own way the economic globalization of which New York was the center. They were drawn by the employment possibilities that the city seemed to harbor and by the networks of families, friends, or associates that constituted so many migratory links between their countries and the shores of the Hudson. As the sociologist Nathan Glazer noted, "Whatever the changes that were affecting New York for the worse in the 1970s, to the immigrant it was still apparently the city of opportunity."[8] In addition to immigrants who left their countries for purely economic reasons, there were Russian Jews, Dominicans and Haitians who were fleeing Soviet anti-Semitism or the dictatorial regimes of Rafael Trujillo and his successors, and François Duvalier and his son

Jean-Claude. All in all, more than a million foreigners settled in New York after 1965.

The large number of new arrivals came to curb the demographic decline and redesign the metropolis's social geography. New York was now a city of minorities, but no one group dominated the others. In 1970, New York counted 7.9 million inhabitants, 63 percent of whom were white, 19 percent black, 16 percent Latin American (of which nearly two-thirds was Puerto Rican) and one percent Asian immigrants. Thirty years later, among the 8 million residents, 35 percent were white non-Hispanic, 24.5 percent were black (a third of whom were foreign-born), 27 percent Latin American (less than a third of whom were Puerto Rican) and 9.8 percent Asian.

Unlike their predecessors, immigrants in the 1970–1990s avoided Manhattan and settled directly in Brooklyn, Queens, Staten Island or the New York suburbs. Thus new ethnic enclaves were formed: Crown Heights and East Flatbush became West Indian centers, Washington Heights a partly Dominican neighborhood; Flushing and Sunset Park accommodated Chinese immigrants, Chinatown expanded, and the mass arrival of Russian Jews gave Brighton Beach, soon nicknamed "Little Odessa," a certain renewed vitality. Another form of segregation then evolved, since Asian immigrants could often settle wherever they liked, and that was not the case with Afro-American or West Indian Blacks or with Latin American immigrants. On the contrary, areas like Canarsie or Howard Beach, on Brooklyn's Atlantic coast, remained white strongholds.

The massive decline in New York's white population was one of the consequences of the weakening of the working class that had been the backbone of whole districts in the Bronx, Brooklyn, and Manhattan until the 1950s. A half century later, the white population consisted mostly of professionals or constituted the city's middle- and upper-level management. Blacks and Puerto Ricans, women in particular, occupied intermediate-level jobs in the service sector, while newly arrived immigrants from Asia, Latin America and the Caribbean largely found less skilled and less well-paid positions, from

restaurant dishwashers to car and floor cleaners to hospital and apartment-building employees. Others began specialized small businesses—Korean groceries, Chinese
restaurants, Asian newspaper stands, or West Indian taxi
services. And finally, many new immigrants, a large portion of them Asian or Latin American women, found
poorly paid work in the industrial sector that had survived closings and relocations—in the clothing or leather
industries, for example.

Thus, unlike certain highly qualified immigrants coming from Asian countries, Afro-American and West Indian
blacks and Latin American immigrants found themselves
excluded once again from most of the best-paying jobs
in the postindustrial economy, just as African-Americans
had been excluded from industrial jobs during the period
when such work led to a rise in social status. But a portion
of the black population and, to a lesser extent, the Latin
American population certainly saw the situation improve.
Some were able to get public-sector jobs, and a small
middle class of managers and businessmen formed. Economic and social disparities continued to grow throughout the 1980s and 1990s, however, because significant
increased wealth for some (tied especially to stock-market
speculation) and moderate gains for others were accompanied by growing poverty for all those excluded from the
economic system—as evidenced by the spectacular rise in
New York's homeless population and the reemergence of
tuberculosis.

The social and demographic reconfigurations that New
York experienced did not come about without difficulties,
first of all between the white population and blacks or
Puerto Ricans. During the summer of 1959, *Newsweek*
stressed the seriousness of racial tensions in a special
report, "Metropolis in a Mess," that described an incident
that had taken place a few days earlier. A drunken Puerto
Rican woman had provoked a scandal in a Harlem restaurant, and her arrest by two white police officers led to an
altercation with a passing black man that degenerated
into the beginning of a race riot. The affair came to a halt
thanks to the intervention of Sugar Ray Robinson, the
boxing champion, but the next day the New York Police

Commissioner, Stephan Kennedy, tactlessly declared that a race riot "would be more destructive than an A bomb." *Newsweek* seized upon the affair and concluded from it, "This is New York City, the world's greatest metropolis, the cultural center of the United States—and yet, so turbulent, so fraught with tensions, that a drunken woman in a Harlem restaurant can be compared to the trigger of an atomic bomb."[9]

Five years later, in the summer of 1964, the anticipated riots broke out, following the death of a young black killed in Harlem by a police officer on July 16. In Harlem, Bedford-Stuyvesant and Brooklyn, demonstrations multiplied, resulting in more than 140 injuries and leading to more than 500 arrests. Beginning in 1965, the War on Poverty launched by President Lyndon B. Johnson, combined with costly but effective efforts by the new New York mayor, the liberal Republican John Lindsay, partially defused economic and racial tensions. New York remained calm while the Watts district in Los Angeles erupted in 1965, and while racial violence broke out in many cities, notably Newark, in the summer of 1967.

After 1970, these racial tensions were accompanied by others, setting blacks, Puerto Ricans, and recent immigrants groups against each other. The growing inequality among New Yorkers during the 1980s exacerbated these difficulties. Racial incidents increased: one young black, Michael Griffith, was killed by white teenagers at Howard Beach in 1986, and another one, Yusuf Hawkins, in Bensonhurst in 1989. In the summer of 1991, a young West Indian child, Garin Cato, was run over and killed in the Crown Heights neighborhood in Brooklyn by a car driven by an Orthodox Jew. The incident provoked a riot that resulted in a second death, of a visiting Hasidic Jew from Melbourne, Australia, Yankel Rosenbaum. Other conflicts, like those that set Korean grocers and African-Americans against each other in some neighborhoods, were largely the result of economic rivalries.

Despite these moments of crisis, immigrants "New Yorkized."[10] Each group and even each individual adapted to New York life, but neither groups nor individuals abandoned their traditional structures, whether familial or reli-

FIGURE 50
Racial riots in Harlem (July 22, 1964)
© Keystone

gious, much less their eating habits. Integrating new arrivals into the metropolis was once again the order of the day, even though it had taken a back seat from 1930 to 1970, when America had closed its doors to immigration candidates.

COALITIONS AND RECONFIGURATIONS

Half a century of such profound changes in the place of blacks and immigrants in New York had overturned the rules of the political game.

Within a few months of each other, World War II and Fiorello La Guardia's third and final term as mayor came to an end. The mayor's seat seemed within the Democrats' grasp, as long as they managed to rebuild the coalition that had assembled Irish and Jewish voters at the beginning of the century. They were a strong force, but that assumed that the paid Tammany Hall officials did not give in to the temptation of corruption, because the memory of scandals from the Walker era and the electoral disaffection that had followed and led to La Guardia's victory in 1933 were still fresh in everyone's mind.

The lesson was well understood by William O'Dwyer. Born in Ireland, O'Dwyer migrated to New York in 1910 at the age of twenty, and studied law after trying his hand at various occupations, including police officer. Honest and competent, he was elected Brooklyn's District Attorney in 1939, before challenging La Guardia unsuccessfully in the 1941 municipal elections. He distinguished himself during the war and won over Jewish and Irish voters upon his return, as well as a significant portion of blacks and Italians. After years of exile, Tammany happily returned to City Hall in 1945.

But the joy of those who were part of the Democratic machine was short-lived. Over the course of the next fifteen years, and despite the presence of an able leader, Carmine DeSapio, the first Italian to win this post, Tammany's hold over New York politics continued to weaken. Its loss of influence was due, to a large extent, to the aspirations of a new generation of Jewish politicians, who were no longer content to play a secondary role in municipal affairs. Mobilized to support successive White House candidacies by the progressive Democrat Adlai Stevenson in 1952 and 1956, they organized themselves locally within political circles and associations, and demanded reforms. Recognizing the danger, DeSapio championed more progressive positions than in the past. Thus the 1953 and 1957 municipal elections witnessed the victory of Democrat Robert F. Wagner, Jr., son of the well-known New Deal senator Robert F. Wagner, Sr.

But in the early 1960s, the coalition fell apart. Black New Yorkers, rallying around the very charismatic Adam Clayton Powell, demanded greater political recognition, while the former state governor, the Liberal party candidate Herbert Lehman, decided to rely on the support of reformist circles. All this led Wagner to announce his break with Tammany Hall on February 3, 1961, and his desire to see DeSapio step down. In the fall, Wagner won the Democratic primary election against the Tammany candidate, and then, with the support of the Liberal party, the municipal election in November 1961. The votes he garnered came especially from New York Jews, African-Americans, and Puerto Ricans, as well as the liberal contingent of the Irish electorate. Utterly humiliated, DeSapio was beaten in his own Greenwich Village district. That was the end of Tammany Hall, and of the historic alliance between Irish conservatives and Jewish liberals within the Democratic party.

A new period began in the political history of New York. Marked by a new coalition primarily made up of Jews, blacks, and Puerto Ricans, the municipality was bound together by a shared liberal ideology and a deep attachment to the civil rights movement, then at its height throughout the country. Moreover, during the 1965 and 1969 municipal elections, liberal voters did not hesitate to form an alliance with their former adversaries to bring to power a Republican, John Lindsay, who seemed to better embody their ideals than his Democratic opponents, Abraham Beame and Mario Procaccino.

But this liberal moment was as brief as it was eventful. The social and racial unrest that New York experienced at the time, notably the huge transportation strike in 1966 and the teachers' strike in 1968, as well as demonstrations against the Vietnam War, the bad economic situation, and especially the radicalization of the civil rights movement contributed to a growing rift between blacks and Jews. Lindsay's concern for expanding minority participation was certainly manifested in the election of a black, Percy Sutton, and a Puerto Rican, Herman Badillo, to the head of the Manhattan and Brooklyn boroughs, and in the establishment of community development programs. But the mayor's blatant support for blacks distanced many white voters and municipal employees. In particular, many New York Jews then abandoned the camp of those they characterized as "limousine liberals" and drew closer to the conservatives. The coalition of the past gave way to racial polarization. In the 1969 municipal elections, Lindsay was reelected by a narrow margin, with 40 percent of the vote, but his two conservative opponents together won 60 percent of the vote.

The municipal elections in the 1970s witnessed the

victory of conservative Jewish candidates. Elected in 1973 with the votes of Catholics and Jews against Herman Badillo, who was supported by blacks and Puerto Ricans, Abraham Beame became New York's first Jewish mayor, and also the one in charge of the city during the 1975 fiscal crisis, after having been the city's top financial authority for years. Subsequently, his political career never recovered, especially since a spectacular general power outage in July 1977, and the looting that followed in black neighborhoods, confirmed the impression that Beame was not equal to the task.

In the fall of 1977, it was a Democrat—a former liberal and now a conservative, Edward Koch, the son of Jewish garment workers, who became mayor. He won the Democratic primary, defeating Mario Cuomo, the Democratic lieutenant governor of New York State, the Liberal candidate Bella Abzug, and representatives of the black and Puerto Rican minorities, Percy Sutton and Herman Badillo. Wanting to accommodate his old and new friends, Koch rapidly decided to abandon Manhattan liberals and rely especially on the support of conservative white voters from Brooklyn, Queens, and Staten Island of Jewish, Italian, or Irish origin. He also cultivated the business circles— the David Rockefellers and Donald Trumps—whom he counted upon to rectify New York's economic situation. Koch was energetic, skillful and personable. Very popular, he was reelected in 1981, with the combined support of Republicans and Democrats, and by three quarters of the New York electorate; and he easily won a third term in 1985.

Nevertheless, in a city where blacks, West Indian immigrants, Latin Americans and Asians were more and more numerous, the coalition that had formed around Ed Koch was very fragile. Blacks and liberals, some of whom had voted for him because of his liberal past, became increasingly alienated. The mayor seemed worn out by his position of power and weakened by the scandals and corruption that involved some of his close associates. In 1989, the outgoing mayor was beaten in the Democratic primary by Manhattan's borough president, David Dinkins, who, on November 7, became the first black mayor of

New York. Dinkins was elected by an extremely slim margin over Republican Rudolph Giuliani. His success, thanks to the minorities and the indispensable support of the Jewish and Catholic electorate's liberal contingent, demonstrated that black and Latin American voters had growing clout in New York politics, even if, in order to win, minority candidates had to depend upon their capacity to build alliances with a portion of the white voters.

In 1993 and 1997, Giuliani's victory did not undermine the formula: even while relying on conservative voters who had long supported Koch, Giuliani attracted a fraction of the minority vote large enough to win. Victory continued to depend upon elaborate compromises by candidates to resolve the dual tensions of ideology (between liberals and conservatives) and race that permeated the city.

NEW YORK IN 2000

At the dawn of the twenty-first century, twenty-five years after barely avoiding bankruptcy and experiencing a painful economic reconversion crisis, New York presented a dynamic image. Unemployment was at its lowest, Wall Street was experiencing the longest period of growth in its history, crime had declined, and the optimism of New Yorkers seemed to have returned. Better yet, over the course of the last quarter century, New York had found the intellectual, human, and financial resources—despite the 1987 stock-market crash—to redefine its place in the global economy. No doubt this glowing report must be qualified by noting the rise in social inequalities, racism, tensions between communities, and police violence encouraged by the authoritarian politics of Mayor Giuliani. Still, "the city feels more livable than it did twenty-five years ago," noted one observer. "It has managed to outlive its own death."[11]

10

NEW YORK, NEW YORK!

The December 28, 1944 premiere of *A Day in New York* at the Adelphi theater on Fifty-fourth Street was a triumphant success. The next day in the *New York Times*, Lewis Nichols gave an enthusiastic review of this musical that recounts the New York adventures of three sailors on a spree during a brief leave, from the Brooklyn Navy Yard to Times Square, from the subway to the museum, from Manhattan to Coney Island.

A Day in New York had a run of 436 shows, and in 1949 Metro-Goldwin-Mayer made it into a film (*On the Town*) with Gene Kelly and Frank Sinatra. For the first time on a Broadway stage, blacks and whites danced side by side. Even more than the quality of Leonard Bernstein's music or Jerome Robbins's choreography or Betty Comden and Adolph Green's libretto, the success of the show, intense and full of humor as it was, came from the way in which it conveyed New York's magnetic attraction.

Like the characters who break into the famous song, *New York, New York*, America and the world felt the irresistible magnetism of the metropolis on the shores of the Hudson. New York was collecting the dividends from the cultural and artistic investments it had made between the wars. Painters and intellectuals, choreographers and writers, architects and directors, actors and composers, journalists and fashion designers, dancers and musicians gave it an exceptional creative intensity.

THE NEW YORK MAGNET

Greenwich Village regained its bohemian atmosphere in the 1940s. Its bars and studios were frequented by the New York School painters—Jackson Pollock, Mark Rothko, Willem De Kooning, Claes Oldenburg, Franz Kline, Arshile Gorky, Robert Motherwell, and others. Even though they were dubbed abstract expressionists, they did not constitute a true "school" or movement and strongly defended individualism in art.

Nevertheless, they had things in common. To varying degrees, all of them had been influenced by European artists exiled to the United States, and particularly the surrealists like Dali, Breton, Tanguy, or Masson. All of them were also indebted to the New Deal's Federal Art Project, which had drawn them to New York. They were strongly supported by the critics Clement Greenberg and Harold Rosenberg, who were very aware of the cultural and aesthetic stakes set by their painting, and again by the director of the Museum of Modern Art, Alfred Barr, who acquired their works.

Reacting against the social realism of the Depression years, they claimed a kind of cosmopolitan modernity that they conveyed in an abstract language. In 1943, Peggy Guggenheim's very new gallery, Art of This Century, sponsored the first show of works by Jackson Pollock, who was quickly nicknamed "Jack the Dripper" because of his poured-paint technique. Success was immediate, for the gallery owner as well as the artist. "Is he the greatest living painter in the United States?" asked a 1949 article in *Life*. Within a few years, Pollock's running paint, Mark Rothko's colored rectangles, the works of Kline, and many others made New York the capital of modern painting.

The quest for modernity was taken up again by the poets John Ashbery and Frank O'Hara. Both of them tried to seize the movement and the rhythm of New York in the manner of the painters, earning them the same label of New York School. "The most interesting experiments were being done in painting and therefore one wanted to keep up with them if only to have an example of what one might try to do in one's own art," Ashbery willingly acknowledged.[1] The composer John Cage, famous in the 1940s for his *Sonatas and Interludes for Prepared Piano*, soon launched into musical experimentations like the memorable silent piece from 1952, *4'33"*. The choreographers Merce Cunningham and Paul Taylor also opted for abstraction. Breaking with the trend embodied by Martha Graham, they proclaimed a modernity that was supposed to explore the depths of the soul.

As for the jazzmen of the 1940s, they moved away from the prewar swing of the big bands, and invented be-bop, which was more reflective and introspective. The saxophonist Charlie "Bird" Parker, the trumpet player Dizzy Gillespie, the pianist Thelonious Monk, and others met up at Minton's and at Monroe's in Harlem, at the Royal Roost, the Village Vanguard, the Five Spot, and of course at Birdland, which opened on Broadway in 1949. From there, within a few years, be-bop invaded Fifty-second Street, *the* street for New York jazz. Miles Davis was making his debut then, and already his or John Coltrane's *cool jazz* was on its way.

In literature, where the modernist temptation was nothing new, the claim for a marginal position and the quest for a subject came back into play—contrary to Dos Passos and the modernists of the 1920s, who tried to eliminate all provincialism. The protagonist was no longer New York, as in *Manhattan Transfer*, but New Yorkers—at least certain New Yorkers. The feeling of exclusion and of being different was often a dominant theme among Jewish writers, from Alfred Kazin to Bernard Malamud, including a visitor who passed through in the 1950s, Saul Bellow, a Canadian from Chicago. All these authors were marked by their families' immigrant experience and by the Holocaust. Malamud let Yiddish flow into his collection of short stories, *The Magic Barrel*; Grace Paley described the Lower East Side before the war in *The Little Disturbances of Man*. Kazin, the author of a history of American literature, *On Native Grounds* (1942), and many volumes of memoirs, retraced his childhood in *Return to Brooklyn* (1951): "We

FIGURE 51
Jazz musicians performing at Birdland
© Bettmann/CORBIS

were the end of the line. We were the children of immigrants who had camped at the doors of the city, in New York's toughest, most remote, most mediocre ghetto. . . . They were New York, the Gentiles, America; we were Brownsville—*Brunsvil*, as the old people said." New York was a foreign city that had to be made one's own. But the gulf often seemed unbridgeable. "One of the longest journeys in the world is the journey from Brooklyn to Manhattan," remarked Norman Podheretz.

No doubt it was even a longer journey to arrive at the heart of New York coming from James Baldwin's Harlem (*Go Tell It on the Mountain*, 1953) or Paule Marshall's Brooklyn (*Brown Girl, Brownstones*, 1959). In his 1952 novel, *Invisible Man*, Ralph Ellison made New York the background for an inner education. Black writers struggled against their culture's lack of recognition, all of them claiming a heritage, cultural values, and autonomy, and expressing their desire to resist oppression and segregation. Baldwin, Ellison, and Marshall were inspired by the African-American experience of New York in their own time, a variation on the course set by the writers of the Harlem Renaissance twenty-five years earlier.

The various literary and artistic debates also rejected the modernist trends that had prevailed before the Second World War. In 1951, J. D. Salinger's *Catcher in the Rye* demonstrated, *sotto voce*, a kind of existential malaise embodied in its main character, Holden Caulfield. More overtly rebellious, the "Beat" movement appeared in the 1940s at Columbia University, where Jack Kerouac, Allen Ginsberg, and William Burroughs were then studying. Rejecting conventions, conformity, and materialism, the Beats were attracted by mysticism and Zen Buddhism, and fascinated by experiences of the extreme, whether it was a matter of sexuality or drugs. The "Beat Generation," whose advent the critic John Clellon Holmes proclaimed in the *New York Times Magazine* in 1952, was not a "lost generation," despite its instinctive individuality and defiance of the norm.[2]

New York was long its preferred place. As the new bohemians, the Beats took over in their turn the lofts, cafés, bookstores. and clubs in the Village. Kerouac published *The Town and the City* in 1950; Burroughs published *Junky* three years later. The White Horse Tavern, the Five Spot, and many other places hosted poetry readings and musical or literary jam sessions. The metropolis lent itself to all their experimentations, including a proclaimed return to authenticity manifested, in 1955, in Ginsberg's poem, "Howl."

The Beats made it onto *Life*'s front cover in 1959. They were part of a wider movement aimed at rediscovering creative spontaneity in all artistic domains. On the New York scene, the off-off-Broadway movement sparked enthusiasm, centering on Stella Adler, the high priestess of the Stanislavski method, as well as the Actors' Studio, a drama school founded in 1947 and directed by Lee Strasberg beginning in 1951. Julian Beck's and Judith Malina's Living Theater, also created in 1947 and established in the

heart of the Village, quickly abandoned the classic reper-
toire to launch avant-garde plays instead. Ten years later,
the photographer Robert Frank and the painter Alfred
Leslie inaugurated the "new American cinema" in their
film, *Pull My Daisy*, devoted to the Beats, with Kerouac,
Ginsberg, Gregory Corso, and Peter Orlovsky in a New
York loft. Finally, in the mid-1950s, the painters Robert
Rauschenberg and Jasper Johns reacted against abstract
expressionism. Their collages and compositions, inspired
by the work of Marcel Duchamp, who lived in New York
from 1956 to 1967, reflected their vision of a paradoxical
city where superimpositions abounded.

LIBERALISM AND ANTICOMMUNISM

In comparison with this incredible ferment, the city's
intellectual life seemed just as rich, but less diffuse. It was
dominated by those Irving Howe, in 1968, would dub
"New York intellectuals"—in fact, a group with quite
fluid boundaries, who expressed themselves just as much
in the universities as in the intellectual reviews. They
considered themselves first of all as the theoreticians of a
liberal, anticommunist, and consensual moment. This
was "the end of ideologies," announced one of them, the
sociologist Daniel Bell, in 1960. This was a long way from
the prewar years when New York was "the most interesting part of the Soviet Union," according to the critic
Lionel Abel.[3]

When the icy climate of McCarthyism took hold, many
intellectuals, distancing themselves from the left and the
Marxism of their youth, discovered that they belonged to
a shared American culture. The impression of alienation
disappeared. Intellectuals ceased "considering themselves
rebels and exiles," wrote the *Partisan Review* in 1952.

For the most part, these intellectuals were the children
of Jewish immigrants, and their feeling of belonging to
the American scene was also tied to the decline of anti-
Semitism in the wake of the Holocaust. Henceforth, New
York universities recruited many Jewish professors, in stark
contrast with their prewar inclinations. One of the greatest figures at Columbia was Lionel Trilling, the first Jew

appointed instructor in English in 1939, thanks to the urgent intervention of the university president against the advice of many of his colleagues. Abandoning the policy of quotas also opened doors much more widely than in the past to Jewish students who wanted to pursue law, medicine, arts and letters, or the sciences.

The symposium "Our Country and Our Culture," organized by the *Partisan Review* in 1952, marked the renunciation of social criticism by many intellectuals. Affirmation replaced protestation, noted *Time* magazine in 1956, in an issue devoted to intellectual life in the United States.

At Columbia, New York University, and the New School for Social Research, this mind-set was conveyed in new trends in sociology, history, literary studies, and political science. The historian Richard Hofstadter set out to examine "the common climate of American opinion" in a study of the political tradition in the United States that would soon become a classic.[4] Sociologists Daniel Bell and Nathan Glazer pursued their interest in social status. Lionel Trilling described the intellectual and political itinerary of his generation in a 1947 novel, *The Middle of the Journey*. Three years later, in *The Liberal Imagination*, which enjoyed considerable success, he underlined the literary stakes of this evolution.

During these cold war years, the consensus seemed fairly general regarding the virtues of the United States and its role in "defending the free world." General MacArthur, dismissed by President Truman for insubordination during the Korean War, was given an enthusiastic reception by millions of New Yorkers in April 1951. In reality however, these new liberals were divided. The major fault line appeared in their attitudes toward communism. The most virulent anticommunists, often coming from the postwar communist left itself, began to mobilize in the 1940s. In 1951, they assembled within the American Committee for Cultural Freedom, founded by the philosopher James Burnham, the writer James T. Farrell, the historian Arthur Schlesinger, and the philosopher Sidney Hook. Liberals such as Daniel Bell, Diana Trilling, Irving Kristol, William

FIGURE 52
Parade and confetti on Broadway: New York welcomes
General MacArthur (April 1951). © L'Illustration/Keystone

Phillips (of the *Partisan Review*) or Elliot Cohen (of *Commentary*) occupied important positions, side by side with true conservatives like Burnham or Farrell.

United by their fear of communism, they wanted to fight against what they perceived as an anti-American conspiracy. But few embraced the extremist positions of Senator Joseph McCarthy, denounced by Hofstadter a few years later in a brilliant essay on *The Paranoid Style in American*

Politics. Considering the excesses of McCarthyism a threat to the liberalism of which they deemed themselves the guardians, most of them attempted with difficulty to define an anticommunism that was not anti-intellectual.

The president of the American Committee for Cultural Freedom was Sidney Hook, a professor at New York University, whose path reflected that of many intellectuals of his generation. A former student of John Dewey at Columbia, where he wrote his doctoral thesis on the metaphysics of pragmatism, Hook was an expert on Marxism. He had put an end to his difficult association with the communists in the early 1930s, and then moved closer to Trotskyism. After the Moscow trials, he gradually abandoned his Marxist positions and became one of the most militant spokesmen for anticommunism. In 1953, Hook published an essay explicitly entitled, *Heresy, Yes—Conspiracy, No.* "Heresy"—the right of an American to publicly state ideas contrary to those of the majority—seemed to him a matter of the freedom of expression guaranteed by the First Amendment to the Constitution, but conspiracy—any secret movement seeking to subvert society, such as communism for a start—must be fought.

Suspicion ruled the day. A veritable witch-hunt unfolded in New York. In 1949, the Alger Hiss affair made big headlines: a journalist, Whittaker Chambers, formerly a communist, testified before the House Un-American Activities Committee (HUAC) that he had had access in the 1930s to confidential documents belonging to the State Department. His informer, he said, was Alger Hiss, who had since become a high government official and a diplomat, and who presided over the Carnegie Endowment for International Peace. Implicated, Hiss denied all ties with Chambers, but his explanations were contradictory. At the end of his trial in New York, Hiss was sentenced to five years in prison for false testimony. The affair confirmed, if there was still any doubt, that the anticommunists meant to act on what they said. In the summer of 1950, two New Yorkers, Julius and Ethel Rosenberg, were arrested for spying for the Soviet Union, and then tried and condemned to death. They were executed at the New York State Prison at Sing

Sing on June 19, 1953, despite the support they received from around the world.

It was in this tense climate that Sidney Hook, in that same year of 1953, called for the dismissal of teachers from the city schools who invoked the Fifth Amendment—"No person shall be compelled, in any criminal case, to be a witness against himself"—in refusing to respond to questions about their alleged ties with the Communist Party. Twenty-four teachers were dismissed; another thirty or so resigned.

In this context, few New York liberals continued to defend free speech against Senator McCarthy and his chief collaborator, the New York lawyer Roy Cohn. At Columbia, the historian Henry Steele Commager tried to do so, and incurred vicious attacks from Sidney Hook and Irving Kristol, who accused him of exhibiting a naive and morally misplaced sympathy toward communism and thus playing indirectly into McCarthy's hands. The philosopher Hannah Arendt, who had lived in New York with her husband Heinrich Blücher since 1942, and who had examined *The Origins of Totalitarianism* in 1951, reiterated that the American democracy could not with impunity resort to totalitarian ways of doing things. "The United States, this republic, the democracy in which we live, is a living thing that cannot be either contemplated or categorized, as the image of a totally invented thing can be: democracy cannot invent itself," warned Arendt courageously in a review of *Witness*, the autobiography of Whittaker Chambers, Alger Hiss's accuser. "As a living thing, dissension belongs to it as much as consensus . . . If you try to "render America more American" or make it into a model of democracy according to a preconceived idea, you can only destroy it."[5]

All these debates nurtured numerous critical reviews—Philip Rahv's and William Phillips's *Partisan Review*, or *Commentary*, launched immediately after the war by the American Jewish Committee and edited by Elliot Cohen. New York was also one of the hot spots for harsh conservative criticism of the pervasive liberalism. In 1955, William F. Buckley founded his *National Review* there; it quickly became one of the principal organs of conservatism, and then of neoconservatism. Besides anticommunism, his warhorse until the fall of the Berlin wall, Buckley staked out positions hostile to the civil rights movement and desegregation, before developing a more pragmatic vision over the course of the 1960s. In New York, he actively supported Barry Goldwater's presidential bid in 1964. The following year, he garnered an unexpected number of votes during his own campaign for New York mayor.

On the left, some had harsh criticism for the period's consensus and the repentance of former radicals from the 1930s. *Dissent*, founded in 1954 by Irving Howe and Lewis Coser, served as their mouthpiece. Howe, who later taught literature at City University, felt no affinities with what he characterized as the "age of conformism." His reservations were echoed by the Columbia sociologist C. Wright Mills. Independent-minded, he cultivated nonconformism and denounced the frustrations of white-collar workers and the hypocrisies of liberalism in *White Collar* (1951) and *The Power Elite* (1956). For his part, Michael Harrington, who rejoined the socialist movement in the 1950s and was long active in Dorothy Day's Catholic Worker Movement, published a striking analysis of poverty in 1962, *The Other America*.

CALLED INTO QUESTION

New York's place in American culture became more relative beginning in the 1960s. The New York intellectuals had lost their quasi-monopoly over intellectual life. The civil rights movement, the opposition to the Vietnam War, and the expanding counterculture all called authority into question in ways that seemed to them incomprehensible or unacceptable, even as some of them were called into service by Presidents Kennedy and Johnson—such as Daniel Patrick Moynihan, Nathan Glazer, and Arthur Schlesinger. *Commentary*, under the direction of Norman Podheretz, its editor since 1960, joined the conservative camp. Lionel Trilling, Daniel Bell, and Richard Hofstadter were scathing in their criticism of the student movement. Many sided with the conservatives, following Bell and Podheretz.

Their weakening hold on the country's intellectual life translated into the advent of other ways of thinking. The *Partisan Review*'s loss of influence and the conservative turn of its colleague *Commentary* created a space quickly occupied by two weekly reviews appearing in 1955 and 1963 respectively, the *Village Voice* and the *New York Review of Books*. The official organ of the nascent counterculture, the *Voice*, where Norman Mailer officiated, immediately showed great talent for investigative journalism. More academic, the long reviews and critical essays of the *New York Review* served as a sounding board for the ideas of the New Left and helped to call into question the postwar liberal paradigm. Each in its own way, the *Voice* and the *New York Review* echoed a wave of revolt and a desire for freedom that swept over students in New York, now more numerous than ever. Whether it was a matter of civil rights, student uprisings, or the New Left, the metropolis's capacity for ferment gave these different 1960s movements a wider audience and scope.

The civil rights movement was born in the 1950s around political-religious figures like the pastor of the Abyssinian Baptist Church of Harlem, Adam Clayton Powell, Jr., or the Baptist pastor of the Siloam Presbyterian Church in Bedford-Stuyvesant, Milton Galamison. Despite its New York base, the National Association for the Advancement of Colored People (NAACP) led a national struggle, marked by the Supreme Court ruling, *Brown v. Board of Education of Topeka* (1954), that made school segregation illegal. The unrest and violence that accompanied this decision's implementation in the South in the 1960s prompted many New Yorkers, white and black, to join the civil rights movement and participate in the various marches organized in Mississippi and Alabama.

Other movements were more radical, for example the militant Nation of Islam, an organization that benefited from strong support among New York's blacks. In 1964, the Congress for Racial Equality (CORE) organized a boycott of New York schools to protest their *de facto* segregation, mobilizing hundreds of thousands of elementary and high school students.

Activism went beyond the civil rights movement. The "underground" press echoed the expansion of the counterculture. Taking its cue from the *Village Voice*, the *East Village Other* registered the antiestablishment atmosphere of St. Mark's Place and the Tompkins Square Park neighborhood, with its bookstores and cafés.

Vietnam was on everyone's mind. On April 15, 1967, between one and two hundred thousand people demonstrated in the New York streets against American policy, in a mass rally in answer to an appeal from the Spring Mobilization Committee to End the War in Vietnam (the Mobe). In Central Park, many hundreds of demonstrating youths burned their draft cards.

Soon, on their Morningside Heights acropolis, Columbia students mobilized, organized, and split into divisions. The movement started small, but it grew in the spring of 1968. Under the leadership of Mark Rudd, a group decided in April to occupy the campus, to protest the ties between the university and the CIA, which financed its Institute of Defense Analysis, and also to protest the university's plans for expanding the campus into Morningside Heights without regard for the interests of blacks in that neighborhood. For two weeks, Columbia became the heart of the American student movement, with visitors from the radical left, like Susan Sontag, Norman Mailer, and Dwight Macdonald, rushing to the scene, as well as the African-American radical militant Stokely Carmichael. On April 30, Columbia authorities had the campus forcibly evacuated by the police. Seven hundred people were arrested, and the students immediately decided upon a strike, which lasted until the summer. Columbia joined the University of California at Berkeley in the movement's history. Richard Nixon, then a presidential candidate, saw the events of April as "the first major battle in the revolutionary struggle to seize control of the universities."

It was then that the psychedelic culture promoted by Timothy Leary drew more and more followers, as the *Rat* and the *East Village Other* attested to between 1968 and 1970. Folk music took over the streets and clubs in the Village, where Bob Dylan, arriving from his home state of Minnesota in 1961, lent his voice to the protest movements. Announcing change ("The Times They Are a-Changin'" or "Blowin' in the Wind"), his songs and those of other singers, such as Leonard Cohen, Lou Reed, Joan Baez, or Paul Simon, embodied the counterculture, which reached its height with the Woodstock rock-music festival, organized in April 1969, in the town of Bethel in northern New York State.

A year later, New York was ablaze once again. The Weathermen (an allusion to a Bob Dylan song), a revolutionary faction growing out of one of the many splits in the Students for a Democratic Society movement, launched several actions involving armed struggle. In 1970, they attacked the house of a judge and the police headquarters. In March 1970, three of them were killed in the bombing of a Greenwich Village house while handling explosives.

For many years, New York was the center of a new feminist movement. In 1963, Betty Friedan published her famous *The Feminine Mystique* there, in which she denounced "the problem that has no name," the malaise of women imprisoned in their homes. Associations and groups proliferated, nurtured by rich student fodder. Some feminists distinguished themselves from the student movement, which they reproached for assigning them a secondary position. Conferences, gatherings, meetings, and demonstrations followed one after another. In 1966, the National Organization of Women was founded and its New York branch became particularly active. Organizations then appeared that advocated more militant activism, like the New York Radical Women, or, in 1968, the WITCH group (Women's International Terrorist Conspiracy from Hell). On September 7, 1968, radicals and "witches" disrupted the Miss America pageant in Atlantic City, and a few weeks later, they launched a spectacular campaign on Wall Street.

By the end of the 1960s, the whole spectrum of the feminist movement was represented in New York, from moderate reformists to SCUM militants (Society for Cutting Up Men). In August 1970, the fiftieth anniversary of the Nineteenth Amendment, which gave women the right to vote, provided the occasion for a huge demonstration on Fifth Avenue. In 1972, Gloria Steinem founded *Ms.* magazine, while Helen Gurley Brown made the respectable *Cosmopolitan* into a feminist magazine celebrating sexual liberation. Feminist attitudes often prevailed over concerns for old proprieties.

The same was true of the homosexual movement. The relative tolerance shown toward homosexuals in the 1920s gave way to much more repressive attitudes after World War II. In reaction, some homosexuals began to organize, notably within the New York branch of the Mattachine Society, established there in 1955, four years after the creation of its parent organization in Los Angeles. On June 27, 1969, a police raid on a Greenwich Village bar, the Stonewall Inn on Christopher Street, provoked a riot that spread throughout the neighborhood. In the months that followed, the Gay Liberation Front appeared, and then the Alliance of Gay Activists, which, along with other organizations, organized the movement on the local and national levels. Bars, clubs, and other places for meeting and socializing, newspapers (*Come Out*, 1969) and gay and lesbian associations proliferated. The anniversary of the Stonewall rebellion was the occasion for the Gay Pride parade, the symbol of liberation and a new kind of freedom. Beginning in 1971, groups agitated for a municipal order forbidding discrimination based on sexual preference and, after a fifteen-year-long effort, obtained its adoption in 1986. The emergence of this new special-interest group on the New York political scene led, in the early 1990s, to the election of a lesbian to the New York State House of Representatives, and of a gay activist to the city council. Both of them had their political base in Greenwich Village.

Beginning in 1980, this affirmation of sexual identity, individual or collective, was confronted with the tragedy of AIDS. The epidemic ravaged the art and entertainment world, causing tens of thousands of deaths in New York, particularly among homosexuals and drug users. AIDS unleashed violent condemnations of the homosexual population, but also strengthened its solidarity and its capacities for organizing. At the beginning of the epidemic, when medicine and public health offered nothing, Gay Men's

Health Crisis, an activist organization founded by the play-wright Larry Kramer in 1982, created a network for infor-mation, social and legal aid, and companionship. Thanks to donor support, notably from the New York artistic commu-nity, the association managed a million-dollar budget and employed more than a hundred paid staff within fifteen years of its creation. Other groups soon appeared, like ACT UP (AIDS Coalition to Unleash Power). Founded in 1987, this group struggled against both the epidemic and what they considered insufficient action on the part of public authorities, scientists, and pharmaceutical laboratories. They used spectacular, sometimes violent methods, always meant to attract the attention of the public.

At the heart of all these various revolts and protests, New York symbolized the new morality that transformed American society beginning in the 1960s, and that Woody Allen, shrewd connoisseur of New York bars and clubs, would affectionately mock and chronicle in his films like *Annie Hall*, *Interiors*, or *Manhattan*. The sexual revolution transformed behavior as families left the city for its sub-urbs. More than at any other time in its history, New York, and especially Manhattan, became a city of young people, many of whom were single. The economic comeback of the 1980s and 1990s further enhanced the appeal of New York nightlife, which became the domain of "yuppies" (young urban professionals)—countless young people who spent their days in the business world getting rich. Often short-lived, restaurants, nightclubs, and hot spots succeeded each other, responding to a growing demand for newer and more engaging distractions.

THE ARTS ON THE MOVE

In their own way, artists expressed these upheavals. In the early 1960s, Marcel Duchamp inspired Pop Art, which extended the ideas of Jasper Johns and Robert Rauschen-berg and constituted a radical reaction against abstract expressionism and its enthusiasts, Clement Greenberg and Harold Rosenberg. Pop Art took bodily hold of the ambi-ent consumerism for which New York served as capital.

Ironic and obliging, cruel and opportunistic, Roy Lichten-
stein, Andy Warhol, and their friends celebrated American
society's banality and everyday objects by holding them
up to ridicule. "I am all for art that gets mixed up in the
daily mire but leaves it clean," proclaimed Claes Oldenburg in the statement accompanying his work, *The Street:
A Metamorphic Mural*.

Warhol made his 1963–67 studio, The Factory, a former
hat-making shop on Forty-seventh Street, into one of New
York's creative centers. He shot avant-garde films, welcomed the musicians from the Velvet Underground, and
produced his pieces there. Pop Art was, by definition,
commercial, and the movement's artists could only be
pleased by the interest gallery owners and art dealers
almost immediately showed in them—Leo Castelli, Sidney Janis, and many others. Warhol gave Coca-Cola bot-
tles and Campbell soup cans a place in art history. Licht-
enstein, whose work was first shown in Leo Castelli's
gallery in 1961, mocked himself when he painted his
1962 *Masterpiece*, in which a sophisticated young woman
exclaims, "Why Brad darling, this painting is a MASTER-
PIECE! My, soon you'll have all of NEW YORK clamouring
for your work!"[6]

Other artists explored different paths, like minimalism,
following the example of Frank Stella's various series. Ques-
tioning the art-market principle, some became interested
in performance and the ephemeral gesture, and in redefining the very idea of representation. The whole city became
material. Arriving in New York in 1956, Claes Oldenburg
used urban rubbish in his creations. Christo planned to
envelope New York apartment buildings in immense pieces
of cloth. In 1975, Red Grooms set up *Ruckus Manhattan*, a
gigantic city-wide performance. Mural frescoes multiplied
under the influence of Jason Crum, Allan D'Arcangelo and
Robert Wiegand, who originated the City Walls group in
1970.

The 1960s and 1970s also witnessed the appearance of
all kinds of artistic forms tied to various political and community protests. In early 1967, several hundred artists
protesting the Vietnam War mobilized and organized a
series of political art shows in New York. Avant-garde

theater groups (off-off-Broadway) threw themselves into politics and experimented with improvisation. Ellen Stewart founded La Mama Experimental Theater in 1963. The Living Theater, which formerly operated in a more poetic vein closer to Cocteau, now inspired many counterculture troupes: the Open Theater, for example, or Peter Schumann's Bread and Puppet Theater, whose actors, mounted on stilts, paced New York's streets and parks, adopting a very agitprop style, mixing street art and puppetry.

The oldest protests, and also the most visible ones, involved the affirmation of an authentic black culture, and in New York, an important spokesman was the playwright Leroi Jones. Under the name of Amiri Baraka, he played an essential role in defining a committed African-American art and in denouncing what black artists like Romare Bearden perceived as white domination. In the image of the Spiral group, created by Bearden and other artists after the huge march on Washington in the summer of 1963 to defend the concept of an authentic black culture, groups, conferences, and shows proliferated as black artists continued working to gain recognition for their works and the importance of the black tradition.

In 1969, the Metropolitan Museum devoted an exhibition to Harlem, emphasizing the sociohistorical context and shortchanging the presentation of works by black artists. A long controversy followed. The Whitney Museum triggered another one when it organized a show on the art of the 1930s and omitted black artists, who then organized an alternative show meant to restore the balance at the Harlem Studio Museum, created in 1968. The show held at the Whitney in 1971 on contemporary black artists did not resolve the controversy. But in the 1970s, African-American art became much more visible, as demonstrated by the 1974 opening of a first-rate gallery exclusively devoted to African-American art, Just Above Midtown, at a prestigious Fifty-seventh Street address.

With the rising influence of these antiestablishment art forms, New York's artistic geography changed. In the south Bronx, particularly devastated by the economic crisis and public-authority urban policies, new cultural forms emerged within the Afro-American and Afro-Caribbean communities. Graffiti appeared on walls and in subways, while break dancing—that jerky, acrobatic dance style—and rap attracted young blacks. Their marginal position did not last long: hip-hop, which soon permeated films like Spike Lee's *She's Gotta Have It* and *Do the Right Thing*, penetrated the commercial sphere and found a national audience. But its rapid commercialization did not mitigate the feeling of social revolt that originally defined it.

As in the past, Harlem remained the heart of African-American visual arts. There, artists like David Hammonds or Adrian Piper sought forms of expression different from those employed by white artists in the same period. In their sculptures and installations, they denounced, sometimes virulently, art's alleged universality.

Finally, in south Manhattan, the SoHo district became well-known for its artistic experimentations. In its studios and galleries, installations and happenings were common currency. Post-minimalism could be found side by side with photorealism, conceptual art, performance art, or graffiti. In the late 1970s and early 1980s, these alternative spaces accommodated the meteoric careers of artists like Keith Haring or Jean-Michel Basquiat, both of whom died of AIDS at the height of their creativity.

These years were notable for the speed of such artists' success. The audience for art, made up of amateurs and collectors, had expanded extraordinarily since the time of abstract expressionism. One result of the success of this avant-garde art was that SoHo became gentrified and rents skyrocketed. Many artists had to withdraw into the neighboring districts of TriBeCa (Triangle Below Canal) and NoHo (North of Houston). They were soon replaced by thousands of young urban professionals who wanted to live in SoHo lofts, and by restaurants, shops, and still more galleries.

IN THE HOUSE OF THE WORLD

New York writers were less concerned with revolt and experimentation. Many explored the consequences of the

city's transformations. Jewish novelists pursued their variations on the apparently inexhaustible theme of assimila-
tion, but now, rather than emphasize the differences, they
described success or failure in adapting. From *Good-Bye
Columbus* to *American Pastorale*, not to mention the hilari-
ous *Portnoy's Complaint*, Philip Roth offered many such
scenarios to his readers' imaginations, while Joseph Heller,
the famous author of *Catch-22*, an absurdist novel about
World War II that developed a cult following among the
Vietnam War generation, provided caustic descriptions of
the contradictory demands on his New York Jewish intellectual heroes in *Good as Gold*.

These novels, as well as those by Paul Auster, Jerome
Charyn, or Don DeLillo, each showed in its own way the
spectacular changes experienced by the various cultures
that had still made New York a city of neighborhoods in
the late 1930s. Canarsie, noted a *New York Herald Tribune*
journalist in 1963, had formerly been "a special place of
homeyness and friendliness. *Fraindlichkeit* is the way
Yiddish-speaking residents described it. *Amicizia* is the
Italian word for the same thing. It was Brooklyn of an earlier century, and little Old New York in its most idyllic
form."[7] After the mass departure of residents from these
neighborhoods in the 1950s, local cultural solidarity, in
Brooklyn as in the Bronx, tended to disappear.

One of the most powerful symbols of this evolution was
the 1957 departure of Brooklyn's baseball team, the
Dodgers, for Los Angeles. At that time, the Dodgers helped
cement Brooklyn's identity together. By the late 1930s,
they had become a formidable opponent, and in the 1940s
and 1950s had garnered successes, many times making it
to the American championship finals, the World Series.
Although they lost every time to their great New York
rivals, the Yankees, for all those years they embodied the
pride of a borough. The Dodgers were also the first professional team to put an end to the tradition of racial segregation that reigned in baseball. Thus, their image was
closely tied to their 1947 decision to take on the African-
American player Jackie Robinson, a figure lauded by some,
hated by others and famous throughout the country. Soon
Robinson was followed by other African-Americans like

Don Newcombe or Roy Campanella. As for the Yankees, they finally signed a black player, Elston Howard, in 1955.

The Dodgers' peak was their final victory against the Yankees on October 4 in the 1955 World Series. Brooklyn was swept up in an impressive wave of popular enthusiasm that night. But two years later, Walter O'Malley, the owner of the Dodgers, chose to leave Brooklyn. The Ebbets Field stadium seemed too small to him with its 35,000 seats, the municipality was not ready to help him, and professional baseball had entered into a capitalist era when local attachments counted for less than they had in the past. Despite demonstrations that brought out thousands of protesters in spring 1957, O'Malley chose California. In February 1960, a page of history definitely turned for Brooklyn and its residents when Ebbets Field was demolished.

Despite the apparent weakening of New York localism, the idea that New York was a melting-pot came into question in the late 1950s. In its own way, the musical *West Side Story* proclaimed that ethnic identities and conflicts had hardly disappeared in the metropolis. Whatever the social and demographic changes, the vitality of black, Italian, Jewish, Puerto Rican and Irish cultures was evident. In a famous essay that appeared in 1963, *Beyond the Melting Pot*, Nathan Glazer and Daniel Moynihan bluntly affirmed that the melting pot "did not work," by demonstrating "the role of ethnicity in the tumultuous, varied and endlessly complex life of New York."[8]

In addition to its black cultures, New York counted ethnic white cultures, rediscovered following Glazer and Moynihan's study. Beyond the New York melting pot, in fact, Jews, Italians, and Irish recreated community structures in peripheral neighborhoods like Canarsie, where they settled when they left the ethnic enclaves of the first generation—Brownsville or East New York, Williamsburg or Bedford-Stuyvesant, Crown Heights, or South Brooklyn. The Italian-Americans of Bensonhurst honored Santa Rosalia, the patron saint of Sicily, each September, while the streets of Astoria attested to the presence of many Greek immigrants, and Greenpoint streets bore indications of a significant Polish population. Elsewhere, community identity was less easily discernible, but no less important. Belonging to an association, reading a certain newspaper (the Polish *Nowy Dziennik*, the Greek *Proini* or *Ethnikos Kerux*, etc.), or participating in a festival defined the symbolic framework of identities claimed and affirmed within specific contexts.

More spectacular was the emergence of other forms of cultural practices associated with the arrival of hundreds of thousands of Asian, Latin American, and Caribbean immigrants to New York, following Congress's adoption in the mid-1960s of laws encouraging immigration. Of course, there were also Europeans, like the some 20,000 Irish immigrants who settled in New York in the 1950s and 1960s, or the Hasidic Jews in Brooklyn. But the majority did not come from Europe, and in once again making New York a metropolis of immigrants, they transformed its cultural life.

In the mid-1950s, the Puerto Ricans created a huge organization, El Congreso del Pueblo, which united several dozen village, or small-town, organizations to respond to all the needs of immigrants. Beginning in 1958, the Puerto Rican Parade, which was held one Sunday each June along Fifth Avenue, brought together members of dozens of local and neighborhood associations, and political or cultural organizations, as well as hundreds of thousands of spectators.

This type of parade took up an old practice of immigrant groups, illustrated by the Saint Patrick's Day Irish parade. Brooklyn's West Indian *Carnival* was a very different matter. Each year beginning in 1969, in early September during the Labor Day holiday, it assembled more than a million participants from the metropolis's various West Indian groups. In a charged atmosphere, concerts, dances, and stands of all kinds cropped up along Eastern Parkway. "Today, whenever I visit my old neighborhood of Bedford-Stuyvesant and walk along Fulton Street or Nostrand Avenue, its twin commercial hubs, I have to remind myself that I'm in Brooklyn and not in the middle of a teeming outdoor market in Saint George's, Grenada or

Kingston, Jamaica, or on some other West Indian island," noted the novelist Paule Marshall in 1985. "Because there, suddenly, are all the sights and sounds, colors, smells and textures of the entire Caribbean archipelago, transplanted intact to the sidewalks of New York."[9]

Like their European predecessors, these immigrants created West Indian enclaves in Manhattan, Brooklyn, Queens, and the Bronx. Jamaicans, Trinidadians, Guyanans, Barbadians, and other anglophones rarely settled in Manhattan, preferring Crown Heights, East Flatbush, East New York, or Jamaica and Cambria Heights in south Queens. The Dominicans, Cubans, and other hispanophones clustered instead in Washington Heights, northwest Manhattan, or the Bronx. As for the Haitians, creolophones and francophones, some lived in Manhattan, but many lived in Brooklyn and Queens, like the West Indian anglophones.

In all these districts, ethnic stores and restaurants multiplied, not to mention a very active press (the weekly *New York Carib News*, founded in 1981, and the monthly *Everybody's*, started in 1977, both had circulations of over 60,000; the weekly *Haïti-Observateur* earned a national and international readership), and hundreds of organizations, sometimes regrouped within a central institution, like the Council of Haitian Centers, which united the Haitian community centers of Brooklyn, Queens, and Manhattan. Baseball (especially for Dominicans and Cubans), soccer (Colombians), and cricket (West Indian anglophones) clubs played an important role, as did mutual aid and political societies. No less essential was the place of religion. Haitian Catholics participated in ceremonies organized each year by East Harlem Italians in honor of Our Lady of Mount Carmel, while many other West Indians were drawn to voodoo and Afro-Cuban *santeria*. These latter increasingly appealed to West Indian immigrants as well as Afro-Americans and Puerto Ricans in search of a spirituality with African references, because they offered an alternative religious framework, and thus a form of cultural identification.

The arrival of hundreds of thousands of Chinese prompted Chinatown's expansion in Manhattan at the same time as many newcomers settled in Brooklyn,

Queens, and especially in Flushing. Chinatown's ethnic economy absorbed a large portion of the new arrivals, who gave new energy to community structures. Alongside traditional societies, often composed of immigrants from the same region or extended family, developed Sino-American organizations directed more toward the struggle against discrimination and more inclined to help immigrants become integrated into New York. In Chinatown, for example, the Planning Council or the Youth Council implemented social, linguistic, and professional assistance programs. The Chinese presence became continually more significant through the countless Chinese restaurants, dozens of newspapers and magazines, television channels, and stores that flourished in New York, now the great Sino-American metropolis in the United States, even ahead of San Francisco.

To all these influences were added those of Korean, Russian, Filipino, Indian, Ecuadorian, Iranian, Syrian, Lebanese immigrants, etc., who established community institutions in the same way. Once again, New York was characterized by its extreme demographic and cultural diversity. As in the early twentieth century, it counted dozens of foreign-language newspapers, thousands of associations and churches, and constituted one of the major points of convergence for migratory tides coming from all over the planet. More than ever, the dream of New York was shared throughout the world.

THE CULTURAL INDUSTRY

Immediately following World War II, New York's domination over American mass culture was reinforced in the first years of television.

Developing at lightning speed, television was first of all a New York affair, with its NBC (the pioneer, transmitting the opening of New York World's Fair in 1939), CBS, and ABC channels. In the late 1940s and early 1950s, their programs aimed at an urban audience, at that time largely concentrated in the New York metropolitan area. They adopted a New York style, in the image of the first

American television star, Milton Berle, "Mr. Television." They broadcast entertainment shows like Ed Sullivan's explicitly New York "Toast of the Town" and televised game shows. The first televised series, then broadcast live, made good use of the resources of Broadway and often had New York for a setting. "I Love Lucy," the successful series in which Lucille Ball starred (1951–57), took place in a New York apartment, as did "The Honeymooners" (1954–61).

The metropolis was the capital of televised news. "Meet the Press" began its long career there in 1947, and CBS developed the first televised documentaries (like "See It Now" by Edward Murrow, who struggled courageously against McCarthyism). In 1954, ABC broadcast live in their entirety the debates between U.S. Army lawyers and McCarthy, who emerged defeated. Walter Cronkite, who became the anchorman for CBS televised news in 1962, acquired a national reputation.

But in the mid-1950s, with the expansion of television, channels moved closer to the big film studios for production and programming purposes. Soon, films and television series used the sets of Hollywood studios, and Hollywood took control of an important part of production. As a sign of the times, "I Love Lucy" was shot in California, and ABC signed a partnership agreement with the Disney Corporation, and then with Warner Brothers. Quite predictably, the most typically New York aspects of television in 1945–55 rapidly disappeared. Johnny Carson, who took over the "Tonight Show" in 1962, left New York for the studios in Burbank ten years later, while the rise in televised political journalism from Washington presented strong competition to New York as the center for televised news production and broadcasting.

Since the mid-1960s, New York's hold on the television industry narrowed down to two areas. The metropolis retained control over variety shows and series that were New York–based by definition, like the famous "Saturday Night Live," the "Seinfeld" series, or the nighttime shows of David Letterman and Jay Leno. And New York continued to house the headquarters, main offices, and other administrative centers for the television industry and its subcontracting enterprises.

In all other sectors of the mass-culture industry, New York lost its dominant role. Coney Island continued to attract visitors in the 1940s and 1950s, but Luna Park disappeared in 1946, and Steeplechase Park in 1964, a victim of competition from other types of diversions and Disney parks. In the theatrical domain, diversification in offerings and production was particularly significant after the war. Of course, musicals continued to thrive on Broadway thanks to proven formulas, adapted to the current tastes, as in *My Fair Lady* (1956) and especially *West Side Story* (1957). But other large American cities that now wanted to attract acting companies and directors, and had the means to do so, reduced New York's dominance accordingly.

The proliferation of local radio stations helped to diversify the musical genres and develop a recording industry outside of New York, with more flexibility than Tin Pan Alley. Rock and roll, which embodied a form of revolt beginning in the 1950s, put Memphis on the map. The metropolis could only adapt, and transformed many of its prewar movie theaters, severely hurt by television's competition, into concert halls. Thus, in the late 1950s, Brooklyn's Paramount welcomed successful rock groups like the Platters and the Comets. In the 1960s and 1970s however, New York found itself at the heart of new musical forms: after Bob Dylan and the folk music of the years of rebellion, disco invaded the nightclubs, and the famous Studio 54 became its hot spot. In the late 1970s, New York counted some 300 discotheques, where as many as 200,000 people crowded in, struck with the *Saturday Night Fever* described in John Badham's 1977 film starring John Travolta. In a trance, the city danced, except where it preferred the metallic sound of the punk groups that performed at CBGB or the Mudd Club.

In its countless halls and clubs, New York accommodated the musical trends that succeeded each other throughout the 1980s and 1990s. Artists and producers rubbed elbows there, but Tin Pan Alley no longer possessed its past luster, even if New York continued to house the offices of the major record producers, such as MCA (Music Corporation of America), Warner, PolyGram, CBS, BMG, or Capitol-EMI.

In journalism, for the first time, the tendency was centrifugal as well. If the *New York Times* remained the major national reference, followed by the *Wall Street Journal*, whose readership had been growing significantly since 1945, the 1970s and 1980s saw the rise of quality newspapers that were not based in New York, such as the *Washington Post*, which exposed the Watergate scandal, or the *Los Angeles Times*.

CAPITAL OF THE TWENTY-FIRST CENTURY?

Times Square, December 31, 1999. At precisely 11:59, the millennium anthem blasted from the loudspeakers while an enormous crystal globe weighing a thousand pounds slowly descended the length of the pole atop the building at 1 Times Square. At midnight, reported the *New York Times*, "the illuminated globe completed its descent and "2000," that poignant figure, appeared fully lit. Fireworks exploded in the frigid sky and three tons of confetti rained down on the crowds. While thousands of balloons rose lazily into the air, the crowd could not contain itself any longer and let out a wild roar."[10] Dubbed "the global celebration at the crossroads of the world," this event, with its $7 million budget, was the largest ever organized in New York, a veritable "marathon of music, fireworks, confetti and deafening voices"—for twenty-six hours, a thousand artists appeared on a stage that stretched along Seventh Avenue from Forty-fifth to Forty-sixth Streets before a crowd of a couple million spectators.

The Times Square show was not just a New York affair. On December 31, throughout the day, many giant screens installed on Broadway, Eighth Avenue, and the Avenue of the Americas, projected to the crowds images of celebrations from around the world, while scenes from Times Square were simultaneously shown to a billion television viewers worldwide. "It was perfect for television," noted the *New York Times*, "clear color images, reducing everything to a show, including the passing of the millennium."[11] Unlike great New York celebrations in the past, the advent of the year 2000 was not accompanied by any official speeches, and the only declaration from New

FIGURE 53
Times Square, January 1, 2000
© AFP/Matt Campbell

York's mayor, Rudolph Giuliani, was to congratulate himself on the absence of incidents. It was true that the
crowds were carefully controlled by a massive police presence that divided them into well-ordered blocks, according to an almost military arrangement.

Not all New Yorkers were at Times Square. In the tall skyscrapers of lower Manhattan and Midtown, the mood was
not entirely festive, due to the fears surrounding the year
2000 bug, the infamous "Y2K." Executives and computer
experts were on the alert, ready to take on wayward soft-
ware programs or to defend New York's financial district
against hoaxes. Elsewhere in Manhattan and the other boroughs, many celebrations assembled tens of thousands of
people—in the Flushing Meadows–Corona park, in Queens,
or near the Bronx zoo. In Brooklyn, the traditional Saint

Sylvester fireworks display in Prospect Park was accompanied this year by a celebration meant primarily for Brooklynites on the Grand Army Plaza.

The huge Times Square machinery, the mobilization of financial and computer specialists, the more community-oriented gatherings in Brooklyn or the Bronx—all these New York receptions for the year 2000 illustrate the place the metropolis occupied at the dawn of a new millennium. Its brief cultural domination in the 1940s and 1950s when it was the capital of the "American century" had passed. It would have to reckon with rival cities even within the United States itself, like Los Angeles, thus depriving it of the sense of omnipotence that had rarely ebbed until now. Henceforth it would have to learn to compromise, to function within a network, to share its position at the top of the American cultural pyramid, even if it remained a center of global culture and one of the best places from which to observe the world.

Its magnetism still attracts hundreds of thousands of immigrants coming from all over the world, who, in return, nurture it with their energy and dynamism. The power of its industries and its cultural institutions, and the continually renewed intensity of its intellectual life bode well for the metropolis's future. New York is an explosive capsule of multiculturalism and capitalism. That is where its stakes lie for the twenty-first century, in that tension between the power, growth, and flexibility of its economy on the one hand, and the diversity of its cultures, proudly defended or grudgingly tolerated, on the other. The twentieth century has taught New York that it cannot have one without the other.

NOTES

1. THE OCEAN

1. J. Franklin Jameson, ed., *Narratives of New Netherland, 1609–1664* (New York: 1909), 22.

2. E. B. O'Callaghan, ed., *Documents Relative to the Colonial History of the State of New York*, vol. 1 (Albany, N. Y.: 1856), 37.

3. Jameson, ed., *Narratives of New Netherland*, 90.

4. I borrow the examples of Verbrugge, De Wolff, and others, here and in the rest of this chapter, from Oliver A. Rink, *Holland on the Hudson: An Economic and Social History of Dutch New York* (Ithaca, N.Y.: 1986), ch. 7, 172–213.

5. "Letters of Nicacius De Sille," *Proceedings of the New York State Historical Association, with the Quarterly Journal* 18 (1919): 101.

6. Michael Kammen, *Colonial New York: A History* (New York: 1975), 72.

7. "Governor Dongan's report on the state of the province, 1687," in E. B. O'Callaghan, ed., *The Documentary History of the State of New York*, vol. 1 (Albany, N. Y.: 1849), 160.

8. Adolph B. Benson, ed., *Peter Kalm's Travels in North America*, vol. 1 (New York: 1937), 135.

9. Benson, ed., *Peter Kalm's Travels*, vol. 1, pp. 134–35; "Answers of Gov. Andros to Enquiries about New York, 1678," in O'Callaghan, ed., *The Documentary History*, vol. 1, 90.

10. Bayrd Still, *Mirror for Gotham: New York as Seen by Contemporaries from Dutch Days to the Present* (New York: 1956), p. 18.

11. Federal Writers' Program, *A Maritime History of New York* (New York: 1973), 53–54.

12. Carl Bridenbaugh, *Cities in Revolt: Urban Life in America, 1743–1776* (New York: 1955), 69.

13. Gary B. Nash, *The Urban Crucible: Social Change, Political Consciousness, and the Origins of the American Revolution* (Cambridge, Mass.: 1979), 237.

14. La Rochefoucauld-Liancourt, *Voyage dans les États-Unis d'Amérique*, vol. 7 (Paris: 1799), 129.

15. Sean Wilentz, *Chants Democratic: New York City and the Rise of the American Working Class, 1788–1850* (New York: 1984), 38.

16. F[ernagus] de G[elone], *Manuel-guide des voyageurs aux États-Unis de l'Amérique du Nord* (Paris: 1818), 56.

17. La Rochefoucauld-Liancourt, *Voyage dans les États-Unis*

d'Amérique, vol. 7, 123; F[ernagus] de G[elone], *Manuel-guide des voyageurs*, 54; David Hosack, *Memoir of DeWitt Clinton* (New York: 1829), 478.

2. THE COMMENCEMENT OF A TOWN

1. Isaac N. Phelps Stokes, *The Iconography of Manhattan Island*, vol. 4 (New York: 1992), 72.

2. J. Franklin Jameson, ed., *Narratives of New Netherland, 1609–1664* (New York: 1909), 259; Stokes, *Iconography*, vol. 4, 97.

3. Carl Bridenbaugh, *Cities in Revolt: Urban Life in America, 1743–1776* (New York: 1955), 32.

4. Stokes, *Iconography*, vol. 1, 165.

5. Bayrd Still, *Mirror for Gotham: New York as Seen by Contemporaries from Dutch Days to the Present* (New York: 1956), 16.

6. Still, *Mirror*, p. 31; Myra Jehlen and Michael Warner, eds., *The English Literatures of America, 1500–1800* (New York: 1997), 426.

7. La Rochefoucauld-Liancourt, *Voyage dans les États-Unis d'Amérique*, vol. 3 (Paris: 1799), 249, 261.

8. Elisabeth Blackmar, *Manhattan for Rent, 1780–1850* (Ithaca, N. Y.: 1989), 45.

9. La Rochefoucauld-Liancourt, *Voyage dans les États-Unis d'Amérique*, vol. 7, pp. 131–32.

10. La Rochefoucauld-Liancourt, *Voyage dans les États-Unis d'Amérique*, vol. 7, 133.

11. Still, *Mirror*, p. 70.

12. Le Corbusier (Charles Édouard Jeanneret), *When the Cathedrals Were White* (New York: 1964), 47–48.

13. Morton Wagman, "Liberty in New Amsterdam: A Sailor's Life in Early New York." *New York History* 64 (2) (1983): 102.

14. Joyce D. Goodfriend, "Burghers and Blacks: The Evolution of a Slave Society at New Amsterdam," *New York History* 59 (2) (1978): 129–30.

15. Goodfriend, "Burghers and Blacks," 137.

16. Howard B. Rock, *Artisans of the New Republic: The Tradesmen of New York in the Age of Jefferson* (New York: 1979), 90.

17. Frederick Cople Jaher, *The Urban Establishment: Upper Strata in Boston, New York, Charleston, Chicago, and Los Angeles* (Urbana, Ill.: 1982), 163.

18. Cynthia Kierner, *Traders and Gentlefolk: The Livingstons of New York, 1675–1790* (Ithaca, N. Y.: 1992), 132.

19. Jameson, ed., *Narratives of New Netherland*, 259.

20. Wagman, "Liberty in New Amsterdam," 109.

21. Jameson, ed., *Narratives of New Netherland*, 260.

22. "Governor Dongan's report on the state of the province, 1687," in E. B. O'Callaghan, ed., *The Documentary History of the State of New York*, vol. 1 (Albany, N. Y.: 1850), 186.

23. Gerald Francis De Jong, "Dominie Johannes Megapolensis: Minister to New Netherland," *New York Historical Society Quarterly* 53 (January 1968): 25.

24. Bayrd Still, *Urban America: A History with Documents* (Boston: 1974), 67.

25. Jaher, *Urban Establishment*, p. 169; Thomas Bender, *New York Intellect: A History of Intellectual Life in New York City, from 1750 to the Beginnings of Our Own Time* (New York: 1987), 12.

3. THE VENICE OF THE ATLANTIC

1. Frances M. Trollope, *Domestic Manners of the Americans* (New York: 1949), 336–37.

2. Michel Chevalier, *Society, Manners and Politics in the United States being a Series of Letters on North America* (Boston: 1839) 98.

3. Alexis de Tocqueville, *Oeuvres Complètes*, vol. 14: *Correspondance familiale* (Paris: 1998), 81.

4. Bayrd Still, *Urban America: A History with Documents* (Boston: 1974), 83.

5. Still, *Urban America*, 83–84.

6. Chevalier, *Society, Manners and Politics*, 78.

7. Eric E. Lampard, "The New York Metropolis in Transformation: History and Prospect: A Study in Historical Particularity," in Hans-Jurgen Ewers, John B. Goddard, and Horst Matzerath, eds., *The Future of the Metropolis: Berlin, London, Paris, New York* (New York: 1986), 46.

8. Robert Albion, *The Rise of New York Port, 1815–1860* (New York: 1939), 266.

9. Allan Nevins, ed., *The Diary of Philip Hone, 1828–1851* (New York: 1927), vol. 2, 896; Louis Simonin, *Le Monde américain. Souvenirs de mes voyages aux États-Unis* (Paris: 1877), 8.

10. Simonin, *Le Monde américain*, p. 20.

11. Albion, *Rise of New York Port*, 220–21.

12. Ramon de la Sagra, *Cinq mois aux Etats-Unis de l'Amérique du Nord* (Brussels: 1837), 29.

13. D. J. Browne, "Commercial Docks," *The Merchants' Magazine*, vol. 5 (1841), 240.

14. Ernest Duvergier de Hauranne, *A Frenchman in Lincoln's America*, vol. 1 (Chicago: 1974), 22.

15. Mary Beth Betts, "Masterplanning: Municipal Support of Maritime Transport and Commerce, 1870–1930s" in Kevin Bone, ed., *The New York Waterfront: Evolution and Building Culture of the Port and Harbor* (New York: 1997), 43. Olympe Audouard, *A travers l'Amérique* (Paris: 1871), 117.

16. "New York Daguerreotyped," *Putnam's Monthly*, vol. I, no. 2 (February 1853), 132.

17. Bayrd Still, *Mirror, or Gotham: New York as Seen by Contemporaries from Dutch Days to the Present* (New York: 1956), 132–33.

18. Emma Lazarus, "The New Colossus" (1886).

4. THE EMPIRE CITY

1. Bayrd Still, *Mirror for Gotham: New York as Seen by Contemporaries from Dutch Days to the Present* (New York: 1956), 99, 202.

2. Allan Nevins, ed., *The Diary of Philip Hone, 1828–1851*, vol. 1 (New York: 1927), 202.

3. David Hosack, *Memoir of DeWitt Clinton* (New York: 1829), 478.

4. Ira Rosenwaike, *Population History of New York City* (Syracuse, N.Y.: 1972), 49.

5. U.S. Bureau of Statistics, *Tenth Census of the United States, 1880*, vol. 18: *Social Statistics of Cities* (Washington, D.C.: 1882), 531–32.

6. David Schuyler, *The New Urban Landscape: The Redefinition of City Form in Nineteenth-Century America* (Baltimore: 1986), 114.

7. George R. Taylor, "Building an Intra-Urban Transportation System," in Allen M. Wakstein, ed., *The Urbanization of America: An Historical Anthology* (Boston: 1970), 137.

8. Paul Bourget, *Outre-Mer: Impressions of America* (New York: 1895), 29–30.

9. Lady Emmeline Stuart-Wortley, *Travels in the United States, etc., during 1849 and 1850* (New York: 1851), 13; Ernest Duvergier de Hauranne, *A Frenchman in Lincoln's America*, vol. 1 (Chicago: 1974), 19.

10. Charles N. Glaab and A. Theodore Brown, *A History of Urban America* (New York: 1967), 84.

11. Albert Delaporte, "Six Jours aux États-Unis," *Le Monte-Carlo mondain*, vol. 2 (March 1890), 7.

12. Elizabeth Blackmar, *Manhattan for Rent, 1785–1850* (Ithaca, N.Y.: 1989) 183.

13. Adna Ferrin Weber, *The Growth of Cities in the Nineteenth Century. A Study in Statistics* (1899; Ithaca, N.Y.: 1967), 461–62.

14. [George Templeton Strong], *The Diary of George Templeton Strong*, edited and abridged (Seattle, Wash.: 1988), 337.

15. Roy Rosenzweig and Elizabeth Blackmar, *The Park and The People. A History of Central Park* (New York, 1994), pp. 51, 55.

16. Schuyler, *The New Urban Landscape*, 7.

17. Still, *Mirror for Gotham*, 105.

18. Walter D. Kamphoefner, *News from the Land of Freedom: German Immigrants Write Home* (Ithaca, N.Y.: 1991), 372.

19. Kamphoefner, *News from the Land of Freedom*, 411.

20. Edward Pessen, *Riches, Class, and Power before the Civil War* (New Brunswick, N.J.: 1990), 33.

21. *Merchants' Magazine*, August 23, 1850, 248–49.

22. Mary P. Ryan, *Civic Wars: Democracy and Public Life in the American City during the Nineteenth Century* (Berkeley, Calif.: 1997), 110.

23. Michel Chevalier, *Society, Manners and Politics in the United States being a Series of Letters on North America* (Boston: 1839) 161.

24. Glaab and Brown, *A History of Urban America*, 205.

25. William L. Riordon, *Plunkett of Tammany Hall* (New York: 1963), 3.

26. *New York Times*, May 25, 1883.

5. MANNAHATTA

1. Walt Whitman, "City of Orgies"; "City of Ships," *Complete Poetry and Collected Prose* (New York: 1982), 279, 430.

2. Lady Emmeline Stuart-Wortley, *Travels in the United States, etc., during 1849 and 1850* (New York: 1851), 158.

3. *Putnam's Monthly*, 9 (September 2, 1853): 233.

4. Stuart M. Blumin, *The Emergence of the Middle Class: Social Experience in the American City, 1760–1900* (New York: 1989), 151.

5. Alexis de Tocqueville, *Democracy in America*, (New York: 1969), 513.

6. Edward K. Spann, *The New Metropolis: New York City, 1840–1857* (New York: 1981), 213.

7. *Real Estate Record and Guide* (1878), quoted by Robert M. Stern, et al., *New York 1900* (New York: 1983), 307.

8. Alexis de Tocqueville, *Oeuvres complètes*, vol. 14: *Correspondance familiale* (Paris: 1998), 81; Ernest Duvergier de Hauranne, *A Frenchman in Lincoln's America*, vol. 1 (Chicago: 1974), 130, 135.

9. Bayrd Still, *Urban America: A History with Documents* (Boston: 1974), 123.

10. Frances M. Trollope, *Domestic Manners of the Americans* (New York: 1949), 340; Whitman, "The Old Bowery," *Complete Poetry and Collected Prose*, 1186, 1189.

11. Ernest Duvergier de Hauranne, *A Frenchman in Lincoln's America*, vol. 1 (Chicago: 1974), 20–21.

12. Phillip Lopate, ed., *Writing New York: A Literary Anthology* (New York: 1998), 48.

13. Lawrence W. Levine, *Highbrow/Lowbrow: The Emergence of Cultural Hierarchy in America* (Cambridge, Mass., 1988), 66.

14. John F. Kasson, *Rudeness & Civility: Manners in Nineteenth-Century Urban America* (New York: 1990), 238.

15. Stuart M. Blumin, "Introduction," in George M. Foster, *New York by Gas-Light and Other Urban Sketches* (Berkeley, Calif.: 1990), 9.

16. Duvergier de Hauranne, *A Frenchman in Lincoln's America*, vol. 1, 20.

17. Thomas Bender, *New York Intellect: A History of Intellectual Life in New York City from 1750 to The Beginnings of Our Own Time* (Baltimore: 1987), 133.

18. Bender, *New York Intellect*, 265, 276.

19. Charles N. Glaab and A. Theodore Brown, *A History of Urban America* (New York, 1967), p. 56.

20. Tocqueville, *Democracy in America*, 278–79.

21. [George Templeton Strong], *The Diary of George Templeton Strong*, vol. 1 (New York: 1952), 260.

22. Charles E. Rosenberg, *The Cholera Years: The United States in 1832, 1849, and 1866* (Chicago: 1962), 33.

23. Bayrd Still, *Mirror for Gotham: New York as Seen by Contemporaries from Dutch Days to the Present* (New York: 1956), 79.

24. Still, *Urban America*, 83.

25. Horatio Alger, Jr., *Ragged Dick and Mark, the Match Boy* (New York: 1962), 108.

26. Herman Melville, *Moby-Dick*, in Melville, *Redburn: His First Voyage; White-Jacket: or The World in a Man-of-War; Moby Dick; or, The Whale* (New York: 1983), 795.

27. Whitman, "Preface," "Crossing Brooklyn Ferry," *Complete Poetry and Collected Prose*, 5, 312.

28. Gustave de Beaumont, *Lettres d'Amérique* (Paris: 1973), 43.

29. William Crary Brownell, *French Traits: An Essay in Comparative Criticism*, (New York: 1893), 381, 384, 388.

6. GREATER NEW YORK

1. Henry Adams, *The Education of Henry Adams: An Autobiography* (Boston: 1961), 499.

2. Herbert Croly, "New York as the American Metropolis," *Architectural Record* 13 (March 1903): 194.

3. *New York Times*, January 1, 1898: 1.

4. Croly, "New York as the American Metropolis," 204.

5. Robert A. M. Stern, Gregory Gilmartin, and John Massengale, *New York 1900: Metropolitan Architecture and Urbanism, 1890–1915* (New York: 1983), 31.

6. Stern, Gilmartin, and Massengale, *New York 1900*, 63.

7. Stern, Gilmartin, and Massengale, *New York 1900*, 91.

8. Lazare Weiller, *Les Grandes Idées d'un grand peuple* (Paris: 1902), 23.

9. Carol Willis, *Form Follows Finance: Skyscrapers and Skylines in New York and Chicago* (New York: 1995), 19.

10. Le Corbusier, *When the Cathedrals Were White* (New York: 1964), 41.

11. Willis, *Form Follows Finance*, 43.

12. Federal Writers' Project, *New York Panorama* (New York: 1938), 375.

13. Federal Writers' Project, *The WPA Guide to New York City* (New York: 1939), 574.

14. Federal Writers' Project, *New York Panorama*, 328.

15. Leonard Wallock, ed., *New York: Culture Capital of the World, 1940–1965* (New York: 1988), 17.

16. Robert A. M. Stern, Gregory Gilmartin, and Thomas Mellins, *New York 1930: Architecture and Urbanism Between the Two World Wars* (New York: 1987), 729.

7. THE PROMISED CITY?

1. O. Henry, "The Duel" (1910) in Phillip Lopate, ed., *Writing New York: A Literary Anthology* (New York: 1998), 382–83.

2. Jacob A. Riis, *How the Other Half Lives: Studies among the Tenements of New York* (New York: 1957), 18–19.

3. Louis Adamic (1932), quoted by Nancy L. Green, *L'Odyssée des émigrants* (Paris: 1994), 41.

4. Gilles Brochard, ed., *Histoires de New York* (Paris: 1997), 7.

5. Kate Holladay Claghorn, "The Foreign Immigrant in New York City," *Reports of the Industrial Commission on Immigration*, vol. 15 (Washington, D. C.: 1901), 473, 474.

6. Nancy L. Green, *Ready-to-Wear and Ready-to-Work: A Century of Industry and Immigrants in Paris and New York* (Durham, N. C.: 1997), 53.

7. *New York Panorama* (New York, 1938), p. 446.

8. Jean-Louis Cohen, "L'Oncle Sam au pays des Soviets," in Jean-Louis Cohen and Hubert Damisch, eds., *Américanisme et modernité: L'art américain dans l'architecture* (Paris: 1993), 406–407.

9. Robert A. M. Stern, Gregory Gilmartin, and Thomas Mellins, *New York 1930: Architecture and Urbanism Between the Two World Wars* (New York: 1987), 369.

8. THE LIGHTS OF THE CITY

1. James L. Baughman, "Take Me Away from Manhattan: New York City and American Mass Culture, 1930–1990" in Martin Shefter, ed., *Capital of the American Century: The National and International Influence of New York City* (New York: 1993), 118.

2. Paul Morand, *New York* (Paris: 1930), 161, 279.

3. Ellen M. Snyder Grenier, *Brooklyn: An Illustrated History* (Philadelphia: 1996), 194.

4. George Chauncey, *Gay New York: Gender, Urban Culture, and the Making of the Gay Male World, 1890–1940* (New York: 1994), 33–34, 248.

5. Federal Writers' Project, *New York Panorama* (New York: 1938), 311.

6. Federal Writers' Project, *New York Panorama*, 294.

7. Federal Writers' Project, *New York Panorama*, 284–85.

8. William R. Taylor, *In Pursuit of Gotham: Culture and Commerce in New York* (New York: 1992), 120.

9. Taylor, *In Pursuit of Gotham*, 123.

10. Gilles Brochard, ed., *Histoires de New York* (Paris: 1997), 252.

11. Gilbert Osofsky, *Harlem, The Making of A Ghetto: Negro New York, 1890–1930* (New York: 1996), 182.

12. Le Corbusier, *When the Cathedrals Were White* (1937; New York: 1964), 45; Bayrd Still, *Mirror for Gotham: New York as Seen by Contemporaries from Dutch Days to the Present* (New York: 1956), 295.

9. THE PHOENIX

1. *New York Times*, August 22, 1948, p. 1.

2. Simone de Beauvoir, *L'Amerique au jour le jour* (Paris:

1954), 13; Claude Roy, *Le Rivage des jours*, 1990-1991 (Paris: 1992), 216-17.

3. Robert A. M. Stern et al., *New York 1960: Architecture and Urbanism Between the Second World War and the Bicentennial* (New York: 1998), 29.

4. David Vogel, "New York City as a National and Global Financial Center," in Martin Shefter, ed., *Capital of the American Century: The National and International Influence of New York City* (New York: 1993), 66.

5. Daniel Bell, "The Three Faces of New York," *Dissent* (winter 1961): 229.

6. Stern et al., *New York 1960: Architecture and Urbanism*, 139.

7. Stern et al., *New York 1960: Architecture and Urbanism*, 261.

8. Nathan Glazer, "The New New Yorkers," in Peter D. Salins, *New York Unbound: The City and the Politics of the Future* (New York: 1988), 58.

9. "Metropolis in a Mess," *Newsweek*, July 27, 1959, p. 29.

10. Nancy Foner, "New Immigrants and Changing Patterns in New York City," in Nancy Foner, ed., *New Immigrants in New York* (New York: 1987), 12.

11. Phillip Lopate, "Trauma, Apocalypse, Boom, Aftermath: New York City in the Last Twenty-Five Years," in Ric Burns and James Sanders, with Lisa Ades, *New York. An Illustrated History* (New York: 1999), 547.

10. NEW YORK, NEW YORK!

1. William Packard, ed., *The Craft of Poetry: Interviews from the* New York Quarterly (New York: 1974), 130.

2. John Clellon Holmes, "This is The Beat Generation," *New York Times Magazine*, November 16, 1952.

3. Lionel Abel, "New York City: Remembrance," *Dissent* (summer 1961): 255.

4. Richard Hofstadter, *The American Political Tradition and the Men Who Made It*, 2nd ed. (New York, 1973), xxxvi.

5. Cited by Elisabeth Young-Bruehl, *Hannah Arendt. Biographie* (Paris: 1999), 356-57.

6. Leonard Wallock, ed., *New York: Culture Capital of the World, 1940-1965* (New York: 1988), 13.

7. Jonathan Rieder, *Canarsie: The Jews and Italians of Brooklyn against Liberalism* (Cambridge, Mass.: 1985), 15.

8. Nathan Glazer and Daniel P. Moynihan, *Beyond the Melting Pot: The Negroes, Puerto Ricans, Jews, Italians and Irish of New York City*, 2nd ed. (New York: 1970), xcvii.

9. Cited by Ellen M. Snyder Grenier, *Brooklyn! An Illustrated History* (Philadelphia: 1996), 55.

10. "For 2000, Rave Reviews All Around After an Anxiously Anticipated Opening Night," *New York Times*, January 2, 2000.

11. "Twirling Globe Stops to Greet 2000, One Midnight After Another," *New York Times*, January 1, 2000.

BIBLIOGRAPHICAL ESSAY

———••••———

Rather than offering a complete bibliography of New York City history—an impossible task—this essay should serve as a grateful acknowledgment of debt. It emphasizes those books that were most useful to me, omitting, for lack of space, collections of sources and, with a few exceptions, journal articles. Unless otherwise indicated, the place of publication is New York.

GENERAL WORKS

Many works approach the history of New York City from a perspective of partial or complete synthesis. Besides the old but indispensable books of James Grant Wilson, ed., *The Memorial History of the City of New York* (1892–93), and especially of Isaac Newton Phelps Stokes, *The Iconography of Manhattan Island, 1498–1909*, 6 vols. (1915–28), see Edwin G. Burrows and Mike Wallace's work, monumental in all respects, *Gotham: A History of New York City to 1898* (1999), as well as Ric Burns and James Sanders, with Lisa Ades, *New York: An Illustrated History* (1999), and George J. Lankevitch, *American Metropolis: A History of New York City* (1998). On Brooklyn, see Ellen M. Snyder Grenier, *Brooklyn: An Illustrated History* (Philadelphia: 1996).

Always useful are the analyses assembled during the 1930s within the framework of the Federal Writers' Project, *The WPA Guide to New York City: A Comprehensive Guide to the Five Boroughs of the Metropolis—Manhattan, Brooklyn, the Bronx, Queens, and Richmond* (1939; new ed., 1992), and from the same authors, *New York Panorama: A Companion to the WPA Guide to New York City* (1938; new ed., 1984), as well as John Kouwenhoven, *The Columbia Historical Portrait of New York: An Essay in Graphic History* (1953; new ed., 1972) The two recent guides I have most used are Elliot Willensky and Norval White, *AIA Guide to New York City* (San Diego, Cal.: 1988), and Carol von Pressetin Wright, *Blue Guide New York: Atlas of Manhattan, Maps and Plans* (1991). Finally, Bayrd Still, *A Mirror for Gotham: New York as Seen by Contemporaries from Dutch Days to the Present* (1956), Phillip Lopate, ed., *Writing New York: A Literary Anthology* (1998), and Kenneth T. Jackson and David S. Dunbar, eds., *Empire City: New York City Through the Centuries* (2002) offer invaluable collections of observations and literary works on New York.

The historian is fortunate to have access to some excellent working tools: besides the specialized journals *New-York Historical Society Quarterly* (1917–1980), *New York History* (1919–   ), and now the *New-York Journal of American History* (2003-), there is the essential *Encyclopedia of New York City*, edited by Kenneth T. Jackson (New Haven: 1995). The Social Science Research Council and the Russell Sage Foundation are responsible for the publication of five, now indispensable, collective works: John H. Mollenkopf, ed., *Power, Culture, and Place: Essays on New York City* (1988); John H. Mollenkopf and Manuel Castells, eds., *Dual City: Restructuring New York* (1991); William R. Taylor, ed., *Inventing Times Square: Commerce and Culture at the Crossroads of the World* (1991); David Ward and Olivier Zunz, eds., *The Landscape of Modernity: Essays on New York City, 1900–1940* (1992); and Martin Shefter, ed., *Capital of the American Century: The National and International Influence of New York City* (1993). For two important interpretations, see Thomas Bender, *The Unfinished City: New York and the Metropolitan Idea* (2002), and Eric E. Lampard, "The New York Metropolis in Transformation: History and Prospect. A Study in Historical Particularity," in Hans-Jürgen Ewers, John B. Goddard, and Horst Matzerath, eds., *The Future of the Metropolis: Berlin, London, Paris, New York. Economic Aspects* (1986), 27–110.

Many books cover all or part of New York history from a particular thematic perspective. Its demographic evolution is described in Ira Rosenwaike, *Population History of New York City* (Syracuse, N.Y.: 1972); immigration is dealt with in Frederick M. Binder and David M. Reimers, *All the Nations Under Heaven: An Ethnic and Racial History of New York City* (1995); the intellectual life is covered by Thomas Bender, *New York Intellect: A History of Intellectual Life in New York City from 1750 to the Beginnings of Our Own Time* (Baltimore: 1987). The growing role of the suburbs has been analyzed by Kenneth T. Jackson, *Crabgrass Frontier: The Suburbanization of the United States* (1985), and the place of Central Park by Roy Rosenzweig and Elizabeth Blackmar, *The Park and the People: A History of Central Park* (Ithaca, N.Y.: 1992).

PART I: THE PROVINCE (1620–1820)

One may begin with Michael Kammen, *Colonial New York: A History* (1975), and, for a global perspective, with Carmen Bernand and Serge Gruzinski, *Histoire du Nouveau Monde*, 2 vols. (Paris: 1991 and 1993). The debate over the commercial dynamism of the Dutch colony, started by Simon Hart, *The Prehistory of the New Netherland Company* (Amsterdam: 1959), has been renewed to a large extent by Oliver S. Rink's interpretation, *Holland on the Hudson: An Economic and Social History of Dutch New York* (Ithaca, N.Y.: 1986). Very useful, too, is Joyce D. Goodfriend, "The Historiography of the Dutch in Colonial America," in Eric Nooter and Patricia U. Bonomi, eds., *Colonial Dutch Studies: An Interdisciplinary Approach* (1988), 6–32.

On the economic history of New York in the seventeenth and eighteenth centuries, in addition to Jacob Price's important article, "Economic Function and the Growth of the American Port Town," *Perspectives in American History* 8 (1974): 123–86, the volumes by John J. McCusker and Russell R. Menard, *The Economy of British North America, 1607–1789* (Chapel Hill, N.C.: 1985), and Stanley L. Engerman and Robert E. Gallman, eds., *The Cambridge Economic History of the United States. Volume I: The Colonial Era* (1996), the major reference is Cathy Matson, *Merchants and Empire: Trading in Colonial New York* (Baltimore: 1998).

On relations with Amerindians, see Bruce G. Trigger and Wilcomb Washburn, eds., *The Cambridge History of the Native Peoples of the Americas. Vol. I: North America* (1996); Denys Delâge, *Bitter Feast: Amerindians and Europeans in Northeastern North America, 1600-64* (Vancouver, B.C.: 1993); Thomas E. Norton, *The Fur Trade in Colonial New York* (Madison, Wis.: 1974); Allan Trelease, *Indian Affairs in Colonial New York: The Seventeenth Century* (Ithaca, N.Y.: 1960); and "Dutch Treatment of the American Indian," in Howard Peckham et al., *Attitudes of Colonial Powers Toward the American Indian* (Salt Lake City: 1969); and Bruce G. Trigger, *Natives and Newcomers: Canada's "Heroic Age" Reconsidered* (Kingston, Ont.: 1985).

For analyses of colonial society, see especially Thomas Archdeacon, *New York City, 1664–1710: Conquest and Change* (Ithaca, N.Y.: 1976); Patricia U. Bonomi, *A Factious People: Politics and Society in Colonial New York* (1971), and *The Lord Cornbury Scandal: The Politics of Reputation in British America* (Chapel Hill, N.C.: 1998); Carl A. Bridenbaugh, *Cities in the Wilderness: The First Century of Urban Life in America, 1625–1742* (1938), and *Cities in Revolt: Urban Life in America, 1743–1776* (1955); Anne-Marie E. Cantwell and Diana diZerega Wall, *Unearthing Gotham: The Archaeology of New York City* (New Haven, Conn.: 2001); Joyce D. Goodfriend, *Before the Melting-Pot: Society and Culture in Colonial New York* (Princeton, N.J.: 1991); Virginia Harrington, *The New York Merchant on the Eve of the Revolution* (1935); Leslie M. Harris, *In the Shadow of Slavery: African Americans in New York City, 1626–1863* (Chicago: 2003); Graham Russell Hodges, *Root and Branch: African Americans in New York and New Jersey, 1613–1863* (Chapel Hill, N.C.: 1999); Stanley Katz, *Newcastle's New York: Anglo-American Politics, 1732–1753* (Cambridge, Mass.: 1968); Gary B. Nash, *Urban Crucible: Political Consciousness and the Origins of the American Revolution* (Cambridge, Mass.: 1979); *Robert Ritchie, The Duke's Province: A Study of New York's Politics and Society, 1664–1691* (Chapel Hill, N.C.: 1977); Nan A. Rothschild, *New York City Neighborhoods: The 18th Century* (San Diego, Cal.: 1990); and Joseph S. Tiedemann, *Reluctant Revolutionaries: New York City and the Road to Independence, 1763-1776* (Ithaca, N.Y.: 1997).

The post-revolutionary period is explored in the classic work by Sidney I. Pomerantz, *New York, An American City, 1783–1803: A Study of Urban Life* (1938), as well as in more recent works by Elizabeth Blackmar, *Manhattan for Rent, 1785–1850* (Ithaca, N.Y.: 1989); Jeanne Chase, "New York. Du port à la ville; la construction de l'espace urbain, 1750–1820," *Annales, Economies, Sociétés, Civilisations* 44, 4 (juillet-août 1989): 793–819; Paul A. Gilje, *The Road to Mobocracy: Popular Disorder in New York City, 1763–1834* (Chapel Hill, N.C.: 1987); William Pencak and Paul A. Gilje, eds., *New York in the Age of the Constitution* (1992); Howard B. Rock, *Artisans of the New Republic: The Tradesmen of New York in the Age of Jefferson* (1979). On the end of slavery, see Shane White, *Somewhat More Independent: The End of Slavery in New York City, 1770–1810* (Athens, Ga.: 1991).

PART II: QUEEN OF THE NEW WORLD (1820–1890)

On the transformations in the New York economy over the course of the first half of the nineteenth century, see the classic book by Robert G. Albion, *The Rise of New York Port, 1815–1860* (1939). The impact of these changes on New York City's hinterland is well described in the books by Paul E. Johnson, *A Shopkeeper's Millennium Society and Revivals in Rochester, New York, 1815–1837* (1978), and Mary P. Ryan, *Cradle of the Middle Class: The Family in Oneida County, New York, 1790–1865* (1981).

On the New York economy in the second half of the century, see Sven Beckert, *The Monied Metropolis: New York City and the Consolidation of the American Bourgeoisie, 1850-1896* (2001) and on the port the reference work by Jean Heffer, *Le Port de New York et le commerce extérieur américain, 1860–1900* (Paris: 1986). The New York port's physical changes are analyzed in the collection edited by Kevin Bone, ed., *The New York Waterfront: Evolution and Building Culture of the Port and Harbor* (1997).

The development of New York's industrial function and its social effects are at the heart of books by Christine Stansell, *City of Women: Sex and Class in New York, 1789–1860* (1986); Richard B. Stott, *Workers in the Metropolis: Class, Ethnicity, and Youth in Antebellum New York City* (Ithaca, N.Y.: 1990); and Sean Wilentz, *Chants Democratice: New York City and the Rise of the American Working Class, 1788–1850* (1984). The crystallization of a middle class is examined by Stuart M. Blumin, *The Emergence of the Middle Class: Social Experience in the American City, 1760–1920* (1989), and the New York elite by Frederic Cople Jaher, *The Urban Establishment: Upper Strata in Boston, New York, Charleston, Chicago, and Los Angeles* (Urbana, Ill.: 1982).

Immigration is analyzed by Robert Ernst, *Immigrant Life in New York City, 1825–1863* (1949), and by Jay P. Dolan, *The Immigrant Church: New York's Irish and German Catholics, 1815–1865* (Baltimore: 1975). On the Irish, see Ronald H. Bayor and Timothy J. Meagher, eds., *The New York Irish* (Baltimore: 1996). On the Germans, Stanley Nadel, *Little Germany: Ethnicity, Religion, and Class in New York City, 1845–1880* (Urbana, Ill.: 1990).

On spatial, social, and political transformations, see the synthesis by Clara Cardia, *Ils ont construit New York: Histoire de la métropole au XIXe siècle* (Geneva: 1987); Edward K. Spann, *The New Metropolis: New York City, 1840–1857* (1981); as well as Robert A. M. Stern, Thomas Mellins and David Fishman, *New York 1880: Architecture and Urbanism in the Gilded Age* (1999). On the African-Americans, besides Harris, *In the Shadow of Slavery*, and Hodges, *Root and Branch*; see George E. Walker, *The Afro-American in New York City, 1827–1860* (1993). Urban changes are studied by Blackmar, *Manhattan for Rent, 1785–1850*; Stanley K. Schultz, *Constructing Urban Culture: American Cities and City Planning, 1800–1920* (Philadelphia: 1989); David Schuyler, *The New Urban Landscape: The Redefinition of City Form in Nineteenth-Century America* (Baltimore: 1986); and David M. Scobey, *Empire City: The Making and Meaning of the New York Landscape* (Philadelphia: 2002).

For analyses of social and political tensions in the nineteenth-century metropolis, see Tyler Anbinder, *Five Points: The 19th Century New York City Neighborhood that Invented Tap Danse, Stole Elections, and Became the World's Most Notorious Slum* (2001); Iver Bernstein, *The New York City Draft Riots: Their Significance for American Society and Politics in the Age of the Civil War* (1990); Amy Bridges, *A City in the Republic: Antebellum New York and the Origins of Machine Politics* (1984); Edward Pessen, *Riches, Class, and Power: America Before the Civil War* (Lexington, Ky.: 1973); Mary P. Ryan, *Civic Wars: Democracy and Public Life in the American City During the Nineteenth Century* (Berkeley, Cal.: 1997); and David Ward, *Poverty, Ethnicity, and the American City, 1840–1925: Changing Conceptions of the Slum and the Ghetto* (1989).

On cultural changes, Melvin L. Adelman, *A Sporting Time: New York City and the Rise of Modern Athletics, 1820–70* (Urbana, Ill.: 1986); Gunther Barth, *City People: The Rise of Modern City Culture in 19th-Century America* (1980); Stuart M. Blumin, "Explaining the NewMetropolis: Perception, Depiction and Analysis in Mid-Nineteenth Century New York City," *Journal of Urban History* 11 (1984): 9–38; Christine M. Boyer, *Manhattan Manners: Architecture and Style, 1850–1900* (1985); George G. Foster, *New York by Gas-Light and Other Urban Sketches* (Berkeley, Cal.: 1990); Timothy J. Gilfoyle, *City of Eros: New York City, Prostitution, and the Commercialization of Sex, 1790–1920* (1992); Carl F. Kaestle, *The Evolution of an Urban School System: New York City, 1750–1850* (1973); John F. Kasson, *Rudeness & Civility: Manners in Nineteenth-Century Urban America* (1990); and Lawrence W. Levine, *Highbrow/Lowbrow: The Emergence of Cultural Hierarchy in America* (Cambridge, Mass.: 1988).

PART III: METROPOLITAN MODERNITIES (1890–1940)

For a general interpretation of the period, one can refer to Kenneth T. Jackson, "The Capital of Capitalism: the New York Metropolitan Region, 1890–1940," in Anthony Sutcliffe, ed.,

Metropolis, 1890–1940 (Chicago, 1984), pp. 319–53, as well as essays included in Taylor, ed., *Inventing Times Square*; and Ward and Zunz, eds., *The Landscape of Modernity*. Also very useful are the works of Robert A. M. Stern, Gregory Gilmartin, and John Massengale, *New York 1900: Metropolitan Architecture and Urbanism, 1890–1915* (1983);Stern et al., *New York 1930: Architecture and Urbanism Between the Two World Wars* (1987); and Keith D. Revell, *Building Gotham: Civic Culture and Public Policy in New York City, 1898-1938* (Baltimore: 2002)

On the corporate sector and the emergence of the white-collar world, one can begin with the works of Alfred D. Chandler, Jr., *The Visible Hand: The Managerial Revolution in American Business* (Cambridge, Mass.: 1977), and Olivier Zunz, *Making America Corporate, 1870-1920* (Chicago: 1990). On skyscrapers, see especially Carol Willis, *Form Follows Finance: Skyscrapers and Skylines in New York and Chicago* (1995).

For the industrial history of New York in the first half of the twentieth century, lacking a synthesis, see the volumes prepared by the Committee on the Regional Plan of New York and Its Environs, *Regional Plan of New York*, 2 vols. (1929–31); and *Regional Survey of New York and Its Environs*, 10 vols. (1927–31), as well as the article by Richard Harris, "Industry and Residence: The Decentralization of New York City, 1900–1940," *Journal of Historical Geography* 19, 2 (1993): 169–90. Also very useful is the old work by Edward E. Pratt, *Industrial Causes of Congestion in New York City* (1911). For the clothing-industry sector, see Nancy L. Green, *Ready-to-Wear and Ready-to-Work: A Century of Industry and Immigrants in Paris and New York* (Durham, N.C.: 1997); on the struggles of workers, M elvyn Dubofsky, *When Workers Organize: New York City in the Progressive Era* (Amherst, Mass.: 1968).

One will find information on the history of the New York port during this period in Carl W. Condit, *The Port of New York: A History of the Rail and Terminal System from the Beginning to Pennsylvania Station* (Chicago: 1980), and *The Port of New York: A History of the Rail and Terminal System from the Grand Central Electrification to the Present* (Chicago: 1981). On the issue of urban planning, see Schultz, *Constructing Urban Culture*, op. cit., The best analyses of urban planning and regional reorganization efforts are in Robert Fishman's work, "The Regional Plan and the Transformation of the Industrial Metropolis," in Ward and Zunz, eds., *Landscapes of Modernity*, 106–125, and Jameson W. Doig, *Empire on the Hudson: Entrepreneurial Vision and Political Power at the Port of New York Authority* (2001)

On the history of the transportation systems, see especially Clifton Hood, *722 Miles: The Building of the Subways and How They Transformed New York* (Baltimore: 1993), and Clay McShane, *Down the Asphalt Path: The Automobile and the American City* (1994). On Moses's actions, the best reference remains the critical biography by Robert A. Caro, *The Power*

Broker: Robert Moses and the Fall of New York (1974). On the role of La Guardia, see Thomas Kessner, *Fiorello H. La Guardia and the Making of Modern New York* (1989).

On immigration, besides Binder and Reimers, *All the Nations Under Heaven*, and Jacob A. Riis, *How the Other Half Lives: Studies Among the Tenements of New York* (1890), see John Bodnar, *The Transplanted: A History of Immigrants in Urban America* (Bloomington, Ill.: 1985), and in French, Nancy L. Green, *Et ils peuplèrent l'Amérique. L'odyssée des émigrants* (Paris: 1994).

Of the various groups that make up New York's population, the Jews have been studied the most, since the pioneering work by Moses Rischin, *The Promised City: New York's Jews, 1870–1914* (Cambridge, Mass.: 1962). See also Arthur A. Goren, *New York's Jews and the Quest for Community: The Kehillah Experiment 1908–1922* (1970); Jeffery S. Gurock, *When Harlem Was Jewish, 1870–1930* (1979); Andrew R. Heinze, *Adapting to Abundance: Jewish Immigrants, Mass Consumption, and the Search for an American Identity* (1990); Irving Howe, *World of Our Fathers: The Journey of the East European Jews to America and the Life They Found and Made* (1976); and Deborah Dash Moore, *At Home in America: Second Generation New York Jews* (1981).

On the Italians, see Samuel L. Baily, *Immigrants in the Lands of Promise: Italians in Buenos Aires and New York City, 1870 to 1914* (Ithaca, N.Y.: 1999); Miriam Cohen, *Workshop to Office: Two Generations of Italian Women in New York City, 1900–1950* (Ithaca, N.Y.: 1993); Donna R. Gabaccia, *From Sicily to Elizabeth Street: Housing and Social Change Among Italian Immigrants, 1880–1930* (Albany, N.Y.: 1983); and Robert A. Orsi, *The Madonna of 115th Street: Faith and Community in Italian Harlem, 1880–1950* (New Haven, Conn.: 1985).

For comparisons, see Thomas Kessner, *The Golden Door: Italian and Jewish Immigrant Mobility in New York City, 1880–1915* (1977); Elizabeth Ewen, *Immigrant Women in the Land of Dollars: Life and Culture on the Lower East Side, 1890–1925* (1985); and Ronald H. Bayor, *Neighbors in Conflict: The Irish, Germans, Jews, and Italians of New York City, 1929–41* (Baltimore: 1978).

On the African-Americans, see Gilbert Osofsky, *Harlem: The Making of a Ghetto: Negro New York, 1890–1930* (1966); Nathan Huggins, *Harlem Renaissance* (1971); David Levering Lewish, *When Harlem was in Vogue* (1981); Jervis Anderson, *This Was Harlem, 1900–1950* (1982); and Cheryl Lynn Greenberg, *"Or Does It Explode?" Black Harlem in the Great Depression* (1991). For the beginnings of the migration from Puerto Rico, Virginia E. Sanchez Korrol, *From Colonia to Community: The History of Puerto Ricans in New York City, 1917–48* (Westport, Conn.: 1983).

On the impact of the Great Depression, besides Greenberg's book, *"Or Does It Explode?"*, see Barbara Blumberg, *The New Deal and the Unemployed: The View from New York City* (Lewisburg, Pa.: 1979). For an analysis of intervention by the state,

Mark I. Gelfand, *A Nation of Cities: The Federal Government and Urban America, 1933–1945* (1975).

The housing problem has been analyzed by Roy Lubove, *The Progressives and the Slums: Tenement House Reform in New York City, 1890–1917* (Pittsburgh, Pa.: 1962), and by Richard Plunz, *A History of Housing in New York City: Dwelling Types and Social Change in the American Metropolis* (1990).

On political life, see the influential work of David C. Hammack, *Power and Society: Greater New York at the Turn of the Century* (1982).

For the emergence of a commercial culture and a mass culture, one can begin with the analyses included in Barth, *City People*; Thomas Bender and Carl E. Schorske, eds., *Budapest and New York: Studies in Metropolitan Transformation, 1870–1930* (1994); Joan Shelley Rubin, *The Making of Middlebrow Culture* (Chapel Hill: 1992); William R. Taylor, *In Pursuit of Gotham: Culture and Commerce in New York* (1992), and Taylor, ed., *Inventing Times Square*.

On vaudeville, see Robert W. Snyder, *The Voice of the City: Vaudeville and Popular Culture in New York* (1986). The cultural impact of Coney Island has been analyzed by John Kasson, *Amusing the Million: Coney Island at the Turn of the Century* (1978), and the changes in New York nightlife by Lewis A. Erenberg, *Steppin' Out: New York Nightlife and the Transformation of American Culture* (Westport, Conn.: 1981). On the leisure-time activities of the working class, see Kathy Peiss, *Cheap Amusements: Working Women and Leisure in Turn-of-the-Century New York* (Philadelphia: 1986). For a remarkable study of the world and culture of New York homosexuals, see George Chauncey, *Gay New York: Gender, Urban Culture, and the Making of the Gay Male World, 1890–1940* (1994).

The emergence of New York as an avant-garde literary and artistic center has been described, most notably, by Martin Green, *New York 1913: The Armory Show and the Paterson Strike Pageant* (1988). On the hybrid character of New York culture in the 1920s, see Ann Douglas, *Terrible Honesty: Mongrel Manhattan in the 1920s* (1995), and George Hutchinson, *The Harlem Renaissance in Black and White* (Cambridge, Mass.: 1995).

Finally, on the emergence of a cosmopolitan academic culture and New York intellectuals, see Thomas Bender, *Intellect and Public Life: Essays on the Social History of Academic Intellectuals in the United States* (Baltimore: 1993); Alexander Bloom, *Prodigal Sons: The New York Intellectuals and Their World* (1986); Terry A. Cooney, *The Rise of the New York Intellectuals: Partisan Review and Its Circle, 1934–1945* (Madison, Wis.: 1986); and David A. Hollinger, *In the American Province: Studies in the History and Historiography of Ideas* (Bloomington, Ind.: 1985).

PART IV: CAPITAL OF THE AMERICAN CENTURY (1940–2000)

First of all, one can refer to the previously cited volumes published under the aegis of the Russell Sage Foundation: Mollenkopf, ed., *Power, Culture, and Place*, Mollenkopf and Castells, eds., *Dual City*, and Shefter, ed., *Capital of the American Century*; New York's economic development has been analyzed by Roger Waldinger, *Through the Eye of the Needle: Immigrants and Enterprise in New York's Garment Trade* (1986), and *Still the Promised City? African-Americans and the New Immigrants in Postindustrial New York* (Cambridge, Mass.: 1996), and the evolution of the working-class by Joshua B. Freeman, *Working-Class New York: Life and Labor since World War II* (2000)

For a collection of studies on regional economic development, see the nine volumes of the *New York Metropolitan Region Study*, published under the general direction of Raymond Vernon, in particular Edgar M. Hoover and Raymond Vernon, *Anatomy of the Metropolis: The Changing Distribution of People and Jobs Within the New York Metropolitan Region* (Cambridge, Mass.: 1959). Also see Jean Gottmann, *Megalopolis: The Urbanized Northeastern Seaboard of the United States* (1961); and Richard Harris, "The Geography of Employment and Residence in New York Since 1950," in Mollenkopf and Castells, eds., *Dual City*, 129–52.

On the crisis in the 1970s, see Martin Shefter, *Political Crisis/Fiscal Crisis: The Collapse and Revival of New York City* (1985), and on the New York revival, Commission on the Year 2000, *New York Ascendant* (1987); Peter D. Salins, ed., *New York Unbound: The City and the Politics of the Future* (1988); and Saskia Sassen, *The Global City: New York, London, Tokyo* (Princeton, N.J.: 1991).

For spatial and political developments, see Jane Jacobs, *The Death and Life of Great American Cities* (1961); John Hull Mollenkopf, *A Phoenix in the Ashes: The Rise and Fall of the Koch Coalition in New York City Politics* (Princeton, N.J.: 1993); Chris McNickle, *To Be Mayor of New York City: Ethnic Politics in the City* (1993); Charles R. Morris, *The Cost of Good Intentions: New York City and the Liberal Experiment, 1960–1975* (1980); Catherine Pouzoulet, *New York, New York. Espace, pouvoir et citoyenneté dans la ville postindustrielle* (Paris: 2000); Robert A.M. Stern et al., *New York 1960: Architecture and Urbanism Between the Second World War and the Bicentennial* (1998); and Joel Schwartz, *The New York Approach: Robert Moses, Urban Liberals, and Redevelopment of the Inner City* (Columbus, Ohio: 1993).

On recent immigration, see Nancy Foner, ed., *New Immigrants in New York* (1987); Alejandro Portes and Ruben G. Rumbaut, *Immigrant America: A Portrait* (Berkeley, Cal.: 1990); David M. Reimers, *Still the Golden Door? The Third World Comes to America* (1985); and Constance R. Sutton and Elsa M. Chaney, eds., *Caribbean Life in New York City: Sociocultural Dimensions* (1994). For a pioneering analysis of ethnicity in the 1960s, see Nathan Glazer and Daniel Patrick Moynihan, *Beyond the Melting Pot: The Negroes, Puerto Ricans, Jews, Italians, and Irish of New York City* (1963). On the rise of white conservatism, see Jonathan Rieder, *Canarsie: The Jews and Italians of Brooklyn Against Liberalism* (Cambridge, Mass.: 1985).

On cultural changes, see Diana Crane, *The Transformations of the Avant-Garde: The New York Art World, 1940–1985* (1987); Serge Guilbaut, *How New York Stole the Idea of Modern Art: Abstract Expressionism, Freedom, and the Cold War* (Chicago: 1983); Tricia Rose, *Black Noise: Rap Music and Black Culture in Contemporary America* (Hanover, N.H.: 1994); and Leonard Wallock, ed., *New York: Culture Capital of the World, 1940–1965* (1988).

Finally readers who will want to assess the impact and consequences of the September 11, 2001 terrorist attacks against the World Trade Center may begin with Mike Wallace, *A New Deal for New York* (2002), and Michael Zorkin and Sharon Zukin, eds., *After the World Trade Center: Rethinking New York City* (2002).

INDEX

Italic page numbers refer to illustrations.

Cooper, Edward, 126
Cooper, James Fenimore, 79, 82, 111, 130, 150
Copley, John Singleton, 63
Cornbury, Viscount (Edward Hyde), 35
Cornell Medical Center, 269
Corning, Erastus, 70
Corporations, 172–79, 211, 263, 266, 269
Corrigan, Michael, 238
Corso, Gregory, 291
Cortelyou, Jacques, 36–37
Coser, Lewis, 296
Cosmopolitanism, 243–44
Costello, Frank, 216
Cotton Club, 253
Council of Hygiene and Public Health, 108
Counterculture, 296, 297, 298, 303
Cousseau, Jacques, 56
Craft industries, 27–29, 36, 49, 54
Crane, Hart, 252
Cravath, Shearman & Sterling, 211
Credit-verification offices, 83–84
Croker, Richard, 222
Croly, Herbert, 165–66, 167, 168, 247
Cronkite, Walter, 310
Croton River, 108
Crown Heights, 277, 278, 280
Crum, Jason, 302
Cuba, 73, 166
Cullen, Countee, 255
cummings, e. e., 252
Cunard, 174
Cunard, Samuel, 80
Cunningham, Merce, 288
Cuomo, Mario, 284
Curaçao, 6, 10, 12, 47, 51–52
Currier & Ives, 90, 157
Curtis, George William, 151–52
Cuyper, Gerrit Jansz, 10

Dali, Salvador, 287
Dana, Richard Henry, 154
Danbury, Connecticut, 88
D'Arcangelo, Allan, 302
Davies, Arthur B., 250
Davis, Benjamin, 243
Davis, Miles, 288
Davis, Sadie Warren, 239
Davison, Gideon, 158
Day, Benjamin, 151
Day, Dorothy, 296
DeForest, Robert W., 180, 181, 219
De Kooning, Willem, 287
Delafield, John, 69
De Lancey, James, 21, 53
De Lancey, Oliver, 39
De Lancey, Stephen, 57
Delano, Franklin, 134, 189

Delaporte, Albert, 103
De la Sagra, Ramon, 79
Delaware Canal, 68
Delaware River, 6
Delaware Valley, 9
De Leon, Daniel, 242
DeLillo, Don, 305
Democratic Party: and federal aid to cities, 263; and Hewitt, 222; and immigrants, 124; Jacksonian Democrats, 122; and Koch, 284; and partisan politics, 123–24, 281–83; and police, 107; and Tammany Hall, 124, 125–26; and urban elite, 123; and Whitman, 151
Democratic Society of French Republicans, 141
Depau, Francis, 71
DeSapio, Carmine, 282, 283
De Sille, Nicasius, 12
Deutscher Liederkranz, 141
De Valera, Eamon, 241
De Vries, Margaret Harden-broeke, 52
Dewey, George, 166
Dewey, John, 218, 246, 247, 294
Dewey, Thomas E., 216
DeWitt, Simeon, 43
De Wolff, Abel, 10, 12, 15
De Wolff, Dirck, 9, 10
Dickens, Charles, 98, 109, 154
DiMaggio, Joe, 237
Dinkins, David, 284–85
Dix, John Adams, 74
Dominican immigrants, 277, 278
Dongan, Thomas, 15, 35, 60
Dongan Charter, 35, 39
Dos Passos, John, 249, 252, 288
Doublet, Jean, 57
Doucinet, Etienne, 57
Downtown–Lower Manhattan Association, 266
Dows, David, 75–76
Dramatic Line, 71
Dreamland, 227, 230
Dreier, Mary, 212
Drew, Daniel, 71
Dripp, Matthew, 96
Dubinsky, David, 213
Dubois, John, 140
Duchamp, Marcel, 250, 291, 301
Duhamel, Georges, 225
Duke, James Buchanan, 173
Dundy, Elmer, 227
Du Pont Company, 176
Dutch empire, 3–4, 6–8, 10
Dutch immigrants, 57, 58
Dutch Reformed Church, 46, 51, 60
Duvalier, François, 277
Duvalier, Jean-Claude, 277–78
Duvergier de Hauranne, Ernest, 79–80, 103, 136, 144, 150
Dylan, Bob, 298–99, 311

THE COLUMBIA HISTORY OF URBAN LIFE

Kenneth T. Jackson, General Editor